Crime and Society in Twentieth-Century England

Also by Clive Emsley:

Crime and Society in England: 1750–1900, fourth edition
(ISBN: 978-1-4058-5863-2), 2010

Crime and Society in Twentieth-Century England

Clive Emsley

Longman
is an imprint of

Harlow, England • London • New York • Boston • San Francisco • Toronto • Sydney • Singapore • Hong Kong
Tokyo • Seoul • Taipei • New Delhi • Cape Town • Madrid • Mexico City • Amsterdam • Munich • Paris • Milan

PEARSON EDUCATION LIMITED

Edinburgh Gate
Harlow CM20 2JE
United Kingdom
Tel: +44 (0)1279 623623
Fax: +44 (0)1279 431059
Website: www.pearsoned.co.uk

First edition published in Great Britain in 2011

© Pearson Education Limited 2011

The right of Clive Emsley to be identified as author of this work has been asserted by
him in accordance with the Copyright, Designs and Patents Act 1988.

Pearson Education is not responsible for the content of third party internet sites.

ISBN: 978-1-4058-5902-8

British Library Cataloguing in Publication Data
A CIP catalogue record for this book can be obtained from the British Library

Library of Congress Cataloging in Publication Data
Emsley, Clive.
  Crime and society in twentieth-century England / Clive Emsley.
    p. cm.
  Includes bibliographical references and index.
  ISBN 978-1-4058-5902-8 (pbk.)
  1. Crime–England–History–20th century.   I. Title.
  HV6949.E5E473 2011
  364.94209'04–dc22
                                        2010050284

10 9 8 7 6 5 4 3 2 1
15 14 13 12 11

Set by 35 in 10/13.5pt Sabon
Printed and bound in Malaysia (CTP-VP)

For Jenny

Contents

List of photographs and cartoons   viii
List of tables and figures   ix
Preface and acknowledgements   x
Abbreviations used in the notes   xi
Publisher's acknowledgements   xii

1 Introduction   1
2 The pattern of crime   15
3 Criminal lives   39
4 Crime and the young   63
5 Organised crime: professional criminals   87
6 Media narratives   109
7 Expert narratives   131
8 Police and policing   153
9 The courts   177
10 Penal policy and penal experience   201
11 Some conclusions   227

Further reading: further research   235
Index   239

List of photographs and cartoons

The Kray twins with Judy Garland and Mark Herron 47

'The Union Jack Library: The Case of the Chinese Hypnotist' 114

'When we get women on juries' 182

'One law for rich and one for poor' 187

'Cheap cruelty: a comment and criticism' 188

A cartoon of the Dartmoor Mutiny of 1932 214

A prisoner on the roof of HMP Strangeways, 1980 220

List of tables and figures

Tables

2.1 Home Office breakdown of classes of murderers sentenced to death and their victims, 1900–1948   28

4.1 Superintendent Water's list of the most common offences committed in public places by children and young persons, April 1907   65

5.1 Metropolitan Police summary showing the value and variety of foodstuffs lost from store and in transit during 1947   96

Figures

2.1 Ratio of crime to population in thousands 1900–1997   21

2.2 Ratio of crime to population in thousands 1900–1938   22

2.3 Ratio of crime to population in thousands 1940–1997   23

Preface and acknowledgements

Almost a quarter of a century ago I published a book on crime and society in England from 1750 to 1900. Criminal justice history has become increasingly popular since then, yet historians have only just begun to dip into the twentieth century. I know that a number of monographs are about to appear and perhaps, as a result, this book is a little premature but given my advancing years, I reasoned that, if I don't have a go at it now, then I never will. I have also opted to stick to the twentieth century, resisting the temptation to stray much into the new millennium and thus giving myself a reasonably clear cut-off date.

As ever I have benefited enormously from talking to a variety of historians and criminologists in the preparation of this book. Some may not have much experience of researching the twentieth century or even researching British/English history, but they have always been generous with their comments and advice, and willing to share their work and ideas. I particularly want to thank Barry Godfrey, Louise Jackson, René Lévy, Jim Sharpe, Heather Shore, Pieter Spierenburg and Marty Wiener. At the Open University I was lucky enough to work with a group of lively young historians with expertise in crime and policing that is second to none: to Ros Crone, Peter King, Paul Lawrence, Georgie Sinclair, Stef Slater and Chris A. Williams, I owe an enormous debt; and the same goes for Bob Morris and Jim Whitfield who, after careers developing practical expertise in different areas of the criminal justice system, retired to follow academic pursuits. Finally, and by no means least, Alyson Brown, Helen Johnston and John Carter Wood, generously read and commented on a draft of the book and saved me from a number of errors and infelicities – those faults that remain are mine.

The dedication is the same as that of the book that precedes this – to my wife. She now seems to act as a district nurse for ageing relatives as well as the occasional sick grandchild. I don't know how she finds time for me as well – but thanks for everything Jenny.

Abbreviations used in the notes

BJC	*British Journal of Criminology*
CHS	*Crime, histoire et sociétés/Crime, history and societies*
CRO	County Record Office
HO	Home Office Papers in The National Archives, Kew, London
MEPO	Metropolitan Police Papers in The National Archives, Kew, London
MPHC	Metropolitan Police Historical Collection
Oldbaileyonline	The Proceedings of the Old Bailey (1674–1913) available at www.oldbaileyonline.org
OUPA	Open University Police Archive
Parl. Debs.	*Parliamentary Debates*
WO	War Office Papers in The National Archives, Kew, London

Publisher's acknowledgements

We are grateful to the following for permission to reproduce copyright material:

Photographs and cartoons

p. 47 from Getty Images; p. 114 from www.sextonblake.co.uk/IPC Media. © IPC Media; pp. 182, 187 and 188 from British Cartoon Archive, University of Kent/Mirrorpix; p. 214 from John Foulkes. Reproduced by permission of the family of Mrs B.L. Foulkes; p. 220 from Ged Murray.

Tables

Table 4.1 from *MEPO 2/4256, Prevention of crimes amongst school-children, 1907–1937*, Metropolitan Police (Supt. Waters) MEPO2/4256; Table 5.1 from *MEPO 3/3046, Pilferage of rationed foodstuffs at the Port of London: Minutes of Food Security Committee investigations 1948–1949* (Metropolitan Police).

Text

Poetry on p. 17 from *The Truncheon*, IV(1), p. 6 (1947).

In some instances we have been unable to trace the owners of copyright material, and we would appreciate any information that would enable us to do so.

CHAPTER 1

Introduction

It was only towards the end of the twentieth century that academic historians began to take a serious interest in the history of crime and penal policy. Their interest was part of the move to study 'history from below' with the broad aim of understanding better those who had left little trace of their lives; those who, in Edward Thompson's eloquent and much quoted phrase, needed to be rescued 'from the enormous condescension of posterity'.[1] The early research into the history of crime, in which Thompson also played a pivotal role, concentrated particularly on periods when the plebeian classes were under pressure from major economic change, when new kinds of relationships between employer and employee were established at the workplace, when new forms of cash payment were introduced, and when there was a criminalisation of some workplace customs. The research had important resonance with its time. It coincided with a soaring statistical increase in criminal offending and with the growth of academic criminology – much of which was heavily funded by government. And while the historical research owed much to the left-wing and radical perspectives that motivated history from below, it coincided with a significant shift in the political world away from liberal penal policies that had been dominant in liberal democratic societies since the close of the nineteenth century.

There was a further paradox in the developments behind this first flush of criminal justice history. The new research grew alongside increasing interest in the history of the twentieth century and a mushrooming of academic criminology, and yet, surprisingly, there was remarkably little work undertaken on the history of crime and criminal justice in twentieth-century England. Such broad historical assertions as were made tended to be the work of criminologists. Academic disciplines feed off and into one another, and rightly so, but it remains the case that the starting perceptions and the way in which sources are selected, read and interpreted by people in different disciplines can vary enormously. The aim of this book is to explore the history of crime and criminal justice in twentieth-century England. At the risk of offending Welsh readers, I have to confess to subsuming Wales with England, but then the two countries have the same criminal justice system and their annual crime statistics have always been lumped together. Scotland continued to have its own legal system throughout the twentieth century and requires a separate study of its own; and while Northern Ireland continued with an essentially English criminal justice system after the treaty that created the Irish Free State at the end of 1921, its unique history would also benefit from a distinct study. I consider myself to be a historian and that which follows to be a work of English history. I like to think that I have learned much from criminologists, and many of the references in this book are to their work. I like to think also that they, as well as other historians, will find what follows of use.

The starting point for any history of crime has to be the recognition that crime is not an absolute. All societies have norms and develop ways to enforce them. Some of the offences against those norms are condemned by a society's laws and labelled as crimes; as a result the perpetrators are condemned and, generally, subjected to some form of punishment or retribution. Various forms of homicide and various forms of the appropriation of property are commonly singled out in this way and are the most obvious examples of behaviours defined as crimes. But even homicide was only fully categorised as a crime across Europe in the mid-seventeenth century.[2] Moreover there remained individuals and groups that were prepared to endorse killing as a means of furthering political ends or resolving domestic problems or affronts. While England did not experience the extremes of political violence that affected much of continental Europe during the twentieth century, there were political activists, commonly labelled 'terrorists' by politicians, the media and the bulk of the population, prepared to use the bomb and the bullet to achieve their aims. The anarchists who committed robberies and shot police officers that got in their way in the period before the First World War were relatively easy to label as criminals. But the periodic Irish nationalist activity that flared with lethal impact in the aftermath of the Great War, on the eve of the Second World War and in the 1970s and 1980s was less easy to write off in this fashion. When the last IRA campaign concluded in the early 1990s, and before anxieties about the violent activities of militant Islamic extremists, it became apparent that other forms of homicide were being tolerated and even encouraged among some sections of society. Fights about honour had been a constant feature particularly among men and youths within certain poor, working-class districts; some of these fights might, occasionally, result in accidental killing. But some of the new immigrant communities moving into English cities from the 1960s brought with them cultural concepts that condoned killing as a means of maintaining or restoring family honour, especially in matters of gender relations and sexual mores. Indeed, failure to act in such circumstances was stigmatised as an offence among some sections of these communities, and it seems most unlikely that they were unaware of their host state's law that stigmatised such behaviour as criminal.

In a similar fashion, while a majority of the population recognised theft to be a crime and hence acknowledged the validity of the criminal law in stigmatising such behaviour, there could still be ambivalence. Some elements of the workforce considered that they had a right to perks from their jobs even though many perks could be categorised as 'theft' and lead to prosecution. Others thought nothing of defrauding the taxman of small sums, while a few were prepared to defraud him of quite considerable sums generally without acknowledging that this was 'theft' in the eyes of the state and its law. Rationing and shortages during both world wars led to the development of a black market. A survey of attitudes towards the black market, conducted in 1943, found people labelling those involved as 'traitors', 'anti-social and unpatriotic'. Severe punishments were demanded, including flogging and even execution. Yet enormous numbers of ordinary people broke the wartime regulations by buying and selling illicitly. In approaching the black market they appear to have made a distinction between large-scale racketeering and minor offences, such as barter, tipping, under-the-counter and off-ration sales. In reality the dividing line was often hazy and some large-scale offending provided for the smaller exchanges.[3]

Popular disorder is another slippery area partly because, like the all-encompassing word 'crime', it covers such a range of behaviours. An argument that erupts into a fight might end up being categorised under a variety of offences. If a participant is injured, the assailant might be charged with anything from assault to grievous bodily harm. A group of participants might be charged with affray. The participants themselves might not recognise any such offences in their actions. Moreover, in the tough, poor working-class districts of the first half of the twentieth century, few of the men injured in such disorder would have relished appearing in court as an injured party; rather, they probably hoped for the opportunity of bettering their assailant on a future occasion. In addition to using their discretion in deciding on a criminal charge, the police themselves were often deeply involved in this tough, masculine culture and fought with their fists, batons, lead-weighted capes and even illicit weapons in preference to using the law. The culture of aggression and toughness continued among young men, and to a much lesser extent among young women, on many of the new estates that were built after the Second World War on the ruins of the old working-class streets. The police, however, were given less and less leeway by their superiors to meet community machismo with their own.

Rioting is a variant of popular disorder. The incidence of riot was not great during the twentieth century though, by its public nature, it was almost certain to attract wide media coverage. The temptation for the authorities and for conservative commentators was to blame agitators, often external to the community involved, for instigating disorder and a 'hooligan element' for carrying it out. Some of the most notable riots in twentieth-century England, however, emerged out of demonstrations in which the participants were protesting about what they considered to be wrongs. When Luton Town Hall was sacked during the Peace Day celebrations of 19 July 1919, the riot was ignited by the decision of the town's elite to exclude ordinary, working-class veterans from the festivities. The violence in Cable Street, east London, in November 1936 was the result of the local community's determination to prevent a march by the British Union of Fascists through an area of predominantly Jewish settlement. Rioting in the inner cities during the early 1980s has been attributed to aggressive policing towards Afro-Caribbean communities and to a more general feeling of hopelessness and powerlessness among the youth of these areas. The problem is complicated still further by the fact that behaviour by the authorities can provoke trouble, indeed occasionally it can constitute what would, if committed by others, be labelled and prosecuted as riot. In Birkenhead in September 1932, for example, the local police appear to have rioted in a poor working-class district that had been protesting about proposals to reduce public assistance. On 18 June 1984 pickets from the National Union of Mineworkers faced police at Orgreave Coking Plant in south Yorkshire. As a result of what was subsequently called the battle of Orgreave 95 pickets appeared in court charged with riot. The case collapsed; there were subsequent allegations that the 'battle' was set up by the authorities, and the allegations seemed to have some backing from the words of the police commander who told the court during the trial, if there was to be a battle, he had wanted it 'on my own ground and on my own terms.'[4]

Offences such as disorder and riot might depend on the eye of the beholder, or rather on the discretion of those functionaries of the criminal justice system who observed an incident, reported it and made the decision to arrest and to prosecute under what they considered to be the appropriate legal category. But behaviours very different from these offences, and different from homicide and theft, have also been designated as crimes by particular societies at particular times. Until the last third of the twentieth century, for example, the law in England made homosexual activity between consenting male adults a crime punishable by imprisonment. In the early 1950s a senior officer of Metropolitan Police in central London used 'male perverts' as a synonym for male homosexuals.[5] A few years later the parliamentary debates over changing the law revealed how firmly many still held to the old norms. Field Marshal, Viscount Montgomery of Alamein, fearful for the moral fibre of the nation's youth, told the House of Lords that the reforming Sexual Offences Bill should be renamed 'a Charter for Buggery', and this was even after the Air Force Minister, Lord Shackleton, had explained that homosexual activity was 'disgraceful conduct' and that the armed forces would still be able to dismiss any 'undesirable person' guilty of such conduct.[6] Thereafter, and until the end of the century, while homosexual activity among consenting adults was legal in civilian life it remained a serious offence within the armed forces and hence against the norms enforced by military law.

Different historical contexts can also generate different concerns about crime in general as well as concerns about, or awareness of different forms of offending. Witchcraft was a concern in the early modern period, but it was scarcely a worry in the more rationalist, secular twentieth century. However, a legacy of the earlier period, the Witchcraft Act of 1723, was found useful by the authorities during the Second World War to prosecute mediums whose seances were feared to have a deleterious impact on public morale. Jane Rebecca Yorke and, more notably, Helen Duncan – 'Hellish Nell' – claimed to be able to make contact with servicemen who had recently been killed. In addition about her impact on morale, 'Hellish Nell' created serious alarm among the authorities when she appeared to have information about warships that had not yet been officially released to the public; and such alarm became acute in 1944 during the weeks leading up to the D-Day landings. The prosecution of the two 'witches' under 200-year-old legislation caused some disquiet at the time, and their offences were rarely the kinds of thing that, in the mid-twentieth century, were considered as constituting crime. The use of the law in this instance was as a wartime expedient.[7]

As is discussed at greater length in the chapters that follow, the two world wars of the twentieth century were considered by those living through them to have had an impact on crime. Offences by juveniles, for example, were believed to have risen during the wars and there was fear of violent crime committed by brutalised veterans in their aftermath. Similarly, there were assumptions that the economic hardship of the Depression fostered law breaking, particularly various forms of theft. The growth of an articulate and vociferous women's movement during the 1960s heightened the awareness of domestic violence and of rape. These were already both punishable at law, but the new climate and the conscious-raising agitation by women's groups removed much of the stigma attached to the victims who came forward to point the finger at their assailants. It was almost certainly this new awareness and confidence, rather than any change in the incidence of sexual offending, that led to the massive growth in the statistics for these offences in the second part of the century.

Increasing calls for gender equality across the century also had an impact on both criminal justice institutions and the ways in which laws were enforced. Perceived gender difference, for example, structured the ways in which women were employed as police officers for almost three-quarters of the century; it also structured the way in which offenders were dealt with by the criminal justice system. Class and ethnicity also had significant impact. The concept of class declined as a tool of social analysis at the end of the twentieth century alongside the growing recognition of gender and ethnicity, yet class remained an important instrument of perception for many who lived during the century. During the 1920s Cecil Chapman, a barrister and stipendiary magistrate, explained crowd hostility towards the police and attempts to rescue prisoners as the result of 'a general perception of the law being an artificial creation by society for the protection of the rich and the repression of the poor.'[8] Immigrants, and especially those who were not white or who did not sound English or look English in styles of dress or hair, were commonly stigmatised. This was the situation for Jewish and other central European refugees that entered the country in the generation before the First World War; it was the same for the Afro-Caribbean, African and Asian migrants who settled in the second half of the century. In 1999, following the clumsy, insensitive and failed police investigation into the murder of a black teenager, Sir William Macpherson, a retired high court judge, criticised the Metropolitan Police for 'professional incompetence, institutional racism and a failure of leadership by senior officers.'[9] It was the term 'institutional racism' that caused the most shock to the police and, possibly also, to a national complacency that was largely ignorant of the way that many black and Asian people felt themselves to be considered by a key element of the criminal justice system.

As well as different contexts contributing to different perspectives on crime and changing perceptions of social groups shaping institutions and law enforcement, there were also instances when a particular offence was taken to be a tocsin warning of a general malaise within society. One of the most striking examples of this in twentieth-century England was the way in which, in 1993, the murder of two-year-old James Bulger by two ten-year-old boys prompted sensationalised media soul-searching about a 'moral vacuum' in the nation. The Bulger murder was shocking, but it was not unique as is evidenced by the case of Mary Bell, the 11-year-old who had strangled two small boys some three decades earlier. Descriptions of such offenders as 'evil' might have served to satisfy an immediate social need for a simple explanation; but 'evil' and 'monsters' are sensational labels, ultimately shallow and largely meaningless as serious explanations for behaviour. And it was the same with attempts to use such incidents as pointers to, or symptoms of a wider malaise in society. A simile is a simile for all that, and in such cases it probably says more about the perceptions of the beholder than providing any useful explanation for, or meaningful symptomatic description of a society's ills.[10]

Concerns about society as reflected in the reaction to the murder of James Bulger, and particularly concerns about the criminal justice system, were considerably different from what they had been a hundred years before. Most educated Victorians in England considered their society to be a leader in economic, political and social development. Such beliefs pervaded their understanding of the English criminal justice system. At the close of the nineteenth century, statistically crime in England appeared to be in decline or, at least, levelling out. Quite unselfconsciously the Victorians and Edwardians commonly described their police as 'the best in the world'. Proposals to codify English criminal law and procedure were debated in parliament between 1834 and 1849 and again between 1878 and 1883. Bills had been introduced; and each time a mixture of judicial criticism and an apparent conservative preference for a range of laws with space for judicial interpretation, led to their failure. Edmund Burke's notion of England's exquisitely evolving constitutional system was largely accepted across the political spectrum and was applied to the law as much as to the wider forms of government. Nevertheless, while law-making and penal practice tended to swing between emphases on reformation in one period and punitive retribution in another, towards the close of the century, and particularly following the Gladstone Committee Report of 1895, a new, broadly liberal penal system began to emerge. There were problems: in particular there were concerns about how to deal with those categorised as 'habitual criminals'; moreover in the decade before the First World War the statistics of crime began to rise slightly. There is no historical consensus about exactly how the liberal penal culture and the abatement of imprisonment developed in the early twentieth century, or about the speed of change.[11] Nevertheless, the English entered the twentieth century largely confident in the strength, success and progressive movement of their criminal justice system.

Confidence in the criminal justice system and, in spite of occasional problems or scandals, faith in the police survived the First World War, the Depression and the Second World War. Crime, criminal justice reform and significant changes in penal policy were scarcely visible on the agenda of any political party as it sought the popular vote during general elections. The sole mention of the topics in the inter-war period came in Stanley Baldwin's Conservative Party Manifesto for 1924. Here, under the heading 'Women and Children', Baldwin declared his intention to see the Probationary Service 'developed', to increase the number of women police and to ensure that 'the penalties for assaults against women and children [were] made adequate to the offence'.[12] Militarist Prussia and then the so-called 'totalitarian' states of both the left and the right were seen as benchmarks against which the ideal of a liberal, progressive Britain was measured and found to be good. Campaigns to abolish corporal and capital punishment, both successful in the aftermath of the Second World War, were seen as a continuation of progressive, humanitarian policies begun during the Enlightenment and driven by a succession of dedicated, far-sighted reformers. This broad interpretation of the history of policing and of penal change was determinedly Whig. After the Second World War, however, the confidence began to falter. This was fostered, in part, by a sharp upturn in the statistics of crime as well as by a loss of faith in social progress and by strident intellectual challenges to the status quo.

Writing at the beginning of the 1990s Andrew Rutherford, the chair of the Howard League for Penal Reform, an academic and former member of the Prison Service, suggested that there were three broad credos espoused by individuals working in the criminal justice system. Those who generally disliked offenders and viewed them with moral condemnation adopted what he called the punishment credo. They wanted the minimum of restrictions on those charged with pursuing and managing criminal offenders; if unchecked, Rutherford maintained, this credo could lead to the degradation of those convicted of criminal behaviour. The efficiency credo, in contrast, prioritised expedience and pragmatism. Moral mission and moral judgements were secondary to ensuring effective management, and this could lead to a reliance on the system because it appeared to work, even at the expense of what some might consider just and fair. The first credo was largely pessimistic, the second was largely neutral, while the third – the caring credo – was optimistic. The caring credo insisted on openness and accountability and involved a liberal and humanitarian attitude towards suspects, the accused and prisoners.[13] Rutherford did not suggest that these credos might be seen as broadly functioning across society as a whole, yet it seems fair to argue that they do exist in this way, sometimes overlapping and generally with one credo dominant in the thinking of those responsible for the criminal justice system. Moreover such overlapping and contesting credos fits well with what has become, perhaps the most influential theorising of the modern criminal justice system – that of David Garland.

Garland has described the first two-thirds of the twentieth century in Britain as a period of penal welfarism. During these years crime, together with a cluster of other matters such as education, the family, health, poverty, work, were seen as social issues that needed to be dealt with by social-work professionals using expert techniques. In the case of crime the basic axiom was that the necessary measures were, as far as possible, to be positive and rehabilitative rather than negative and retributive. The underlying assumption was that growing affluence, combined with social reform, would significantly reduce crime. In the final third of the century, however, penal welfarism gave way to a culture of control. A soaring increase in the statistics of crime, combined with a succession of blows to the economy with concomitant unemployment and decaying inner cities led both the liberal élite and the educated middle class to loose faith in the old reformist ideals. In the new culture of control, as defined by Garland, penalty, policing and prevention became central to the whole way of life, particularly in Britain and the United States, the countries which form the main focus of his work. In both countries there were recurrent panics about violent crimes linked with demands for harsher penalties and, at the same time, there were new systems of prevention and extensive observation.[14] Returning, once again, to a broad and simplistic application of Rutherford's schema to society as a whole, it is as if the caring credo was replaced by the punishment credo. Yet considering Rutherford's credos as functioning simultaneously, with different credos becoming dominant at different periods, ensures that the retributive element is recognised as continuing, if often muted, during the period of penal welfare. Similarly the rhetoric of care persisted, again often muted, under the shrill culture of control. The efficiency credo also remained ever present, although efficiency developed a new kind of significance from the 1980s.

Towards the end of the century, as Keynesian welfarism yielded to a resurgent neo-liberalism, the component parts of the criminal justice system were required to demonstrate the value that the state and its citizens were getting for their investment. Targets were set to measure achievement. Accountants, auditors and official regulators were brought in to make assessments. Unquestionably this helped to iron out some abuses, but it also imposed new layers of bureaucracy. This bureaucracy, in turn, was considered a burden by many of those that worked in state institutions and who were required to write reports on their activities and to measure their success against the new targets. The police service, the courts, penal institutions and organisations experienced the new assessments, demands and regulations like other parts of the public sector. Targets were met, or perhaps it might be fairer to suggest that, at times, the evidence was manipulated in a way to imply that the targets were met. But, while much of the old trust and faith in the criminal justice institutions may have been misplaced, the illustrations of failure that the targets and measurements revealed, and the way in which they were seized upon by some populist and partisan sections of the media, helped significantly to undermine such trust and faith as still existed in these same institutions.[15]

The Conservative government of Margaret Thatcher played a major role in establishing the importance of assessing value for money and quality control in the public sector. It also played a major role in the new culture of control. In the general election of 1979, which brought Thatcher to power, the Conservatives made much of law and order as a crucial political issue. In spite of Conservative rhetoric, promises and increased funding for the criminal justice system, however, the statistics of crime continued to rise, reaching a peak in the mid-1990s. Even so, in 1992 the Labour Party lost its fourth general election in a row, and this prompted a major rethink of party strategy and the formulation of the idea of New Labour. Among the key issues within New Labour's raft of policies was a determination to challenge the Tory government's assertion that it had a monopoly on listening to the victims of crime and had the best policies for dealing with crime and criminal offenders. Early in 1993 the Shadow Home Secretary, Tony Blair, published 'Why crime is a socialist issue' in the *New Statesman*. The article virtually coincided with the shock of the James Bulger murder. It announced:

The Tories have given up on crime. Not just their policies but their philosophy has failed . . . Labour's commitment is to match popular concern with a constructive and broad-based programme of action.

Blair declared that: 'We should be tough on crime and tough on the underlying causes of crime.' Labour, he promised, would listen to victims, put policing back into the hands of local communities, modernise the courts and the criminal justice system, and even applaud the government if it came up with sensible reforms.[16] The Conservatives found themselves forced to respond, and they did so most forcefully at their party conference later in the year. A report suggesting prison reform, and a subsequent White Paper, *Custody, Care and Justice*, were shelved and the Home Secretary, Michael Howard, announced a package of twenty-seven measures 'to prevent crime . . . to help the police chase criminals . . . to make it easier to convict the guilty . . . to punish them once they [were] found guilty.'[17] There followed a period in which the two sides continued to ratchet up the rhetoric of responding to crime with tough, retributive policies. The mid-1990s witnessed the statistics of crime beginning to level out and, in some instances, to fall, but this had little effect on the rhetoric. In 1997 New Labour won the General Election and launched a wave of criminal justice initiatives and legislation, together with a new wave of targets and requirements for criminal justice institutions to adopt the practices of accountants, auditors and corporate lawyers. It has been pointed out that, in the ten years following this election victory New Labour passed 53 Acts of Parliament dealing with crime, criminal justice and punishment; this was ten more than had been passed during the previous one hundred years. In the process it created at least 1,000 new criminal offences.[18] By the end of the century the prisons were bursting.

While this book is a work of history, the issues are explored thematically rather than in a steady chronological progression. Any form of academic political and social study is messy and has to recognise that there is always a dialogue between interpretations and responses. Increases in the statistics of a particular offence, for example, might encourage policy change; equally changes in policy can affect the recording of offending behaviour within the statistics. Similarly, ideas about the causation of particular crimes cannot be readily separated from policing and penal policies; and criminal justice policy in the twentieth century particularly has been closely linked with broader social policy. To make the content manageable the book is divided roughly into three. The first part deals broadly with the kind of evidence that exists for levels and types of crime, and for those identified as offenders. The media, social commentators, police and politicians, as well as the general public often speak of 'criminals' as if these were an identifiable group existing outside of society and following a distinct criminal lifestyle. During the twentieth century there were some individuals who chose to break the law as a means of earning their daily bread, yet a brief consideration of the variety of behaviours defined as crimes demonstrates the sheer range of such behaviours. The serial burglar, who may have considered himself as equipped with some form of skill and professionalism, was very different from the serial rapist whose motivation was, most likely, a perverted assertion of masculine power. The youth who, following the expansion of the late twentieth-century night-time economy, got very drunk and severely assaulted a fellow might face the same charge as an enforcer in one of the racecourse gangs of the inter-war period. Yet their social origins and way of life could be poles apart; and while for the former the assault might be a single offence, never repeated, the latter was most likely a veteran street-fighter who indulged also in other forms of offending.

The second part of the book, Chapters 6 and 7, addresses the way in which twentieth-century crime was mediated by various forms of media and by different kinds of expert. Sensational crime has always been a staple of newspapers and other types of media. One noticeable element here is how fiction and supposedly non-fiction sometimes employed the same tropes. Moreover some of those claiming to be experts on crime, especially many among the police officers and the former offenders who wrote of their 'true crime' experiences, crafted their memoirs (or allowed their ghost writers to craft their memoirs) similarly. Other forms of expert, specifically the academic criminologist whose numbers grew enormously in the second half of the century, drew attention to this but the academic's portrayal of crime never gave the same frisson and, while it may have reflected the reality of the petty nature of most criminal offending and of who was stigmatised, who was arrested and processed through the criminal justice system, it failed to dislodge the lurid and the sensational.

The final section of the book, Chapters 8, 9 and 10, deals with principal components of the criminal justice system: the police, the courts and the different penal sanctions employed across the century. It charts the ways in which these components changed as a result of pressures, both internal and external, and as a result of shifts in the broader economic, social and political culture. A very brief chapter then rounds the whole off with some concluding remarks.

References and notes

1 E.P. Thompson, *The Making of the English Working Class*, London: Gollancz, 1963, p. 12.

2 Pieter Spierenburg, *A History of Murder: personal violence in Europe from the Middle Ages to the present*, Cambridge: Polity Press, 2008.

3 Ina Zweiniger-Bargielowska, *Austerity in Britain: rationing, controls, and consumption 1939–1955*, Oxford: Oxford University Press, 2000, pp. 157–9.

4 Neil Gordon Orr, 'Keep the home fires burning: peace day in Luton, 1919', *Family and Community History*, 2, 1 (1999) pp. 17–31; John Stevenson and Chris Cook, *The Slump: society and politics during the depression*, London: Jonathan Cape, 1977, pp. 207–8; *The Times*, 4 November 1985, p. 13, letter from Professor John Bohstedt, one of the leading analysts of riotous behaviour in eighteenth- and early nineteenth-century England; Clive Emsley, 'Police forces in England and France during the inter-war years', in Clive Emsley and Barbara Weinberger (eds), *Policing Western Europe: politics, professionalism and public order, 1850–1940*, Westport, CN: Greenwood Press, 1991, p. 170 and n. 44; Seumas Milne, *The Enemy Within: the secret war against the miners*, London: Pan Books, 1995, pp. 371–2.

5 MEPO 2/9367, Report from Chief Superintendent Walters, 30 October 1952.

6 *Parl. Debs. (Lords)*, 24 May, 1965, col. 648 and 21 June, 1965, col. 342.

7 Malcolm Gaskell, *Hellish Nell: last of Britain's witches*, London: Fourth Estate, 2001.

8 Cecil Chapman, *The Poor Man's Court of Justice: twenty-five years as a metropolitan magistrate*, London: Hodder and Stoughton, 1925, p. 153.

9 Sir William Macpherson, *The Stephen Lawrence Inquiry: report*, Cm 4262-1, London: HMSO, 1999, para. 6.34.

10 Clive Emsley, *Hard Men: violence in England since 1750*, London: Hambledon, 2005, pp. 9, 180 and 184. See also, Gitta Sereny, *The Case of Mary Bell: a portrait of a child who murdered*, new edition, London: Pimlico, 1995; and see below, chap. 4, pp. 80–1.

11 Victor Bailey, 'English prisons, penal culture and the abatement of imprisonment, 1895–1922', *Journal of British Studies*, 36, 3 (1997) pp. 285–324.

12 Iain Dale (ed.), *Conservative Party: general election manifestos, 1900–1997*, London: Routledge, 2000, p. 35.

13 Andrew Rutherford, *Criminal Justice and the Pursuit of Decency*, Oxford: Oxford University Press, 1993, chap. 1.

14 David Garland, *Punishment and Welfare: a history of penal strategies*, Aldershot: Gower, 1985; *idem, The Culture of Control: crime and social order in contemporary society*, Oxford: Oxford University Press, 2001.

15 Geoffrey Hosking, 'Trust and distrust: a suitable theme for historians?', *Transactions of the Royal Historical Society*, 16 (2006) pp. 95–115.

16 Tony Blair, 'Why crime is a socialist issue', *New Statesman and Society*, 29 Jan. 1993, pp. 27–8.

17 *Evening Standard*, 6 Oct. 1993, p. 1. Howard's speech was picked up and reported in detail in all of the daily and the Sunday papers.

18 Ian Loader, 'Has liberal criminology "lost"?', the Edith Saville Memorial Lecture, 2007. My thanks to Professor Loader for permission to cite material from this.

CHAPTER 2

The pattern of crime

Alarge number of the questions that are most commonly posed about the history of crime and about the pattern of crime from year to year, and decade to decade, are ultimately statistical. How much was there? Was it increasing or decreasing? Did it increase or decrease as a result of specific economic or political events or processes? Did it increase or decrease over time as a result of shifting cultural and social attitudes and behaviours? On the face of it the questions are simple; but offering answers is fraught with difficulty not least because the available statistics are so contentious and themselves raise so many questions. Do they really provide a reflection of the pattern of crime? Or, given the ways in which they are collected and categorised by people working in the criminal justice system, do they reflect little more than the shifting agendas and policies of sections of that system?

By the beginning of the twentieth century judicial statistics had been collected for almost a century, although the kind of data then being assembled had only been settled in the mid-1850s. Local police forces were required to transmit to the Home Office annual returns of crimes that had been reported and the effectiveness of the police follow-up; local courts were required to submit details of offenders brought before them and the types of sentences passed. In the Home Office the data was aggregated, checked and then published with an introduction that drew attention to any matters that appeared to stand out in the annual figures. The introductions might also include discussions of longer-term relationships between crime and economic, political or social developments such as world war or economic depression. In 1928, for example, a particularly extensive introduction made the assumption, and then proceeded to develop it with figures, that a 'huge rise in offences of "breaking-in" ' in country districts was 'a by-product of the coming of the motor vehicle'. A few pages further on it explored the question of whether, as a result of late nineteenth-century educational reforms, 'criminals nowadays use brain rather than brawn'. Seven years later, specifically because of the Home Secretary's appointment of a committee to examine the use of corporal punishment by the courts, there was detailed comment on recent employment of the sanction.[1]

The problems with the judicial statistics begin with the very division of the offence categories; 'crime', as discussed above in the introductory chapter, covers a variety of different behaviours. There is little to link a premeditated, violent assault culminating in murder with an opportunist theft from a shop display stand, but both are defined by the law as crimes. John Wainwright, who served for 20 years in the West Yorkshire Police before embarking on a career as a successful crime-writer, made the point about how his force used the broad category of 'crime' to their own ends in the middle of the century.

If, for instance, a house was broken into and some contents were stolen, it was obviously a crime, and treated as such. But if, after a fortnight, that housebreaking was still classified as 'undetected', something had to be done to make the crime statistics look healthier. So, if you then saw a youngster using a catapult against glass in the street-lighting, you would book him. Not merely because he was doing something wrong, but also because that, too, was a 'crime' and the broken glass of the street-lamp countered the house-breaking: one 'undetected' balanced by one 'detected'. On the graph – on every graph all the way up to the top office – these were merely 'crimes'. A stolen milk-bottle was no less important than an office-breaking; wilful damage to a flower-bed could compensate on paper for rape.[2]

This suggests that, whenever possible, it would be more sensible to dis-aggregate the broad numbers and focus down on particular forms of offence. Indeed, this is what the divisions in the Judicial Statistics claim to do, but there remain questions about what the figures for particular offences actually show. The Home Office expected the various police forces to list all the crimes reported to them, but the police could have their own agenda and present their figures in the light that they wished. Thus, for the first third of the twentieth century Metropolitan Police stations had a Suspected Stolen Book and many of the items listed there were never transferred to the official lists of reported crimes. These books were abolished on 1 June 1932; in the year following there was a significant increase in the figures for reported larceny and the Commissioner put much of the increase down to this abolition.[3]

There may have been some sense in the Suspected Stolen Book since people who had reported a single precious item to have been stolen might have been too embarrassed, on discovering that it had merely been mislaid, to go to the police station to report it 'found'. But, more seriously, by listing some reported thefts as merely 'suspected stolen' the police could make their success rate look better, and criticism that the police had failed to detect offences was never far from the minds of senior police officers. The rank and file, who knew the reality of the streets, may have been rather more sceptical. Shortly after the Second World War a poetic Essex police officer addressed the matter of poor police detection rates in the force's magazine:

Those Home Office mystics,
Who compile the statistics,
Concerning detections of crime,
Have been much perplexed,
That the figures annexed,
Show a tendency now to decline.

For the policeman-poet the answer was simple: policemen, like other sensible, respectable members of the working class, had allotments that gave them much to worry about over the summer.

What this data collected,
Of crimes undetected,
Has sadly omitted to show,
Is the great concentration,
Shown at a Police Station,
On how to make vegetables grow.

Take the chap on the street,
On a night duty beat,
With hundreds of doorknobs to try,
Can he give his attention
To crime and prevention
While his onions are smitten with fly?[4]

In the last quarter of the century the police were expected to demonstrate that they were providing value for money. They were also expected to measure their performance against centrally imposed targets. In such circumstances there was a great temptation to imply favourable clear-up rates and to conceal offences – as police slang had it, to 'cuff' them, as a conjuror supposedly hides cards up his sleeve.

Tangentially it is important to note that there were several other institutions involved in preventing and prosecuting crime that did not have to send their statistics to the Home Office. These included the British Transport Police, formed in 1949 out of the remaining railway police forces, the Ministry of Defence Police, established in 1971 from the civilian constabularies responsible to the War Office, the Admiralty and the Air Ministry, and the UK Atomic Energy Police, established in the 1950s to protect nuclear installations. By the turn of the millennium these three police institutions were recording around 80,000 offences annually between them. Some of these offences did appear on the official Home Office statistics, since local forces increasingly included on their own returns any incidents in their district that involved the British Transport Police and any offences that involved joint operations with one of the non-Home Office institutions. It was the same with cases of benefit and tax fraud investigated by the Inland Revenue, Customs and Excise and the Benefits Agency. The latter agencies kept records of the number of offenders given financial penalties outside the criminal courts and the amounts of revenue saved or clawed back; they did not keep details of the total number of offences brought to their notice.[5]

If the police had their own agenda for some offences and occasionally used dubious discretion in the collection and massaging of the crime statistics, private individuals also had agendas when it came to reporting, or not reporting offences. A few women, victims of domestic violence, went to the police not to bring charges against a violent partner but apparently in the hope that the police might dissuade their attacker from further such abuse. 'The parties are husband and wife' ran an entry in the Refused Charge Book for the police station on the Isle of Dogs in March 1910, 'and at the station the complainant declined to charge.'[6] Such entries were not uncommon; after all, a successful prosecution for such an assault in this period could cost a poor working-class family dear if the principal breadwinner was imprisoned, albeit for only a week or so. Many other women probably made no complaint and hence not even a surviving police station Refused Charge Book has any record of their suffering. Male victims of domestic violence could be too embarrassed to report attacks. Men injured in fights often saw it as a matter of their honour and masculinity not to make a complaint to the police and not to bring charges. This was particularly apparent in inter-gang conflicts such as those between the strong-arm men working for certain bookies on racecourses during the inter-war period. As ex-Detective Superintendent John Gosling explained in his memoirs, it was impossible to get a complaint, and hence a prosecution, even if the police had witnessed the violence.

I had seen, let us say, Jack chivving Harry – but my evidence was useless. If I pulled in Jack, Harry would swear on oath that it wasn't Jack who did it. The gangs like to fight their own battles.[7]

Manifestly the statistics do not give the overall level of crime, and since the nineteenth century students of crime statistics have been acutely aware of the 'dark figure', that is the difference between the number of crimes reported to the police and the number of crimes actually committed. There is no way of assessing the dark figure and whether or not it varies from year to year. In 1964 the distinguished criminologist Leon Radzinowicz estimated that 'crimes brought into the open and punished represented no more than 15 per cent of the great mass actually committed.' Some of his colleagues called this an informed guess; others called it mere spe-culation. In a chapter on the dark figure written ten years later, he stuck to his estimate.[8] But such an estimate, however informed, also makes the assumption that, probably, people report offences committed against them in roughly the same numbers year on year. An equally rational assumption is that the police have roughly the same agenda in the way that they record crime year on year and that brief upturns or downturns are to be expected when laws change and when police practices change. But, informed or not, rational or not, these remain assumptions and hence the continuing debate about what the statistics mean and particularly whether they reveal any genuine patterns in criminal activity.

Howard Taylor has described the administration of criminal justice developing from the mid-nineteenth century into an increasingly imper-sonal and routine system almost lacking in purpose. He argued that the bureaucrats responsible for the system applied rules of averages to bud-gets, prison quotas and the other elements within the system. Moreover, he suggested that the regulation of the budgets had an increasing influence on the statistics of crime. Cash limits restricted the money available for pro-secutions with a knock-on impact for the amount of crime recorded and followed up. He suggested that a further element had a similar impact in the first part of the twentieth century. Wartime pressures and changes in licensing regulations led the hard-pressed police to cut their focus on drunks and vagrants. Following the police strike of 1918 and the sub-sequent increase in police pay, there were pressures both central and local to cut police numbers so as to save money. The police, in consequence, fought back by increasing the number of serious offences that they recorded in order to make crime control more of a political issue, to make their own position more secure and to make police budgets, numbers and policies major competitors for resources against other developing social services. Central government, Taylor maintained, had no problem with this since, while the police were redefining themselves, first and foremost, as crime fighters, they had also given up the pursuit of the old regulatory offences such as drunkenness, vagrancy, school attendance and petty assault for the more financially lucrative pursuit of motor traffic offenders who could afford fines.[9] The problem with Taylor's arguments is that they also rely heavily on assumption. He was unable to find any clear evidence of Treasury limits on criminal justice budgets that restricted the reporting and prosecuting of crime. Nor does he explain how nearly 200 hundred police forces colluded to achieve a result favourable to themselves in the half century or so following the Great War. But this is not to deny that institutions can profoundly affect the criminal statistics. Indeed, subsequent work has suggested that the victims of some suspicious deaths in the late nineteenth century – infants, strangers and foreigners, prostitutes, poor women with alcohol problems, asylum inmates – were often not considered worthy the time and effort of a serious police investigation.[10]

The importance of the way in which the police and other criminal justice institutions could shape the annual statistics began to be stressed by academic criminologists during the 1970s.[11] From 1982 the official statistics were periodically supplemented by the British Crime Survey (BCS). The survey carried out under the auspices of the Home Office involved both questionnaires and interviews with a sample of several thousand adults. The rationale was that by asking a sample of the public if they had been the victim of a crime in the preceding twelve months, and if so, what sort of crime and whether they had reported it to the police, the responses might be extrapolated to provide a fuller picture of the overall pattern of offences. Eight such surveys had been conducted by the year 2000. They showed a pattern similar to that of the official statistics – specifically, a rise to a peak in the early 1990s, with a slight downward trend from the middle of the latter decade. Various flaws were identified in the BCS, specifically that they did not capture sufficiently the extent of sensitive crimes, and particularly sexual and domestic offences. Yet the British Crime Survey was increasingly reckoned to be a more reliable assessment of the pattern of crime and to provide some clue to the dark figure. By the turn of the century it was viewed as a much better measure of crime than the police recorded statistics.

For all the problems and reservations, however, the annual judicial statistics provide a starting point for discussion. Moreover, while academics in particular might query the validity of the crime statistics and enjoy the luxury of being able to make careful analyses of long-term trends, others do not. A newspaper editor's task is to sell newspapers and the eye-catching headline and speedy précis of the more exciting aspects of crime has always tended to take precedence over any careful, nuanced assessment of the statistics. It is the same with the editor of a radio or television news programme; a limited time slot exists for each item and this discouraged the delivery of lengthy, considered analyses in preference to short, pithy accounts that were designed to hold an audience. And, as the twentieth century progressed, politicians increasingly were obliged to respond, or to challenge their opponents over short-term fluctuations in the statistics that may, over time, have meant very little. Hence the statistics of crime commonly provided a basis for media and political debate, and a benchmark by which policy was assessed, made and remade. Both the ferocity of the debates and the benchmarks have varied over time and have always been greatly influenced by the economic, political or social context.

The statistics in Figures 2.1, 2.2 and 2.3 give overall crime figures adjusted to take account of population growth. Figure 2.1 charts the pattern across the century; Figures 2.2 and 2.3 close in on shorter periods to give a clearer idea of fluctuations. The twentieth century began with a

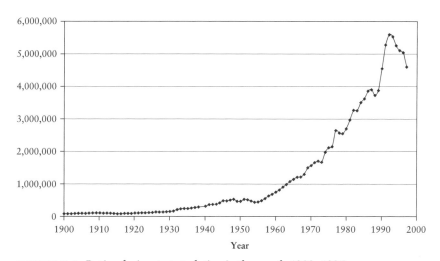

FIGURE 2.1 *Ratio of crime to population in thousands 1900–1997*

Source: Constructed from the annual crime figures given in the *Judicial Statistics* and from the population details provided by the Census office (Office for National Statistics)

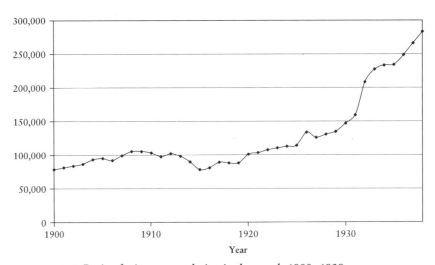

FIGURE 2.2 *Ratio of crime to population in thousands 1900–1938*

Source: Constructed from the annual crime figures given in the *Judicial Statistics* and from the population details provided by the Census office (Office for National Statistics)

broad feeling of satisfaction about the pattern and the direction of crime. The overall statistics suggested that there had been a general levelling out of crime since the 1850s. Breaking the overall figures down, the major exception appeared to be burglary, the figures for which ran somewhat counter to the overall pattern. There was a very slight increase in the statistics for all crimes before the First World War. The increase is barely perceptible in Figure 2.1, but becomes much clearer in Figure 2.2 as a result of the shorter time bracket. During the war, following a pattern detected during earlier conflicts, the overall figures dipped very slightly. In the inter-war period crime began to increase; the pattern was relatively steady during the 1920s with a slightly sharper upward turn in the 1930s. There were no figures for 1939 but, as demonstrated by Figure 2.3, the increase was maintained during the Second World War. Figure 2.3 also shows that, allowing for the occasional rise and dip, the crime statistics levelled out during the late 1940s and early 1950s, but from the mid-1950s there was a marked upward turn that continued unremittingly for the next 40 years.[12] New legislation and new ways of recording and categorising various offences could have an impact upon the figures. The Theft Act of 1968, for example, extended the offence of burglary and the old offences of house- and shop-breaking disappeared. At the end of the 1990s a number of summary offences, particularly involving assault and harassment, began to be included in the published statistics. This inclusion led to an increase in the statistics of more than a quarter of a million in the instances of violence

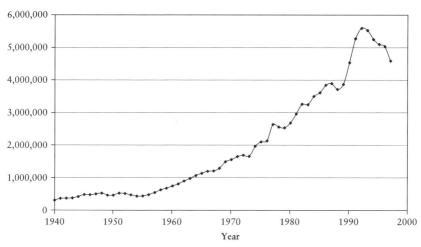

FIGURE 2.3 *Ratio of crime to population in thousands 1940–1997*

Source: Constructed from the annual crime figures given in the *Judicial Statistics* and from the population details provided by the Census office (Office for National Statistics)

against the person. The statistics given in the three figures printed here thus end in 1998 so as not to cloud what is generally acknowledged as an overall decline in crime detected as beginning in the mid-1990s and continuing into the new century.

When the crime statistics were published at the dawn of the new century both the Home Office and the press hailed the downturn in crime as a triumph. Even among the quality press, however, the headlines demonstrated the confusion about the best way to interpret such figures over time. 'Largest fall in crime for twenty years', declared *The Guardian*. *The Daily Telegraph* proclaimed: 'Eighty year crime rise "is reversed"'; and *The Times* made the same figures look even better: 'Crime starting to fall after a hundred years'.[13]

There are an infinite number of variables that it is difficult to allow for in the overall pattern of the statistics. Police foot patrols were stretched more and more in the early part of the century and declined considerably as the police became mechanised in the period after the Second World War and the number of specialised roles increased. Did the declining presence of the beat constable limit the options of poorer victims in being able to report offences? Did the increase in the number of telephones available in people's homes, and then at the very end of the century the availability of mobile phones, provide increasing opportunities for reporting offences? What impact did the spread of moveable property insurance have on the reporting of thefts? Or on the fraudulent reporting of thefts?

Equally, it is difficult to link the broad pattern of the crime statistics to the great economic, political and social changes and upheavals of the century and thus to produce an explanation for criminal behaviour that fits easily and logically with other social phenomena. In the first half of the century the country was engaged in two colossal world wars. The recruitment of large numbers of young men into the armed services probably had an impact on the statistics of crime. Young men were always the group in society most likely to be noted for committing criminal offences and, as the introduction to the cumulative statistics for the 1939–45 period commented, 'the number of offences against the ordinary criminal law dealt with by courts martial, such as thefts and frauds . . . must have been considerable.'[14] Many contemporaries believed that the First World War had a significant impact on crime. A perceived increase in juvenile offending was put down to fathers and schoolmasters serving at the front and women replacing them at the workplace, leaving no parents at home and few men in the schools to supervise and discipline children, especially boys. There was also concern that men, brutalised by their experiences at the front would return home and slip easily into violent crime.[15] The evidence of the annual statistics did not confirm these fears although in the introduction to the statistics for 1923 it was suggested that an increase in fraud and commercial dishonesty was 'in many cases assignable to the long continued debasing effects of the war upon conduct and character.' The point was reiterated the following year.[16]

As in the previous conflict, the Second World War witnessed an increase in juvenile offending. Explanations ranged from the removal of parental discipline – fathers at the front, mothers at the factory – to the unruliness of evacuee children. But while the statistics for young people found guilty of criminal offences increased from 1939 to 1941, thereafter, until the end of the war, they declined. The explanation for this is probably to be found in many police forces deciding to replace the prosecution of juveniles by giving cautions.[17]

Evidence from the Second World War suggests that various forms of fraud and misappropriation of military materials were prominent among some servicemen. They knew, for example, that petrol was plentiful for the armed forces, but not for civilians and hence could be sold very profitably on the black market both at home and overseas. Probably the bulk of the offending by service personnel occurred overseas. Soldiers committed crimes for a variety of reasons. Some appear to have committed offences shortly before their unit was sent to the front; it was a way of avoiding danger. Others, often deserters, appear to have engaged in large-scale theft, fraud or vice rackets behind the shifting frontlines as the allied armies liberated Europe. '[I]t is not an exaggeration to say', noted one Army Provost, 'that a majority of long term deserters have civilian criminal records and are skilful and dangerous types.' But it is also tempting to suggest that he would think that anyway. The military in wartime was an exceptional environment and most men that indulged in theft, looting, fraud and worse probably did so only as a result of their ephemeral involvement in a community and culture that faced death and danger as a matter of course and that also enjoyed a novel camaraderie. 'I'm very ashamed of it, but I pinched a wireless set [from an old German lady]', recalled one veteran. 'You get into a certain frame of mind, callousness must come into it because of what you had been going through.'[18] Probably such offending by servicemen in wartime was usually discarded, with the battle-dress, on the return to Civvy Street. As in the aftermath of the First World War, there were once again concerns about returning, brutalised veterans, especially those who had been trained in unarmed combat in the new special forces such as the commandos and paratroops. These concerns were dismissed as unfounded by Sir Harold Scott, Commissioner of the Metropolitan Police from 1945 to 1953, and John C. Spencer who conducted one of the few serious sociological studies of the effects of service life on criminal offending.[19] Towards the end of the century, however, the concept was revived with a particular focus on men who appeared to have suffered psychological problems as a result of military service in the conflicts that arose with the end of empire and especially the Falklands War and the lengthy 'peace-keeping' role of the army in Northern Ireland.[20]

Turning away from wartime, in 1926 there was an increase in indictable offences which the introduction to the annual statistics noted appeared almost entirely in the mining districts and which it attributed to the effects of industrial action in those districts and the General Strike.

In the mining districts, many of the larcenies were thefts of coal or other fuel. Other larcenies may have been committed by thieves who took advantage of the diversion of police from ordinary duties during the stoppage.[21]

During the depression of the inter-war years 'it was fairly generally accepted' that economic factors played a significant role in the causation of crime, but demonstrating clear links between unemployment and offending taxed even the most notable criminologists. In keeping with what he claimed was 'fairly generally accepted', Herman Mannheim produced the tortuous conclusion that:

*Where unemployment and crime both stand at a high watermark, it can
safely be assumed that the latter is largely due to the former; where the
crime figures remain low in spite of much unemployment, certain factors
are obviously at work which counterbalance its evil effects. In other
words, the fact that there is so often much unemployment with little
crime does not prove that, wherever we find a great deal of both, crime
has not resulted from unemployment.*[22]

Unemployment and the economic depression may have contributed to
some of the inter-war increase in crime. Equally, a very general assumption, like that above, can be made for the impact of affluence in fostering
crime among the generation that came to maturity after the Second World
War. According to research conducted for the Home Office by Simon Field:

*Prior to the Second World War, increases in national income were
heavily invested in improvements in the basic necessaries of life, such as
good quality food and housing, heating, lighting and public transport.
Increased expenditures in these areas did little to affect the opportunities
for crime. It is only in the last half century that increasing wealth has
been devoted to more stealable commodities – cars and electronic goods
prominent among them. This feature of the half century may explain why
economic growth during this historical period can be linked so clearly to
rising property crime.*[23]

So it is conceivable that the growth of a consumer society after the Second
World War, in which more and more people had more and more property
that was relatively easy to move, contributed significantly to the rise in
property crime. But here too the evidence tends to make the argument
complex and confusing. The official criminal statistics show a 50 per cent
increase in burglary. Data from the British Insurance Association also
reveals a massive increase in burglary losses suffered by its members.
However, the increase in the scale of insurance company losses may have
been considerably aggravated by the growth of policies during the decade
that promised the cost of a brand new replacement for a stolen item; similarly it is possible that the growth of these policies fostered some growth in
fraudulent claims. The 1970s pre-dated the British Crime Survey, but a
succession of surveys from the Office of Population Censuses and Surveys
that sampled household expenditures and experiences over the decade
suggested, in complete contrast to these other sources, that there had been
little or no change in the incidence of domestic burglary. In the event it may
be that the large increase in the crime statistics was the result of changes in
police methods of recording domestic burglary.[24]

Burglary is one of the more serious ways of illegally appropriating the property of others. Theft in all its forms, together with the handling of stolen goods, accounted for some three-quarters of the offences recorded at the beginning of the century. It remained at about 70 per cent of the total for most of the century, gradually dropping to slightly over one half at the end. But very few thefts involved violence and it was generally only this minority of violent incidents that attracted publicity and that generated most concern among the population. Public anxieties about crime may thus be disproportionately driven by relatively rare cases. The same can be said of that crime which has caused the most sensational headlines, sold the highest number of books and attracted the widest audiences: murder. Murder has also often been used as a benchmark for assessing the degree of violence in a society.[25]

The homicide statistics for the twentieth century include murder, manslaughter and infanticide; the difference between murder and manslaughter depends upon the perceived intent of the perpetrator. The figures suggest that England and Wales were remarkably non-violent. The number of homicides remained at around 300 a year, and was often below this, more or less until the end of the 1960s. By the 1970s the figures were around 450 a year and occasionally even higher. The increase continued into the 1990s when the number of known homicides annually was well into the 700s. The statistics for attempted murder and for threats and conspiracy to murder also show an increase, especially the threats and conspiracy categories during the closing years of the century. The statistics themselves have to be qualified in several ways. First, they need to be set alongside the population. Thus, in the decade of increase from the late 1960s to the early 1980s, the homicide rate went up from around seven deaths per million of the population to around 11. But the statistics need also to be qualified by the outcomes decided by the courts, and over the same period only around one-third of the homicide cases heard by the courts resulted in a conviction for murder; two-fifths were decided as manslaughter; and in the remainder of cases the accused was concluded to have acted on account of diminished responsibility.[26] The term 'diminished responsibility' was introduced in the 1957 Murder Act. It extended the M'Naghten Rules that, since the 1840s, had shaped the way in which courts decided upon a defendant's capacity for rational thought at the time of an offence. Diminished responsibility led to cases of euthanasia and killing because of a morbid jealousy that could be defined as psychosis being defined as manslaughter.[27]

TABLE 2.1 *Home Office breakdown of classes of murderers sentenced to death and their victims, 1900–1948*

Victims	Men	Women
Wives and husbands	209	11
Parents	18	1
Sweethearts, mistresses, lovers	290	4
Children over one year in sexual assaults	30	0
Other children over one year	43	40
Women, other than those above, in sexual assaults	41	0
Men and women during robbery	150	7
Men and women, other than those above, in quarrels or from revenge or jealousy	105	2
After drink	26	0
Police and prison officers	19	0
Miscellaneous	74	1

Source: Anthony Martienssen, *Crime and the Police*, Harmondsworth: Penguin, 1953, p. 166
N.B. Of the 1,002 men sentenced to death above, 611 were executed; of the 66 women, 11 were executed.

As with other forms of criminality men were more likely to be responsible for homicide than women, except in the relatively few instances of infanticide. What was usually unclear from selective media reporting that focused on sensational cases of murder, was the high percentage of homicides that involved members of the same family, people who were otherwise intimate or who were at least acquainted in some way. The reality of this situation in the first half of the century was exposed in a breakdown of murderers and their victims prepared in the Home Office and reproduced in Table 2.1. Studies of the statistics made much later in the century produced similar findings and were in keeping with contemporary victim studies that had concluded that the family was one of the most common sites for interpersonal violence. An analysis of Home Office material relating to homicides between 1997 and 2001 found that almost one-third (31 per cent) could be defined as 'domestic', and three-quarters of these involved a man killing a woman. Of the remaining homicides in the survey, more than a fifth (22 per cent) resulted from a violent clash between young men. Only 7 per cent of the total occurred during the course of another crime and only about one killing in 100 involved gang activity.[28]

Homicide, murder and manslaughter are descriptive words and legal categories. It is the same with the labels applied to other offences, and just as 'murder' can cover an enormous range of very different incidents, so too can 'rape' and 'robbery'. The figures for rape within the criminal statistics are striking. The twentieth century began with around 200 cases a year; the numbers began to fall reaching around 120 a year in the early 1920s and generally fewer than a hundred annually during the 1930s. They began to rise during the Second World War, peaking in 1944 (416) and 1945 (377) before dropping back to around 250 for the remainder of the 1940s. Thereafter, however, the numbers began to increase dramatically; there were around 500 cases each year at the close of the 1950s, over 800 at the end of the 1960s, 1,200 at the end of the 1970s. The numbers then soared to 6,000 by the mid 1990s and continued to rise thereafter. Probably this was not so much an increase in the incidence of rape, but rather an increase in the incidence of women reporting that they had been raped. The persistence of Victorian perceptions of morality meant that there continued to be a tremendous stigma attached to the victims of rape especially in the early part of the century. Rather than confessing publicly to a loss of sexual innocence and having intimate details of their lives probed and exposed by possibly unsympathetic police officers and by the tough, hostile questioning of defence council, embarrassed victims chose to keep silent or else opted to proceed to court with a much lesser charge, such as common assault. It could also suit the accused to plead guilty to common assault in the expectation of a lighter sentence than that for rape and recognising that his victim would go along with this to avoid the harrowing experience of the witness box.[29] At the end of the 1920s Colonel Pulteney Malcolm, the Chief Constable of Cheshire, urged his fellows to consider the problem of the under-reporting of sexual offences. He believed that this was 'due to the objections on the part of some most respectable and law-abiding persons, to young females being forced to appear frequently in Courts of Law and be subjected to continuous and painful ordeals'. But he, and the other chief constables, also made another assumption: that this only happened in the less serious cases of sexual assault.[30] There appears also to have been the belief that rape was an extremely rare occurrence and the assumption that, when a case involved acquaintances, the woman had consented to intercourse. Women police tended to be more sympathetic in their questioning of rape victims but, during the inter-war period and beyond, many of them subscribed to the broad cultural beliefs about sexual behaviour that were common among their male colleagues.[31]

The changing sexual mores, especially from the 1960s, together with the spread of feminist awareness, the growth of 'rape suites' in police stations and a better awareness of the problems among police officers, all appear to have encouraged more victims to come forward and report rape. There were changes in the courts; the Sexual Offences (Amendment) Act of

1976 disallowed any questions about a rape complainant's previous sexual experience without the express permission of the judge. The development of the contraceptive pill meant that, by the final decades of the century, the opportunity for finding consenting sexual partners was probably greater than it had ever been. But just because a woman was taking the contraceptive pill did not necessarily affect her decision to consent to sex with a particular man; similarly, the way that she dressed or the amount of alcohol that she had drunk was no automatic green light regarding availability. During the 1980s and 1990s the terms 'date rape' and sometimes 'acquaintance rape' were employed to characterise the circumstances of a victim who knew her attacker, had gone out with him for a good time, could show no serious marks of violence on her person, but denied that she had given her consent to the sex that occurred. It was left to the police and the Crown Prosecution Service to decide on whether to proceed with a prosecution for rape, and then for a criminal court to reach a verdict on the facts presented to it. The problems were aggravated by some assailants slipping into their victim's drink undetectable drugs such as Rohypnol. Conflicting and muddied evidence was politicised by the insistence of radical feminists that rape was less a criminal offence and more an instrument by which men asserted power and managed to keep women in a state of constant fear and, ultimately, subjection. This did not necessarily mean that all men were potential rapists; rather this perspective saw the fear of rape as a means of control by fathers, brothers and husbands to limit the movement and independence of women.[32]

In May 1983 two young paratroops were convicted of raping a girl in Aldershot Barracks and another four were found guilty of indecent assault. At the time of the attack, in November 1981, the victim had been only 15 years old. She had entered the barracks willingly and the court heard evidence of young women regularly being taken into the barracks even though this was against regulations. But the girl was no willing participant in the events that followed her illicit entry into the men's quarters; she had been held down violently during the assaults with soldiers gleefully crying out 'Gang Bang!'[33] This attack had distant echoes of the date rape problem; however, rape by a group of relative strangers was not typical, and nor were attacks by single, sexual predator who was previously unknown to the victim. The evidence from different victim surveys at the end of the century stressed that, as with murder, the biggest threat of rape came not from gangs or strangers, but from people known to the victim, often husbands or partners. A major problem here, however, was that until the early 1990s and a ruling by the Law Lords, the law maintained that marriage meant that a husband had continual consent for sexual activity with his wife at any time he wished.[34] But in spite of the growth of rape suites, of greater sympathetic awareness among police officers, of restrictions on the cross-examination of victims and of the legal recognition that rape could occur within marriage, there continued to be suspicion among police, prosecutors and sections of the public that many rape accusations were false. Moreover, a very high proportion of complainants that appear to have been genuine victims continued to withdraw their allegations, especially at the initial reporting and investigative stages.[35]

While there is good reason to be aware of the complicated factors shaping the relationship between the statistics of rape, the rise in these figures towards the end of the century appeared shocking to the public. The same could be said about the statistics of robbery. At the beginning of the century the number of robberies ranged between 200 and 300 a year; the figures dropped in the second decade, returned to around 200 in the three years following the First World War, but then fell away again. There was a slight, general increase during the inter-war period and a rise to around 1,000 offences a year in the immediate aftermath of the Second World War. The figures doubled to some 2,000 a year at the close of the 1950s and then began to rise inexorably to a peak of 74,000 in 1995. It seems probable that a significant reason for the increase in the rape statistics was the greater preparedness of victims to report the crime to the police in the closing decades of the century. But it would be difficult to make a similar claim for the even greater increase in the statistics of robbery. The word itself had a specific legal meaning throughout the century; it involved the use, or the threat of force to steal something from a person or institution. The meaning thus encompassed an organised raid on business premises or goods in transit in which the yield could run into many thousands of pounds, such as the so-called Great Train Robbery of 1963, which netted £2.5 million, and the bullion theft at the Brinks Matt depository in Heathrow Airport 20 years later which, much to the surprise of the perpetrators themselves, took ten times that amount. But the meaning also applied to street attacks for relatively small amounts of ready cash, the offence popularly characterised in the media during the 1970s as 'mugging'. The perpetrators of the big robberies were commonly individuals who had made a career of criminal offending and who planned and organised their operations. 'Muggers', however, ranged from the amateur opportunist to those who have been labelled 'addict robbers', a type of offender who robbed to feed a drug habit and who appeared to grow in numbers with the noted increase in opiate addiction in the closing decades of the century.[36] This considerable range in the behaviours encompassed by the legal term 'robbery' make it particularly difficult to detect any broad trends.

The statistics can be disaggregated regionally as well as by offence type. The annual introductions to the official statistics occasionally picked up on regional differences. In 1908, for example, it was noted that there had been a considerable increase in offending in the principal manufacturing and mining districts; building on the assumption that habitual offenders probably varied little from year to year and that white collar offences such as embezzlement and fraud were also fairly constant, the Home Office statisticians concluded that the increase was due to the 'marked depression of trade and an unusual amount of unemployment over the year'.[37] Twenty years later, at the onset of the great depression, similar conclusions were developed between the industrial north and the south of England, and between industrial Glamorgan and Monmouth and the rest of Wales. While crime had increased in the industrial areas, there were interesting qualifications. It appeared that

Industrial depression in the North has not made the incidence of crime among mature men over 30 higher in the North; at many points it is lower. Secondly, there are various indications that, in the South, men and youths of ages 21 to 30 and youths of 16 to 21 are more prone than those in the North to offences of downright lawlessness. But as regards boys under 16, the number found guilty in the North of offences of dishonesty is out of all proportion higher than in the South. It seems that the various conditions arising out of industrial depression in the North are calculated to result in picking and stealing and the like among the very young, while relatively prosperous conditions in the South tempt youths and young men to exploit opportunities of more adventurous species of crime.[38]

Mannheim deployed local figures to explore what he thought to be the important connection between crime and unemployment during the inter-war period. He set figures for Gateshead, South Shields and Norwich against each other but found that the figures for crime and unemployment only coincided here in the case of juvenile delinquency. A comparison of the figures for Leeds and Sheffield created similar problems and he found it 'little short of a miracle that there should hardly have been any increase in indictable offences in Sheffield in years like 1926 and 1931 when unemployment nearly doubled.' His hoped-for relationship appeared to exist in the figures for Birmingham, Liverpool and Manchester. But he was also conscious of the high level of crime in Liverpool that he attributed to its unique nature as a port city with a marked racial and religious mix and a tradition of casual labour on the docks.[39]

While Mannheim was struggling to relate the crime figures with unemployment statistics, Stanley Bishop, a reporter for the populist weekly *John Bull* was making much simpler comparisons for his readers about the 'underworld' of the country's big cities, and drawing much simpler, populist conclusions. Leeds had a smaller population than Sheffield, but a greater crime problem; this, he suggested, was probably because of its cosmopolitan population. Manchester appeared to have 'the largest proportion of commercial swindlers and crooks who live by their wits.' Birmingham had a bigger population than Liverpool, but the latter had three times as many crimes known to the police. Bishop also noted that the Birmingham Police, commanded by the influential Cecil Moriarty whose various instruction books were used for training and guiding police officers across the country, had no cars equipped with radios, no other radios and no telephone boxes. Interestingly, however, he did not make any connection between the lack of modern equipment and the efficiency of Moriarty's men.[40]

Both Mannheim and Bishop tended to take the statistics largely at face value. A quarter of a century later, as police forces were increasingly amalgamated, the criminologists F.H. McClintock and Howard Avison hoped that the reduction in the number of separate, independent forces would make recorded crime more uniform and thus potentially more valuable. However, by setting regional variations alongside each other they produced comparisons which, while not altogether unexpected, constituted useful illustrations of the pattern of crime during the 1950s and early 1960s. All localities tended to follow the national trend of rising crime, but it was the urban areas that had the largest incidence of crime. In particular there were six major conurbations in England and Wales – Tyneside, West Yorkshire, South East Lancashire, Merseyside, the West Midlands and Greater London. These accounted for just over one-third of the population, but almost one-half of recorded crime.[41] In the last 20 years of the century more localised studies further refined these broad regional conclusions. The aim of the new work was to assess the extent to which being the victim of crime varied among different sections of the population. It focused particularly on poor, inner-city areas, and it indicated that problems of assault, burglary and robbery were far greater here than was revealed by, for example, the British Crime Survey.[42] These findings led to developments in the British Crime Survey and to samples that probed the experiences of different age and ethnic groups. But, at the end of the century, these same findings had failed to penetrate much of the media or the consciousness of the respectable and relatively well-off who, while they had less occasion to fear crime than those living in the inner cities, were the most vocal in expressing alarm and calling for vigorous measures.

The criminal statistics do not have the mathematical certainty that people often assume of hard figures, nor do they have the solidity that many of those that present them to the public imply, no matter whether these presenters be politicians, police officers or apparently authoritative and responsible sections of the media. The rough correlation between the criminal statistics published by the Home Office and those of the British Crime Survey suggests that the figures do provide a broad image of the pattern of offending. When properly contextualised, and with all their limitations recognised, the increasingly sophisticated analyses of the figures have added considerably to the understanding of crime and the changes over time. They have helped to provide a greater awareness of who were the likely victims of crime. Statistical information also contributed to a very broad awareness of who committed various crimes; but, like so many others, this issue too has to be probed further in order to establish a more nuanced picture of, for example, those that perpetrated one or two offences and those that opted for a life of crime.

References and notes

1 *Judicial Statistics of England and Wales for 1928*, 1929–30, Cmd. 3581, pp. xii–xvi; *Judicial Statistics . . . for 1937*, 1938–9, Cmd. 5878, pp. xvi–xxiv; **Hermann Mannheim**, *Social Aspects of Crime in England Between the Wars*, London: George Allen and Unwin, 1940, Appendix to Part 1, pp. 90–102 provides a full discussion of the content of statistics that covers their presentation for most of the century.

2 **John Wainwright**, *Wainwright's Beat: one man's journey with a police force*, London: Macmillan, 1987, p. 20.

3 *Judicial Statistics . . . for 1932*, 1933–4, Cmd. 4608, p. viii.

4 *The Truncheon*, IV, 1 (July 1947) p. 6.

5 **Mike Maguire**, 'Crime statistics: the "data explosion" and its implications', in **Mike Maguire**, **Rod Morgan** and **Robert Reiner**, eds, *The Oxford Handbook of Criminology*, 3rd edn. Oxford: Oxford University Press, 2002, p. 336.

6 MPHC, Refused Charge Book, K Division: Isle of Dogs (1909–1960), 13 March 1910; see also, 1 January 1910 and 19 July 1910.

7 John Gosling, *The Ghost Squad*, London: W.H. Allen, 1959, p. 161: see in general, **Clive Emsley**, *Hard Men: violence in England since 1750*, London: Hambledon, 2005, pp. 5–8, 32–5 and 60–5.

8 **Leon Radzinowicz** and **Joan King**, *The Growth of Crime: the international experience*, Harmondsworth: Penguin, 1977, p. 62.

9 **Howard Taylor**, 'Rationing crime: the political economy of criminal statistics since 1850', *Economic History Review*, 51, 3 (1998) pp. 569–90; *idem*, 'The politics of the rising crime statistics of England and Wales, 1914–1960', *CHS*, 2, 1 (1998) pp. 5–28; *idem*, 'Forging the job: a crisis of "modernization" or redundancy for the police in England and Wales, 1900–1939', *BJC*, 39, 1, (1999) pp. 113–35.

10 **John E. Archer**, 'Mysterious and suspicious deaths: missing homicides in North-West England (1850–1900)', *CHS*, 12, 1 (2008) pp. 45–63.

11 Much of the early work in this respect had its origins in the United States. A key investigation drawing attention to the role of institutions, and especially the processes of the police, in shaping the statistics was **A.K. Bottomley** and **C.A. Coleman**, *Understanding Crime Rates*, Farnborough: Saxon House, 1981.

12 For an early, influential analysis of the statistics up to the mid-1960s see **F.H. McClintock** and **N. Howard Avison**, *Crime in England and Wales*, London: Heinemann, 1968, chap. 2.

13 *The Guardian*, 26 November 2001, p. 2; *Daily Telegraph*, 26 November 2001, p. 1; *The Times*, 26 November 2001, p. 14.

14 *Judicial Statistics . . . for 1939 to 1945*, 1946–7, Cmd. 7227, p. 4.

15 See, *inter alia*, **H.T. Waddy**, *The Police Court and its Work*, London: Butterworth, 1925, chap. 11; **H.L. Cancellor**, *The Life of a London Beak*, London: Hurst and Blackett, 1930, pp. 33 and 52–3. **Clive Emsley**, 'Violent crime in England in 1919. Post-war anxieties and press narratives', *Continuity and Change*, 23, 1 (2008) pp. 173–95.

16 *Judicial Statistics . . . for 1923*, 1924–5, Cmd. 2385, p. 10; *Judicial Statistics . . . for 1924*, 1926, Cmd. 2602, p. 6.

17 **Edward Smithies**, *Crime in Wartime: a social history of crime in World War II*, London: George Allen and Unwin, 1982, chap. 10.

18 **Sean Longden**, *To the Victor the Spoils: D-Day to VE Day: the reality behind the heroism*, Moreton in Marsh: Arris Books, 2004, pp. 199 and 241.

19 **Sir Harold Scott**, *Scotland Yard*, Harmondsworth: Penguin, 1954, p. 62; **John C. Spencer**, *Crime and the Services*, London: Routledge and Kegan Paul, 1954; see also, **Alan Allport**, *Demobbed: coming home after the Second World War*, New Haven and London: Yale University Press, 2009, chap. 6.

20 Aly Renwick, *Hidden Wounds: the problems of Northern Ireland veterans in Civvy Street*, London: Barbed Wire, 1999.

21 *Judicial Statistics . . . for 1926*, 1928, Cmd. 3055, p. 5.

22 Mannheim, *Social Aspects of Crime*, pp. 123 and 151.

23 Simon Field, *Trends in Crime Revisited*, Home Office Research Study, 195, London, 2000, pp. 15–16.

24 Keith Bottomley and Ken Pease, *Crime and Punishment: interpreting the data*, Milton Keynes: Open University Press, 1986, pp. 22–4 and 35.

25 See, *inter alia*, Manuel Eisner, 'Modernization, self-control and lethal violence: the long-term dynamics of European homicide rates in theoretical perspective', *BJC*, 41 (2001) pp. 619–38; *idem*, 'Long-term historical trends in violent crime', in Michael Tonry (ed.), *Crime and Justice: a review of research*, 30 (2003) pp. 83–142.

26 Bottomley and Pease, *Crime and Punishment*, pp. 6–8.

27 Ronnie Mackay, 'Mentally abnormal offenders: disposal and criminal responsibility issues', in Mike McConville and Geoffrey Wilson (eds), *The Handbook of the Criminal Justice Process*, Oxford: Oxford University Press, 2002, pp. 467–68.

28 Fiona Brookman, *Understanding Homicide*, London: Sage, 2005, pp. 312–15; Sue Lees, *Ruling Passions: sexual violence, reputation and the law*, Buckingham: Open University Press, 1997, p. 109; Esther Sagara, 'Dangerous places: the family as a site of crime', in John Muncie and Eugene McLaughlin (eds), *The Problem of Crime*, 2nd edn. London: Sage, 2001.

29 Clive Emsley, *Hard Men: violence in England since 1750*, London: Hambledon, 2005, pp. 6–7.

30 OUPA, ACPO Bag (32) 65, Central Conference of Chief Constables 1921–1938, 26 March 1929, p. 3.

31 Louise A. Jackson, *Women Police: gender, welfare and surveillance in the twentieth century*, Manchester: Manchester University Press, 2006, p. 187.

32 The key pioneering study here is Susan Brownmiller, *Against Our Will: women and rape*, New York: Ballentine, 1975.

33 *The Times*, 5 May 1983, p. 3; 6 May, p. 3; 12 May, p. 12; 17 May, p. 2. There was a similar occurrence two years later when a WRAC went into a barrack with 30 paratroops. Thirteen of the paras were charged with rape; after a 25-day trial all were acquitted of rape, although some were found guilty of indecent assault. See Keith Soothill and Sylvia Walby, *Sex Crime in the News*, London: Routledge, 1991, pp. 71–3.

34 This common law assumption was overturned by the ruling *R v. R (Rape: marital exemption)* [1992] 1 AC 599. See also, K. Painter, *Wife Rape*.

Marriage and the Law: survey report, Faculty of Economic and Social Science, University of Manchester, 1991; **S. Walby** and **J. Allen**, *Domestic Violence, Sexual Assault and Stalking: findings from the British Crime Survey*, Home Office Research Study, no. 276, London, 2004.

35 **Liz Kelly**, **Jo Lovett** and **Linda Rogers**, *A Gap or a Chasm? Attrition in reported rape cases*, Home Office Research Study 293, London: Home Office Research Unit, 2005.

36 **Martin Gill**, *Commercial Robbery*, London: Blackstone Press, 2000. The term 'addict robbers' was coined in **John E. Conklin**, *Robbery and the Offender Justice System*, Philadelphia: J.B. Lippincott, 1972.

37 *Judicial Statistics . . . for 1908*, 1910, Cd. 5096, pp. 10–11.

38 *Judicial Statistics . . . for 1929*, 1930–31, Cmd. 3853, pp. xv–xxi.

39 Mannheim, *Social Aspects of Crime*, pp. 135–40; quotation at p. 138.

40 *John Bull*, 15 January 1937, p. 30; 22 January p. 28; 29 January p. 30; 5 February p. 30; 12 February pp. 28–30.

41 McClintock and Avison, *Crime in England and Wales*, chapters 3 and 5.

42 See, for example, **Richard Kinsey**, *Merseyside Crime Survey: first report*, Liverpool: Merseyside Metropolitan Council, 1984; **Trevor Jones**, **Brian Maclean** and **Jock Young**, *The Islington Crime Survey: crime, victimzation and policing in inner-city London*, Aldershot: Gower, 1986; **Adam Crawford**, et al., *Second Islington Crime Survey*, London: Middlesex Polytechnic, 1990.

CHAPTER 3

Criminal lives

On 28 September 1926 George Lawrence appeared before the London Sessions charged with stealing a Gladstone bag and its contents from St Pancras Station. He entered a plea of guilty. It was not Lawrence's first offence. He told the court that his father, a staunch Baptist, had declared him to be 'born a devil.' At the age of 10 years he had been sent to a reformatory school for three years for a theft. But that was 72 years earlier and since then Lawrence had collected another 36 convictions and prison sentences amounting to 53 years. Sir Robert Wallace KC, chairing the sessions, considered it extremely difficult to know what to do with Lawrence. He opted to postpone sentence, and send him to the workhouse. A quarter of a century later, on 4 January 1950, at the Manchester City Sessions, 62-year-old Ernest Lacy was sentenced to 8 years preventive detention for the theft of a suit, valued at £8. The Court of Appeal dismissed Lacy's appeal that, in view of his age, he should only be required to serve a five-year sentence. The court's decision was based on Lacy's record. He had notched up 42 convictions since 1906.[1]

There has long been a popular assumption that criminals start out as petty offenders when juveniles and progress to more serious crimes as they grow older and more experienced. The assumption is not purely English; it goes back at least to the nineteenth century and rests on the belief that individual criminals make career choices and stick with their 'trade' as others pursue more conventional jobs over a lifetime. Such ideas drew upon and fostered the notion of the professional criminal. They also contributed to the search for hereditary traits or common psychological or genetic elements in offenders, something that began in earnest in the nineteenth century.[2] The belief that such hereditary traits could be found recurred throughout the twentieth century as medical and psychological experts sought to identify aberrations in brain functions, chromosomes, nervous systems and so forth. The 'broken windows' theory, proposed in the United States in the early 1980s, echoed the idea that criminals started with petty offences and progressed to bigger things. The theory was seized on and simplified at the end of the century by those advocating the policy of 'zero tolerance' which maintained that, by clamping down on petty offending, more serious criminal behaviour would be prevented.[3] Throughout the twentieth century in England, as well as in other countries, there were habitual offenders who committed their first offences when young. But, as George Lawrence's and Ernest Lacy's criminal careers suggest, they did not necessarily progress to more serious offences. There were also juveniles who ceased offending no later than their early twenties; and there were some individuals who committed their first, and sometimes their only, offences late in life.

Most crime is, and was, undertaken sporadically and opportunistically. Those offenders who offend once and those who, on one or two occasions, commit petty offences over a limited period during their youth do not see themselves as criminals. Most other people probably would not see them as such either. But there are, and were, others who have a much more involved relationship with breaking laws of various kinds. These individuals generally leave a paper trail in criminal justice archives and in the media that it is possible to follow through; partly because of this trail, but more because of their persistence in offending, they tend to be regarded as criminals. These are the individuals that form the basis of this chapter. Other than their persistence in offending, there is not often much else that unites them. Some were gang members who often saw some of their actions as conforming to a kind of code. Others were individuals who seem to have been diverted on to a criminal path by contingent life experiences; and there were some that appear to have embarked deliberately upon a criminal career.

Individuals like George Lawrence and Ernest Lacy were social pests rather than a serious threat. They provided newspapers with occasional space-fillers but few lost much sleep over such petty offenders. The media of all kinds, however, revelled in sensational, but rare crimes, and gruesome murders commonly provided such offences. Serial killers were particularly exciting and while these were few in number, the opportunities for speculating on the mental state of such offenders and their motivation, and for dramatic and lurid reporting and presentation in newspapers, in films and on the television, as well as in 'true crime' books, were second to none. Such killers were labelled as psychopaths or monsters; John George Haigh, for example, the 1949 'acid bath murderer' who claimed to have drunk his victims' blood, was labelled a 'vampire'. Fred and Rosemary West, charged in 1994 on a dozen counts of murder, were grotesque figures that fitted the image portrayed in late twentieth-century cinematic models of sadistic, sexually perverted serial killers. Rosemary West had given birth to eight children and had worked as a prostitute. Fred West had been introduced to unconventional sexual behaviour by his father, had worked for a period in an abattoir, and had suffered a serious head injury. He also had several convictions for petty theft. Yet it was not the case that such serial killers were professional criminals in the popularly imagined sense of progressing from petty offending to their major crimes, although some, like West, had criminal records before they hit the headlines with their murders. Neville Heath, who murdered two women during the Second World War, was a petty thief and fraudster who had been dismissed from the RAF while still a teenager and had served a period in Borstal. Haigh had been in prison for forgery and fraud and had dodged wartime conscription. John Christie who eventually confessed to the murder of six women, including that of his wife, and whose false evidence, a little over three years before his confession, had led to the conviction and execution of the unfortunate Timothy Evans, had served short prison terms for theft, false pretences and violence. During the war, however, Christie had managed to secure appointment as a War Reserve police officer. Denis Nilson, sentenced for six murders of men between 1978 and 1983 in North London, was a quiet, unassuming civil servant and former army cook who had also served for a short time as a police officer. But Nilson had no previous criminal record.[4]

The actions of such killers were analysed and debated by a variety of authors drawing on cultural, gender and psychiatric perspectives.[5] But the reconstruction and investigation of their lives was commonly presented in a popular and rather limited fashion that sought explanations for the behaviour of the individual with the main focus on his (and less commonly her) unique experience and peculiarities, and a relatively superficial sweep through the wider cultural and socio-economic context. Moreover, while such killers inspired press article after press article, book after book, film after film and consequently played a significant role in shaping people's perception of crime and criminals, they were not really individuals who could be said to have been typical of those who had committed murder, let alone those who indulged in the more common, but very different forms of criminal activity.

The criminal gang, like the serial killer, also attracted considerable attention in the media and in the popular 'true crime' literature. Again the stories of such gangs played a significant role in shaping perceptions of criminality, but it was the nature of the true crime genre to chronicle exciting stories and violent careers rather than to provide any systematic analysis of what made some individuals opt for criminal careers. One of the problems here is to separate the criminal gang from the wider community within which a degree of 'ducking and diving' and 'wheeling and dealing' was simply a part of the way of life in poor working-class districts. A series of interviews with people brought up in poor parts of East London from the 1930s to the 1980s revealed important perspectives on attitudes to crime within the community, particularly while it remained relatively static before the rebuilding programmes and the migrations of the 1960s and 1970s. A rough masculinity meant that some young men were ready and eager to fight. Family honour, demands of respectability and a sense of 'we are all in this together' as a community meant that people were quick to condemn anyone who stole from a neighbour or a workmate. Theft from a shop or a company was something else:

You don't break into people's houses and do their gas meters 'cause that's a social crime . . . and that really had a stigma to that. Someone breaking into a warehouse and stealing ten million cigarettes, that's seen on an entirely different level.[6]

Some young men from such communities acquired criminal records and, possibly because of the difficulty of 'going straight' thereafter, possibly because of the buzz that they got from perpetrating offences, they kept at it. Through acquaintance networks such young men might then come together for a major project or cluster of projects. On occasions members of these networks had artisanal skills well-honed over time. The skilled safecracker, who had an intimate knowledge of explosives, would be a prime example.[7] Less skill was needed for stealing and driving the right car for a quick getaway, but individuals would pride themselves on such skills, and be noted for them among their peers. Probably, however, there were many more run-of-the-mill offenders who could turn their hand to several less-skilled tasks and involved themselves in criminal activity believing it to be the best way of making a lot of money as quickly as possible. On occasions some individuals came together with others that they knew personally, or by reputation, for a particular job.

The group involved in the Great Train Robbery of August 1963 provides a good example of a network brought together for a specific job. At the time the audacity of stopping the Glasgow to London mail train and seizing something in the region of £2.6 million was breathtaking. But the gang responsible was not a long-established grouping of clever professionals employing the scheme of a brilliant criminal mastermind. Bruce Reynolds, who organised the robbery, was a housebreaker and thief who enjoyed expensive cars and good living; he also understood the value of careful planning. For the robbery he brought together a dozen or so men with convictions for various forms of theft. Many of the men knew each other, having worked together in two loose groups of offenders. Typical of the robbers, and most notable perhaps for their subsequent histories, were Ronnie Biggs, who had first fallen foul of the law by deserting from the RAF, and Ronald 'Buster' Edwards, who had also disgraced himself as a National Serviceman in the RAF by stealing cigarettes. But for all Reynolds's planning and the gang's extended criminal careers, the Great Train robbers were careless and most were soon caught.[8] And if some of them made extraordinary, romanticised escapes, this probably says less about the brilliance of the offenders than it does about the inefficiency and incompetence of sections of the criminal justice system.

There were also gangs that existed over an extended period. These were often engaged in forms of entrepreneurial activity, such as offering protection or supplying illicit goods. Violence or the threat of violence to warn or intimidate rivals was central to the behaviour of these gangs. Rivals who insulted the entrepreneurs or their henchmen, or publicly challenged them were beaten up, slashed with knives or razors or, very occasionally, murdered for revenge. This violence was deployed to maintain or restore authority and to warn others. It also provided a discourse through which the perpetrators sought to legitimise their actions by appeals to the rules of their supremely masculine community. Thus any individual who was 'bang out of order' knew what punishment to expect; and to maintain the community order, the self-appointed community leaders knew that punishment had to follow any personal slight, offence against the community's norms, or encroachment on their territory.[9]

In the 1920s there were violent confrontations between the gangs that offered protection to bookies on racetracks; the violence spilled beyond the racetracks to streets and pubs with brass-knuckles, knives, razors and guns as much in evidence as fists and boots. In the mid-1960s there was the potential for an exceptional, murderous gang war over disputed territory in London between the Kray brothers of East End and the Richardson brothers south of the Thames. Arms were collected, including machine guns although, allegedly, the hand grenades sought by Ronnie Kray were unavailable. The conflict was averted when, following an unrelated gunfight and death in a south London club in March 1964, the police were able to arrest the Richardsons and break up their gang. The Krays, however, were not prepared to let matters rest entirely. George Cornell had been one of the Richardsons' henchmen; he had also argued with the Krays over the distribution of pornographic films and had dared to call Ronnie Kray a 'fat poof'. Ronnie shot him. Jack 'The Hat' McVittie swindled the Krays and added insult to injury by boasting about it. Reggie Kray planned to shoot him but, when the gun misfired, he resorted to a knife; McVittie's body was never found.[10] Killings as part of the turf wars over drug distribution territory blighted some of the major cities towards the end of the century. The particularly alarming element here was the public way in which the killings had occurred. They often involved shootings from cars; once or twice bystanders or otherwise innocent, potential witnesses were deliberately targeted or, occasionally, caught in the crossfire. In July 2000 the *Manchester Evening News* claimed to reveal 'the true scale of gun law on the [city's] streets . . . in 1999 more criminals fired more guns than in any other year, killing seven people and injuring 43'.[11] Such violence did not usually involve members of the general community other than by accident, but it gave the media opportunities for hyperbole which many readers and viewers accepted uncritically.

Gangs could, and often did, claim a central and influential position within their communities. While the authorities and the media insisted that gangs dominated their districts through intimidation, gang members claimed a code of honour based on ideas of what was and what was not acceptable within their poor, working-class communities. It meant that the gangs might resolve the occasional community outrage such as, for example, children being knocked down by local joyriders. Under the gang's code it was acceptable to rob and burglarise the wealthy and businesses, but not the houses of their own people. And as one member of the so-called 'Salford Firm' explained to an academic in the mid-1990s:

You've not got to be a grass, I mean there's a code in that – when is it right to inform the police about a certain thing, and when it is not correct. You know, if someone rapes somebody or interferes with a kid, or mugs an old lady, as far as the correct-minded thing for people, you know what I mean, the concern – if somebody hands them in then they're not grassing, you know, but if someone goes and says 'so and so has done a ram raid' or 'so and so has done a post office', then it's grassing and it's not acceptable.

'Grassing' might lead to public shaming with an individual's name written on a wall in a public place. It might also lead to a beating, though there could be a code to this, with the gang not assaulting any woman who had grassed, but rather picking on a close male relative.[12]

On occasions ethnicity and family links gave particular strength to such gangs. The racecourse gangs of the inter-war period were commonly identified by district or ethnicity: the Brummagen Boys, the Jewish Aldgate Mob and, perhaps best-known, the Italian gang, the Sabinis. The Sabinis had an Italian father and an Irish mother and were born and bred in Saffron Hill, Clerkenwell. Whatever their name and the distant association with Italy, they were Londoners through and through. Moreover one of the brothers, Joseph, volunteered for the army early in 1916, was wounded in action, invalided out as no longer fit for service, and was acknowledged for good conduct while a soldier. None of this prevented Joseph Sabini from being involved in the shooting of a rival bookmaker, Frederick Gilbert, in 1922.[13]

The press played on the fact that the racecourse violence was committed by 'foreigners' and, during the Second World War, the Sabinis were targeted by the police and two of the brothers were interned, presumably in an attempt to discourage them from their criminal ways. The police insisted that Harry Sabini 'is a dangerous man of most violent temperament and has a heavy following and strong command of a gang of bullies of Italian origin in London'. But, they went on:

We have no knowledge that he has previously engaged in any political activities but . . . he can at best be described as a dangerous gangster and racketeer of the worst type and appears to be a most likely person who would be chosen by enemy agents to create and be a leader of violent internal action against the country.[14]

This says more about Home Office and police assumptions than it does about Harry Sabini. In the nineteenth and early twentieth centuries it was a common assumption in many quarters that criminals were simply individuals on the lookout for opportunities for plunder and that they came into their own during periods of revolution and internal unrest.[15] Quite why an enemy power would want to contact gangsters to foment disorder, always assuming that gangsters could foment disorder, remains an unanswered and largely imponderable question. Similarly, the question can be posed as to why individuals who made their living from protection rackets and bookmaking would want to compromise any profits from their existing enterprises by indulging in the chancy business of stirring up political unrest. A more cynical but ultimately more persuasive conclusion might be that the police were targeting the Sabinis as potential political suspects, either to warn them to limit their criminal activities or else because they knew that they could not make any other charge stick and this was a way of removing them, at least temporarily, from the scene.

A degree of ethnicity and district loyalty may have provided an additional stanchion to some of the drugs gangs at the turn of the century. The news media and, arguably, also the police contributed to the promotion of the idea of Yardie gangs originating from the West Indies as central within much of this entrepreneurial criminality.[16] But, at the close of the century, the police were also involved in seeking to downplay the notions of 'black crime' and, through the introduction of Operation Trident in London in 1998, in trying to combat the black-on-black gun violence linked with gangs.

Criminal gangs often emerged out of poor working-class districts where old ideas of a masculinity dependent on physical prowess and strength continued to predominate. It is significant that many of the principal criminal figures in London during the first two-thirds of the century were known early on for their ability as boxers. For such tough young men, criminal activity appeared often to promise a way out of a bleak lifetime in a dead-end job or in a queue for the dole. The fact that such activity was defined as 'criminal' by the state was probably not given much thought. First and foremost it was a profitable way of making a living; secondly, success gave the men standing in their locality. The leader (or leaders) of a successful entrepreneurial group sometimes aspired to a paternalistic role within his community. Alfred White, the patriarch of the King's Cross Gang in the inter-war period, was reported to have held court in pubs in the Pentonville Road where he strictly prohibited the use of any bad language. White's sometime collaborators, sometime rivals, the Sabinis, were similar; young Anglo-Italian youths in their Clerkenwell patch were not to drink before they were 20 years old and women had to be respected and treated properly. In the 1960s the Kray brothers enjoyed playing the role of philanthropic businessmen, contributing to a wide variety of charities in their native East End; they also enjoyed mixing with a variety of celebrities. But the Richardsons, in contrast, did not demonstrate the same kind of philanthropy for a working-class community. Their father had been a prizefighter and merchant seaman, yet the Richardsons became successful businessmen. Charlie Richardson had a scrap metal firm and overseas investments, while brother Eddie continued to run a profitable wholesale chemist business; crime was a means to bigger profits in other areas.[17]

But while the criminal violence and the murders committed by criminal gangs, like the murders of serial killers, played a significant role in the

The Kray twins with Judy Garland and Mark Herron

One for the family album? The Kray brothers – twins Ronnie and Reggie and their brother Charlie –
were among the last but also among the most celebrated of working-class East End gang leaders. By the
mid-1960s the twins were seeking to present a veneer of respectability through their nightclub. Here they
entertained a variety of celebrities. This image shows them in their hallmark smart suits posing, rather
self-consciously, with the American singer and actress Judy Garland and her husband Mark Herron.
(*Source*: Getty Images)

creation of the popular image of the criminal and his (or less commonly
her) perverted lifestyle, there were relatively few gangland murders. Few
people murdered more than once and few had progressed from petty
offending to offending as a way of life, and so on to murder. As ever, there
was the occasional exception to prove the rule. Sydney Herbert Fox, born
in Narborough, Norfolk in 1900 acquired a criminal record for fraud and
forgery in the immediate aftermath of the First World War. *Supplement
'A'* of the *Police Gazette* also noted him 'as a reputed sodomite'. In 1928
he was jailed for 15 months for stealing jewellery from a married woman
who he may also have tried to murder for insurance money. On his release
he continued his career as a fraudster, but now in company with his
mother. In April 1930 he was charged with murdering his mother in a
Margate hotel, apparently with the intention of collecting the insurance
money payable on her death; he was found guilty and hanged.[18] Fox can be
said to have made a career by his criminal offending. His career was not

typical given the way in which it ended but, in as much as it consisted of a string of offences generally of a similar type, it had similarities with those of others labelled by the state as habitual offenders. The state kept details of such individuals in the paper files of its Criminal Record Office and later, electronically, on the Police National Computer.

The Criminal Record Office was initially housed with the Metropolitan Police in New Scotland Yard. The Prevention of Crimes Act of 1871 required that registers be kept of every person convicted of a crime in the United Kingdom. With the creation of the Central Fingerprint Office in Scotland Yard 30 years later fingerprints were added to the files of photographs and personal descriptions of offenders. From 1913 a Method Index was added in the belief

that there is tendency amongst criminals to do the same thing over and over again in the same sort of way.

This Index was formed . . . with the idea of making systematised use of these well-known facts and exploiting to the uttermost the lack of originality of the average criminal.[19]

The information for the Criminal Records was prepared by the police forces across the country. The Criminal Record Office, in turn, issued the daily *Police Gazette* to all forces in the country. The *Gazette* was free and copies could be supplied sufficient for every Police Station and, in rural counties, for every isolated Police House. It contained details of crimes, of wanted persons, suspect persons in custody, missing persons, property stolen; it was illustrated with photographs of suspects and any-thing else that might assist in an inquiry. In addition to the daily *Gazette* a fortnightly *Supplement 'A'* was circulated in the same fashion. Each *Supplement 'A'* contained details of six habitual offenders, their names and aliases, previous convictions and *modus operandi*; there was a photograph of each offender and, from 1924, their right forefinger fingerprint. Space was provided for a police officer to fill in additional details under an indi-vidual's name and, probably under the watchful eyes of senior officers, many of the *Supplements* were kept up to date in this way. It seems equally probable, however, that many were not.[20] The books offer a unique collec-tion of the careers of habitual offenders. They demonstrate also how these individuals sought to use changing circumstances to their advantage and how petty and pathetic so much persistent offending was.

The *Supplements* describe some nasty, violent offenders. Ernest James Johnstone, born in Belfast in 1905, had a string of aliases and, over the years, amassed a string of convictions ranging from fraud to theft. In 1934 he brutally attacked a fellow hotel guest and stole valuable jewellery. The *Supplement* warned: 'He is of very violent disposition and in the case of robbery with violence . . . for which he was . . . convicted [in 1934], it was only by reason of the fact that his victim died 16 months after the commission of the assault that he escaped the capital charge.' Johnstone was still active in the 1940s.[21] Harry Rix was a Londoner, nearly ten years older than Johnstone; he carried scars on each side of his throat and across his left eye. He was known for breaking into shops and stealing from cars; and he could be violent. The *Supplement* was clear about his methods:

A very clever house and shopbreaker who effects entry by means of celluloid strips, but has not yet been charged with that class of offence. He does not confine his activities to London or the Home Counties but, in company with his wife, Peggy, travels all over the country in a small car. Especially with cases of shopbreaking, he goes to a lot of trouble, previously visiting scene of offence, making enquires, etc., to ensure success.[22]

Violent men like Johnston and Rix sometimes made up the foot soldiers of entrepreneurial gangs. Thomas 'Monkey' Benneworth, for example, was one of the Elephant Gang, rivals of the Sabinis; he had a string of convictions involving theft and receiving in addition to his reputation for violence. In the file that they assembled on what appears to have been a racecourse gang scuffle in Waterloo Road in 1925, the Metropolitan Police noted that Benneworth had a job as a printer with the *News of the World*.[23] Criminal offenders could, of course, have permanent jobs completely unconnected with their criminal offending. Moreover violence was not always a component of serial offending.

A large number of the habitual offenders described in *Supplement 'A'* travelled the country living on their wits. The principal common denominator for such offenders was the way in which they sought to turn the context in which they found themselves to their own advantage. There were fraudsters before the First World War, but the war provided them with new opportunities. With the sole intent of obtaining money, men in army uniforms, sometimes deserters, sometimes not, pretended to be recruiting sergeants or claimed to have been wounded or gassed. Lawrence Andrew Deacon, born in Lavenham Suffolk, was in his mid-thirties when the war broke out. In 1916, claiming to have a degree from an American university, he talked his way into an appointment in a military hospital. Proving to be both intemperate and incompetent, and unable to produce any testimonials, he was quickly dismissed. Undaunted, he passed himself off to a bank manager as a major in the Royal Army Medical Corps; he succeeded in getting a cheque book from the bank and he then proceeded to travel the country claiming to inspect hospitals on behalf of the War Office and paying for his lodgings with his new cheques. He was sentenced to six months imprisonment at Nuneaton Police Court at the end of the year. Deacon resurfaced in the *Supplements* ten years later and during the early 1930s he was active in the West Country collecting convictions for passing fraudulent cheques in Bath, Bristol and Devon, while claiming to be an electrical contractor, an ex-army officer and the son of a clergyman.[24] It was a similar story in the Second World War. Men pretended to be army officers and persuaded gullible hotel managers to cash worthless cheques and to accept similar cheques in payment for rooms. Others posed as Dunkirk survivors, as wounded heroes of glamorous commando raids, veterans of Bomber Command, torpedoed merchant seamen and as anything else likely to ingratiate them with people that might be persuaded to part with money or goods.[25]

Women appear in far fewer numbers in the *Supplements*; nevertheless, men like Lawrence Deacon had their female counterparts. Avis Fitzroy, who was born in Malta in 1877 according to the Criminal Records Office but in 1883 according to her own account, went under a variety of aliases: Lady Mercia Somerset, Mary Rogers, Lady Gypsy Rodgers, the Hon. Ida Falconer, the Hon. Alice Fitzroy Somerset and the Hon. Mrs Cholmondley. In 1917 she was described as 'a clever adventuress' who had 'lived in various parts of the country and has nearly always contrived to enjoy life at the expense of others'. Twenty years later she was still going strong when, travelling under the name of Roma Rodgers, she was sentenced to six months for fraud and attempted fraud.[26]

On the outbreak of the Second World War the criminologist Hermann Mannheim put together information on 1,274 recidivists (1,197 men and 77 women) who had appeared at the Central Criminal Court and at 20 or so quarter sessions between 1915 and 1935. He excluded from his total any individual whose offending was largely confined to forms of vagrancy and begging, and included only those with a minimum of four offences. Some of the offenders that he described had extensive criminal careers and had passed long years in prison. The evidence indicated that, generally, they began their confrontations with the law when young: 59 per cent had their first conviction before they were 22 years old and 13.6 per cent of the men had their first conviction before they were 14. Only a few started their criminal behaviour after the age of 40, and most of these were involved in some form of coinage offences. Also, only a few also stuck to a single kind of offence. 'The average recidivist', Mannheim concluded, 'although mainly concerned with crime against property, also, more often than not, tries his hand in other spheres of criminal law.'[27]

Mannheim's evidence did not enable him to draw any conclusions about why some individuals ceased offending and there has been little historical analysis of what is now commonly called desistence across twentieth-century England. There is some scattered evidence in, for example, the record cards kept on some of the young male offenders subject to the training methods of Borstal institutions.[28] The cards contain a small photograph of the offender, a brief note of his offence and of how he was regarded by both the governor and the chaplain of the institution where he was held. There are short factual statements about his final weeks in prison and what he did once he was released. Some boys did well and, once they got a steady job, they appear to have settled down to a life without offending. The boys appear often to have been encouraged to go to sea; Britain had the largest navy in the world on the eve of the First World War and a significant merchant marine. George Blanchard, who had been sentenced to 20 months for burglary, initially went into the merchant navy as a deck boy in March 1909. He had difficulty in finding a new ship after his first voyage and in the following year he resolved to join the Royal Navy. It was a life to which he thought himself suited; at the end of 1911 he was contemplating signing on for a full 22 years and on the outbreak of the war, when contact with him ceased, he was serving on *HMS Neptune*. Charles Brundell, also known as Greer, served 21 months for larceny. The governor, under whose charge he had been held, was suspicious: 'Gives me the idea of being an "excellent prisoner" which means he is too cute.' The chaplain, however, thought him 'a smart intelligent boy who ought to do well'. Brundell joined the merchant navy on his release in May 1909. He sent money back from different parts of the world requesting that the authorities hold it for him until his return. He kept in regular contact throughout 1910 and 1911, at which point the information on his record card ends. Other stories ended less happily. A boy named Turner from the East End had served 15 months for larceny and receiving. The governor believed that his time in custody had seen him improve and the chaplain thought him 'worth a good chance'. Young Turner was released at the end of 1908, but had little family support other than a grandmother in Bethnal Green to whom he appears to have been close. He wanted to be a carman and when he got such a job working with his own horse and wagon everything appeared to be going well. His foreman was concerned that he sometimes quarrelled with workmates, but his landlady spoke well of him; he was prompt with his rent. But then the horse that Turner had worked with was sold; he complained that the new horse was old, that he could not work with poor horses and he gave up the job. Finding new employment was not easy. In April 1910 his grandmother was not sure where he was living, and she thought that he was helping a man with a barrow. The following Christmas, at Bow Street Magistrates' Court, he was sentenced to 21 days for begging. In 1916 he was charged with stealing money. He was said to have been to sea twice and to have worked on the docks. The following year he could not be traced.

Frederick Burgess was an even sorrier case. Following a three-year sentence for burglary at Lincolnshire Assizes, Burgess was held for some time in Dartmoor Prison and was released in the summer of 1908. The chaplain thought him a weak character, very impressionable and someone who needed to be kept away from bad companions. But bad companions do not appear to have been Burgess's problem. He had difficulty in settling back into work. At first he was reported to be lazy, 'spoiling his chances' and in need of a 'rousing up'. Subsequent reports were contradictory; he appeared to have settled down, then he pawned his clothes, then he was reported to be improving. Early in 1909 he disappeared from his lodgings in Edgware; he was arrested a few days later for having burgled two houses in Slough. Those responsible for supervising him since his earlier release did their best for him; they spoke to the judge at the Bucks Assizes and in May 1909 Burgess was given three years' probation. Once again, for a brief period, he seemed to settle down but almost a month after appearing before the judge in Buckinghamshire he confessed to the rape and murder of a little girl in Hendon. The police thought Burgess a 'mental degenerate'; the jury at the Central Criminal Court thought him insane. He was ordered to be detained at His Majesty's pleasure and sent to Broadmoor Hospital.[29] Burgess was only 20 years old when his criminal career came to an end. There is no doubt that he was a serial offender, but his offending seems to have been the result of severe personality problems rather than any calculated decision to follow a life of crime.

A unique study of recidivism and desistence in Crewe over the period from 1880 to 1940 stands out for its historical analysis of the persistence of offending in families and across generations. The evidence here suggests that there were few hardened recidivists in the town. Unsurprisingly the offenders were predominantly male and they committed a variety of offences. The women picked up in the study were more likely to be drunkards and physically abusive. Overall, however, the differences between offenders and their offences were often greater than the similarities.

There was sometimes a short-term transmission of offending within family groups, but this was never automatic and it generally disappeared within three generations. A steady job, as in the cases of Blanchard and Brundell described above, together with marriage and children all appear to have been significant reforming influences, although the male working-class culture that predominated in the period up to the Second World War fostered heavy drinking which, in turn, contributed to some kinds of offence. It would appear that any reforming element of such behaviour that originated from wives and mothers became more influential only after that war.[30]

Most of the offenders discussed so far were born into the poorer sections of British society. Indeed it is probably true to say that most of the criminal offenders that passed through the courts during the century came from the semi-skilled and unskilled manual groups specified as social classes IV and V in the Registrar General's five-part classification of class by occupation and which, for all its imperfections, was used fairly generally throughout the period. In Victorian England it was common for commentators to identify criminal behaviour as the work of a criminal class situated in what, towards the end of the nineteenth century, was described as the 'residuum' of the working class. The evidence shows that criminal offenders can originate in any social group. White-collar offenders, for example, range across the employment world from financiers and managers to the lowliest clerks; few of these might be situated in the Victorian residuum or the Registrar General's social classes IV and V. If the term 'criminal class' was used less freely in the twentieth century, the perception remained that there were problem families and that such families existed, in part at least, by various forms of criminal behaviour. The evidence from Crewe, noted above, suggests that the transmission of offending was not extensive; yet the existence of the Sabinis, the Whites, the Krays, suggests that the family was a bond for some offenders. Even so, the Sabinis, the Whites and the Krays were exceptional in the scale and relative, if temporary, success of their offending and notoriety.

During the 1940s the term 'problem family' emerged in the discourse of social commentators and it became increasingly popular over the following 10 or 20 years. Moreover the 'problem families' were not characterised by bonding but rather the opposite. They were seen as largely involving broken relationships, absentee fathers, frequent pregnancies, poverty and alcohol, all of which, it was believed, contributed to crime and delinquency. Following the electoral defeat of the Conservative Party under Edward Heath in October 1974, Sir Keith Joseph sought to identify and

revive what he considered to be distinct Tory values behind which a regen-
erated party might revive. He lamented that:

*For the first time in a century and a half, since the great Tory reformer
Robert Peel set up the Metropolitan Police, areas of our cities are
becoming unsafe for peaceful citizens by night, and some even by day.*

The assertion would hardly stand up to serious historical investigation, but
it struck a chord with many in his party. So too did his concluding comments on a central cause of the situation that he described, and for which
he drew on the evidence of a recent study by the Child Poverty Action
Group. There were large numbers of young mothers in social classes IV
and V.

*Many of these girls are unmarried, many are deserted or divorced, or
soon will be. Some are of low intelligence, most of low educational
attainment . . . They are producing problem children, the future unmarried
mothers, delinquents, denizens of our borstals, sub-normal educational
establishments, prisons, hostels for drifters.*

Joseph's comments about the nation's 'human stock' being under threat
and his advocacy of birth control facilities for these young women smacked
of eugenics and, arguably, cost him the leadership of the Conservative Party.
But many shared his conclusions and, by the last decade of the century,
'problem families' were still singled out as the root cause of criminality but
their label had changed to the 'underclass'.[31]

In 1989 the *Sunday Times* brought to Britain the American social
policy analyst Charles Murray to compare Britain's 'underclass' with the
one that he had exposed in the United States. Murray was well aware that
the perception of a dangerous, criminal underclass was not new. However,
he considered that the underclass of the late twentieth century was marked by three key phenomena: illegitimacy, dropping out of the labour
force, and violent crime. Central also were the decline of the family and
the growth of too generous welfare benefits. The problem of illegitimacy,
he believed, was aggravated by such benefits which, while they did not
necessarily encourage young women from the lowest social class to get
pregnant, did not do much to discourage them either. Benefits, Murray
believed, meant the opportunity for accommodation away from parents,
especially with a second or third pregnancy. The growth in the number of
single mothers aggravated the collapse of the family still further since the
boys of such mothers had no civilising and socialising father figure; this, in
turn, worsened the entire underclass problem since marriage was no longer

able to work its civilising and socialising process on many young men. Murray's ideas provoked much support and, equally, much criticism. The support was rooted in the fear of the growth in the figures of crime and in the assumption that too many scroungers were benefiting from the system of state benefits when they should be working or, at least, out looking for work. The critics picked up on a variety of issues, for example, the way in which he had used statistics and the way in which he did not appear to distinguish between those who were poor because of personal inadequacy and those who had suffered serious economic misfortune.[32]

The belief that there were two kinds of poor – those that deserved assistance because their problems of, for example, age or infirmity were no fault of their own, and those who were undeserving because they preferred to scrounge, or slip in and out of crime, often by seeking to defraud the welfare system – was not new in the late twentieth century. Those considered to be 'sturdy beggars' were the objects of much condemnation and judicial sanction in the sixteenth and seventeenth centuries. What was new, however, was the growth of a significant system of benefits to assist those in need. The system had been given a major boost with the creation of the Welfare State in the aftermath of the Second World War. But, as the post-war boom in employment fell away with the economic problems of, especially, the 1970s, the social benefit scrounger, claiming benefits to which he or she was not entitled, became a focus of media and popular outrage. There were individuals and groups of individuals that did set out to defraud the system. But there were others, probably a majority among the offenders, that made false claims because they were desperate, because they were angry, mistrustful and felt degraded by the officials that decided on their claims, because they did not fully understand the system, or perhaps simply because they felt that everyone else was doing it and getting away with it. Distinguishing members of the underclass among such offenders depended, probably, on the initial perceptions of the observer. A study published in the same year as Murray's initial essay on the British underclass made an illuminating comparison between the offenders that defrauded what was then called the Supplementary Benefits system and those higher up the social scale who defrauded the taxman.[33]

Dee Cook had worked as a tax officer for the Inland Revenue and as an executive officer in the Department for Health and Social Security (DHSS) before becoming an academic. Her book on fraudsters and the ways in which they were treated, was consequently based on personal experience as well as academic research. She did not engage with Murray; as the publication of the book virtually coincided with his description of the British underclass, this was hardly possible. But her description of single mothers was far more nuanced than the image of the feckless or calculating underclass girl that got pregnant either by accident or design. She stressed, for example, how the social welfare system still assumed the natural state of the family to be two parents with a male breadwinner when, in reality, permanent emotional and sexual relationships did not necessarily mean marriage or that a man gave money to his female partner. Many single mothers had relationships with poorly paid men; many had been deserted. By the mid-1980s there were a million single-parent families in Britain, most of which were headed by a woman and over half of these women were dependent upon benefits. Moreover, the benefits were increasingly set at what was defined as a poverty line. Most single mothers were caught in a poverty trap aggravated by their class and gender. Interestingly, however, Cook noted also that DHSS officers appeared often to have taken a view of single mothers not greatly dissimilar from Murray. 'I can't understand why people like her think they've a right to rely on the taxpayer for everything', commented one of the officials that she interviewed. Cook also quoted from the opposite side of the benefit table. A single mother who had separated from her husband, for example, complained that the DHSS officers 'wanted all the mucky details . . . who I'd slept with, when and where and how many times. I'm surprised they didn't ask what positions too . . . They didn't want to *help* me.' There were fraudsters: the Smyths of Wolverhampton were an extreme example. As one local newspaper put it in February 1985:

Neighbours spoke today of the spend, spend, spend life-style of a Wolverhampton couple who fiddled £50,000 in social security handouts. Kathleen Smyth and her husband Tom were always rolling in money . . . Kathleen Smyth known as the 'tattooed lady' admitted 12 changes . . . While they were enjoying the good life Smyth, a 19 stone mother of six, drank much of the cash away in pubs and her husband bet heavily on horses.[34]

The Smyths may have had lives that fitted with some perceptions of the criminal underclass, but the press reporting was able to re-emphasise their deviance by stressing their tattoos, their excessive size, their implied drunkenness and gambling. And in the same way that descriptions of serial killers suggested that they were somehow the ultimate form of criminals, so stories like that of the Smyths, by an emphasis on their failure to conform to expectations of gender and decent behaviour, helped to construct a deviant picture apparently typical of those who broke the law by defrauding state benefits.

People who defrauded the benefits system may not have been commonly considered as criminal in the way that the Krays or the Great Train robbers were considered criminal. Nevertheless they were subject to prosecution and it might be said that their existence was often, but not always, being supported by their illegal activities.[35] As noted above, the opportunities for such behaviour, and for the concerns and condemnation, increased with the growth of state assistance and, especially, with the creation of the Welfare State. The concerns and the condemnations fostered the growth of an inspectorate to police the system. At the beginning of the 1960s there were 72 inspectors charged with detecting abuses of the assistance schemes; in 1961 they helped to launch 1,100 prosecutions and allegedly caused more than 900 individuals to surrender their allowances when they found themselves under investigation. By 1988 there were 785 inspectors responsible for launching 395,000 investigations in a year.[36] One major concern was the number of men who refused available work in the belief that they were better off on benefits. The worry, however, appears to have been greater in the minds of those concerned than was the actual incidence of the problem, at least in so far as it can be measured by prosecutions; in 1959 only 79 men were prosecuted for the offence, of whom 55 were found guilty and imprisoned.[37] A much greater problem was the man who claimed unemployment benefit while working on his own account, or even for an employer that was prepared to pay in cash leaving no written record of the man's employment or payment.[38] This points to the other kind of individual whose economic life encompasses criminal activity – the fraudulent employer.

Fraudulent employers and fraudulent business people made significant, illegal profits in a variety of ways. They might simply seek to avoid paying taxes. In the autumn of 1931, for example, *The Times* reported the cases of a City of London hat-maker and a butcher from Kingston-upon-Thames prosecuted for tax evasion going back respectively to 1910 and 1916.[39] Towards the end of the 1930s, as the government sought to increase its revenue to help pay for rearmament, there were editorials and heated debates in *The Times* over the inefficiencies and unfairness of the taxation system, especially the supertax imposed on the very wealthy.[40] In the aftermath of the Second World War the National Insurance Act of 1946 provided for compulsory contributions from employers and employees for unemployment benefit, sickness, maternity and widow's benefits and old age pensions. But in so doing it provided a variety of opportunities for employers and employees to defraud the Treasury. In the 1970s 'the lump', as tax evasion by sub-contractors in the building trade was known, became a particular source of concern. There were similar frauds in Fleet Street where print workers concealed earnings (moonlighting) or simply remained invisible to the Revenue (ghosting). In the summer of 1991 *The Independent* reported that, in the last financial year, 15 employers had been prosecuted for paying their staff low wages and encouraging them to sign on for unemployment benefits; and another 20 cases were awaiting court hearings. Highly paid professionals and businessmen were not immune and through their systems of allowances and expenses, and their knowledge of how to salt money away to avoid tax – usually perfectly legally but sometimes not – they too engaged in fraud.[41]

Brian Charrington and Curtis 'Cocky' Warren, whose activities will be discussed in Chapter 5, had entrepreneurial flair and, even after they had made enormous sums of money, they continued wheeling and dealing on the wrong side of the law. They were settled in a particular economic and social milieu that offered them little advantage in their dealings with criminal justice but they appear not to have wished to move out of it. The press saw them as professional criminals and masterminds of organised crime. Roger Levitt, a City investor, appears to have committed major fraud and lost thousands of pounds of his clients' money. But Levitt was able to plea bargain and, rather than facing a trial that could have led to a sentence of between seven and ten years in prison, he agreed to plead guilty to having misled the City watchdog; he was then sentenced to just 180 hours of community service.[42] Four well-respected and well-connected businessmen were convicted of fraud in the Guinness takeover of United Distillers in 1986. Ernest Saunders, the chairman of Guinness, was sentenced to five years. On appeal the sentence was halved but, in the event, Saunders served only ten months and he was released in June 1991, allegedly suffering from a form of dementia associated with Alzheimer's disease. He made a miraculous recovery and by the mid-1990s was acting as a highly paid business consultant. Gerald Ronson, convicted alongside Saunders, played no such sickness card but, within six weeks of his release he was shaking hands with the Queen Mother at the opera and he remained among the top 500 wealthiest people in Britain.[43] The press and many others were highly critical of Levitt, those connected with the Guinness affair and the way in which they were allowed to work the system, but their offences tended to be seen as a one-off and there was no suggestion of them having pursued criminal careers; the career criminal, whether a pathetic George Lawrence or a 'Cocky' Warren, remained a product of the working class.

Towards the end of the century a major, highly respected firm of accountants estimated that over the 20 years 1976 to 1996 the British Crown had been defrauded by tax evasion alone to the tune of £2 trillion.[44] Businessmen were not normally categorised among those living criminal lives or labelled as professional criminals during the twentieth century. Yet it was possible for the otherwise respectable man who, for example, paid part of his workforce in cash or otherwise defrauded the taxman, to make considerable profit over an extended period. Respectable businessmen and entrepreneurs responded to changing markets and opportunities, as did many of those considered as living criminal lives or labelled as professional criminals. The issue of the professional criminal will be revisited under the heading of organised crime, but first it is necessary to address the issue of where many feared that a criminal career began – with the juvenile offender.

References and notes

1 *Manchester Guardian*, 29 September 1926, p. 12, and 14 February 1950, p. 3.

2 **Clive Emsley**, *Crime, Police and Penal Policy: European experiences, 1750–1940*, Oxford: Oxford University Press, 2007, pp. 155–6, and chap. 10.

3 **James Q. Wilson** and **George L. Kelling**, 'Broken windows: the police and neighborhood safety', *Atlantic Monthly*, March 1982, pp. 29–38. An extended version appeared in **James Q. Wilson**, *Thinking About Crime*, New York; Vintage Books, 1985, chap. 5. For the advocacy of 'zero tolerance' in the late twentieth-century British context see, for example, **Norman Davies** (ed.) *Zero Tolerance: policing a free society*, London: Institute of Economic Affairs, 1997. George Kelling subsequently expressed concern about the way in which his and Wilson's strategy had been reduced to campaigns directed at beggars and squeegee merchants. **Nick Davies**, *Flat Earth News*, London: Vintage Books, 2009, pp. 39–40.

4 See, *inter alia*, **Conrad Phillips**, *Murderers Moon: being studies of Heath, Haigh and Christie*, London: Arthur Barker, 1956; **Molly Lefebure**, *Murder with a Difference: studies of Haigh and Christie*, London: Heinemann, 1958; **Ludovic Kennedy**, *Ten Rillington Place*, London: Victor Gollancz, 1961; **Brian Masters**, *Killing for Company: the case of Denis Nilsen*, London: Random House, 1985; *idem, She Must Have Known: trial of Rosemary West*, London: Doubleday, 1996.

5 One of the most novel and stimulating assessments of Peter Sutcliffe, 'the Yorkshire Ripper', sentenced in 1981 for the murder of 13 women and for attacks on another 7, was by Nicole Ward Jouve, Professor of Literature

at the University of York. Ward Jouve's book linked Sutcliffe with what she perceived to be largely normative gender identification in late twentieth-century Yorkshire. **Nicole Ward Jouve**, *The Streetcleaner: the Yorkshire Ripper case on trial*, London: Marion Boyars, 1988.

6 **Roger Hood** and **Kate Joyce**, 'Three generations: oral testimonies on crime and social change in London's East End', *BJC*, 39, 1 (1999) pp. 136–60; quotation at p. 151.

7 See, for example, **Dick Hobbs**'s account of 'the craftsman' in his *Bad Business: professional crime in modern Britain*, Oxford: Oxford University Press, 1995, pp. 14–19.

8 **Piers Paul Read**, *The Train Robbers: their story*, London: W.H. Allen, 1978. Reynolds was on the run for a period, but returned home to a ten-year prison sentence. On his release he became a minor criminal celebrity publishing an autobiography, *The Autobiography of a Thief*, London: Bantam, 1995. Buster Edwards's life was the subject of a feature film, *Buster* (1988) starring the actor and singer Phil Collins. Ronnie Biggs escaped and spent many years in Brazil again as a romantic, minor celebrity cocking a snook at British authority.

9 **Hobbs**, *Bad Business*, pp. 108–10.

10 **John Pearson**, *The Profession of Violence: the rise and fall of the Kray Twins*, London: Weidenfeld and Nicolson, 1972, pp. 134–8 and 174–8; **James Morton**, *East-End Gangland*, London: Warner Books, 2001, pp. 308–12. These books are in the popular, true crime mould. For a less detailed, but sharper analysis see **Dick Hobbs**, *Doing the Business: entrepreneurship, the working class and detectives in the East End of London*, Oxford: Oxford University Press, 1988, pp. 50–61.

11 *Manchester Evening News*, 3 July 2000, p. 12. For similar problems in Nottingham see, for example, *Nottingham Evening Post*, 14 March and 18 April 2000.

12 **Karen Evans**, **Penny Fraser** and **Sandra Walklate**, 'Whom can you trust? The politics of "grassing" on an inner city housing estate', *Sociological Review*, 44, 3 (1996) pp. 361–80: quotation at p. 372.

13 MEPO 3/1581, Sabini and Birmingham Gangs: shooting affray in Mornington Crescent, October 1922.

14 Quoted in **A.W. Brian Simpson**, *In the Highest Degree Odious: detention without trial in wartime Britain*, Oxford: Clarendon Press, 1992, p. 313.

15 Emsley, *Crime, Police and Penal Policy*, pp. 133, 145, 151 and 228.

16 See, for example, the stories carried by the London *Evening Standard*, 20 May 1992, p. 20; 29 October 1992, p. 14; 11 January 1993, p. 17; 20 May 1993,

p. 18. The Metropolitan Police ran at least one Yardie as an informer and allowed considerable freedom of unlawful action. See *The Guardian*, 6 November 1995, p. T2 and **Nick Davies**, *Flat Earth News*, London: Vintage Books, 2009, p. 78.

17 Pearson, *Profession of Violence,* pp. 103–5 and 134; Morton, *East End Gangland*, pp. 164–5 and 315; **Duncan Campbell**, *The Underworld*, Harmondsworth: Penguin, 1994, chap. 5.

18 *Police Gazette, Supplement A, 1920,* no. 178; *The Times*, 22 February, 13, 14, 17, 18, 19, 20, 21, 22 March and 9 April 1930; **Douglas G. Browne** and **E.V. Tullett**, *Bernard Spilsbury: his life and cases*, London: Odhams, Companion's Library, 1952, pp. 381–90.

19 *Catching Thieves on Paper: the history and purpose of the Criminal Record Office and the 'Police Gazette' and its Supplements,* Issued by the Commissioner of the Metropolitan Police, London: Metropolitan Police, 1936, p. 7.

20 Arthur Almond claimed never to have seen a *Police Gazette* when he served with the Cambridgeshire Force between 1928 and 1930; **Clive Emsley** (ed.), 'The recollections of a provincial policeman: Arthur Ernest Almond', *Journal of the Police History Society*, 3 (1988) pp. 53–66; at p. 58 An article in *John Bull*, 26 March 1949, pp. 16–17, complained that there were police officers who never consulted the *Gazettes* and that in some police stations the pages of old copies were sometimes found to be uncut.

21 *Police Gazette, Supplement A, 1937,* no. 617.

22 *Police Gazette, Supplement A, 1937,* no. 673.

23 MEPO 3.352, Race Gang affray in Waterloo Road, 1925.

24 *Police Gazette, Supplement A, 1917,* no. 176; *1927*, no. 258; *1930*, no. 277 and no. 273; *1931*, no. 340 and no. 583.

25 *Police Gazette, Supplement A, 1942,* nos. 91 and 258; *1943*, nos. 86, 124 and 196.

26 *Police Gazette, Supplement A, 1917,* no. 261, and *1937*, no. 410.

27 **Herman Mannheim**, *Social Aspects of Crime in England Between the Wars*, London: George Allen and Unwin, 1940, chap. 12; quotation at p. 361.

28 Galleries of Justice, Nottingham: AAPSM: 2003: 0892, Prison Record Cards, c.1908–1913.

29 Additional information on Burgess from Oldbaileyonline, t19090719-25.

30 **Barry S. Godfrey, David J. Cox** and **Stephen D. Farrall**, *Criminal Lives: family life, employment, and offending*, Oxford: Oxford University Press, 2007.

31 Sir Keith Joseph's speech was reproduced in full in *The Guardian*, 21 October 1974, p. 7; John Macnicol, 'From "problem family" to "underclass", 1945–95', in **Rodney Lowe** and **Helen Fawcett** (eds), *Welfare Policy in Britain: the road from 1945*, Basingstoke: Macmillan, 1999.

32 For Murray's analysis, which first appeared in the *Sunday Times*, and for a range of criticisms see **Ruth Lister** (ed.), *Charles Murray and the Underclass: the developing debate*, London: Institute of Economic Affairs, 1996.

33 **Dee Cook**, *Rich Law, Poor Law: different responses to tax and supplementary benefit fraud*, Milton Keynes: Open University Press, 1989.

34 Quotations from Cook, *Rich Law, Poor Law*, at pp. 152, 92 and 17 respectively.

35 In July 1999, for example, a grandmother in Birmingham was given a 12-month sentence suspended for two years after falsely claiming nearly £23,000 over a six-year period. Under her married name she claimed to be unemployed; but she worked under her maiden name. She admitted the offence and insisted that she made the false claims because she was in debt but also to help her two nephews since their mother was an alcoholic. The judge accepted that greed had not been her motive in passing sentence. *Birmingham Evening Mail*, 16 July 1999, p. 14.

36 *The Times*, 7 June 1962, p. 9; *The Guardian*, 1 June 1988.

37 *The Times*, 8 May 1961, p. 13.

38 *The Times*, 19 June 1958, p. 2.

39 *The Times*, 11 September 1931, p. 9 and 7 October, p. 11.

40 *The Times*, 11 March 1937, p. 17; 17 July, p. 12; 24 September, p. 13; 24 March 1938, p. 15; 25 March p. 13; 28 March p. 15; 1 April p. 17; 2 April, p. 13 and 5 May p. 9.

41 Cook, *Rich Law, Poor Law*, chap. 3; *The Independent*, 23 August 1991, p. 10.

42 *The Independent*, 13 June 1995; *Parl. Debs. (Commons)* 17 July 1995, c.1303–05.

43 www.thisismoney.co.uk/news/article Article by Patrick Hosking, 'How they live now' from *Evening Standard*, 21 December 2001.

44 **Larry Elliott** and **Dan Atkinson**, *The Age of Insecurity*, London: Verso, 1998, p. 99.

CHAPTER 4

Crime and the young

The statistics suggested that, throughout the twentieth century, most crime was committed by young males in their late teens and early twenties, although the number of young female offenders was increasing towards the close of the century. In addition, often without any basis in the statistical evidence, there were periodic moments of agitation about a supposed wave of offending by the young. The term 'moral panic', often used with reference to such moments, was coined initially with reference to the anxieties generated by violent clashes between youth gangs that, during the 1960s, acquired the names Mods and Rockers.[1] Much of the media and a cross-section of politicians, police officers and conservative social critics repeatedly claimed to find a new depravity and a new lack of respect behind crime committed by the young, and especially by juveniles in their early teens or even younger. Other commentators were concerned at what they saw as vulnerability among young adults and juveniles; this vulnerability contributed to them falling under various influences which, in turn, prompted antisocial activities labelled as criminal. This dichotomy – seeing young adults and juveniles as, alternatively, vicious or victims – continued throughout the century although, in keeping with the broad liberal shift in the approach to crime by the criminal justice elite at the beginning of the century, the generation before the First World War witnessed a significant change in the understanding of offending by the young. Rather than behaviour rooted in a station in life, specifically the offspring of the poor working class, it began to be understood as more connected with a difficult stage of life, namely adolescence.[2] But again, feckless, uncaring and sometimes criminal parents, usually situated in the poor working class, remained popular scapegoats for explaining, in particular, the juvenile offender.

The offences committed by young adults and juveniles ranged from vandalism and petty theft to much more serious crimes and even, very occasionally, to murder. The principle of *doli incapax*, that is that children under a certain age were incapable of evil, went back to the Middle Ages. Recognition of the age of criminal responsibility in children had been elastic and had often been decided by a court's perception of whether or not the child appeared 'hardened'. The separate Juvenile Courts established in 1908 were concerned with offenders between the ages of 7 and 16 years, thus effectively defining the ages at which children were responsible for their behaviour, but sufficiently vulnerable to be kept apart from courts dealing with adults. The Children and Young Persons Act of 1933 raised the age of criminal responsibility to 8 years and the cut-off for the Juvenile Court to 17 years. Thirty years later the age of criminal responsibility was raised to 10. But in the more punitive 1990s the whole principle of *doli incapax* was challenged. In 1994, in the wake of the murder of James Bulger, the Conservative government put the principle under review; and four years later the new Labour government's Crime and Disorder Act effectively abolished it; even children, it was now insisted, should know the difference between right and wrong and act accordingly.

At the beginning of the twentieth century scares about hooligan violence had subsided in the press. In Manchester, where the ferocious Scuttler gangs had fought each other for 30 years or so, the gangs themselves appear to have been in decline. The decline is difficult to explain; while a later, popular tradition often put it down to the flogging of offenders, it was more probably the result of a combination of hard policing, tough prison sentences and new sporting and entertainment outlets for potential Scuttlers in their early teens – specifically street football teams and the new cinema.[3] As the Scuttlers were seen to be fading away in Manchester so, elsewhere, the police were often looking for more preventive policies to reduce delinquent behaviour among the young. This appears to have been the case in Oxford, for example; and in London too Metropolitan Police officers were looking for ways to limit the lesser forms of juvenile offending that did not require a heavy-handed approach. The Superintendent of Southwark Police station drew up a list of the 18 most common offences committed by children and young people in the streets and public places; alongside the offence he wrote the penalty (see Table 4.1). The list is revealing for the pettiness of the offences, but the superintendent suggested that the London County Council have copies printed for display in various elementary schools so as to discourage children from such behaviour. This

TABLE 4.1 *Superintendent Water's list of the most common offences committed in public places by children and young persons, April 1907*

Nature of Offence	Penalty
1. Defacing any wall or building with chalk, etc.	Fine 40 shillings
2. Wilfully breaking, destroying or damaging any building, wall or fence, etc.	" 40 shillings
3. Wilfully breaking, destroying or damaging any tree, shrub, or seat in any public walk, park or garden	" 40 shillings
4. Throwing or discharging any stone or other missile to the damage or danger of any person	" 40 shillings
5. Making a bonfire	" 40 shillings
6. Throwing or setting fire to any firework	" 40 shillings
7. Wilfully and wantonly disturbing any inhabitant by pulling or ringing any door bell	" 40 shillings
8. Knocking at any door without lawful excuse	" 40 shillings
9. Wilfully extinguishing the light of any lamp	" 40 shillings
10. Flying a kite to the annoyance of passengers or inhabitants	" 40 shillings
11. Playing at any game to the annoyance of inhabitants or passengers	" 40 shillings
12. Making or using any slide upon ice or snow in any street or thoroughfare to the common danger of passengers	" 40 shillings
13 Riding behind carts, carriages etc. without the driver's consent	" 5 shillings
14. Throwing stones at a railway train (or endangering the safety of passengers on railways)	" £10 or 40 shillings or whipping according to age
15. Gambling with any coin, card, etc.	1st offence 40 shillings 2nd " £5
16. Depositing the rind of any orange, banana or other fruit in any street or public place	" 40 shillings
17. Throwing, placing or leaving any bottle, broken glass, nail or other sharp substance in such a position as to be likely to cause injury to passengers or animals, or damage to property	" 40 shillings
18. Place or throw any stones, dirt, wood, refuse or other material on any part of a tramway	" £5

Source: MEPO2/4256

would 'thus prevent them coming in contact with Police in undesirable ways'. The LCC decided not to implement the proposal.[4]

While the Edwardian police dealt with child stone-throwers and the declining fighting gangs, an influential theory was propounded, initially on the other side of the Atlantic, that significantly developed the concept of adolescence and singled it out as a particularly difficult period of life and one during which criminal behaviour was most likely. G. Stanley Hall's two-volume work had a title that could scarcely have been more inclusive: *Adolescence, Its Psychology and Its Relations to Physiology, Anthropology, Sociology, Sex, Crime, Religion and Education.* His argument was that each individual was compelled to follow the development of the human race from primitive behaviour to rational civilisation. The child was the primitive; the adult enjoyed the civilised state; in adolescence the individual was pulled in both directions and the ensuing storm and stress meant that this period of life saw the individual most likely to commit crime and was when the most vicious, long-term criminal careers commenced. This suggested to Hall the need carefully to control and direct youth.[5] In England, Hall's work coincided with another issue seen as contributing to juvenile offenders and which vexed a range of social commentators. The 'boy labour' problem was picked up in a Royal Commission, in various Home Office Reports and in the General Report of the 1911 census. The concern was that many boys left school at around 10 to 14 years and were tempted into dead-end jobs – what the Census Report called 'blind alley occupations'.[6] These jobs – generally working as messengers or newsboys – were seen as necessary in poor working-class families for boosting the weekly budget. But for the respectable commentator free from the difficulties of such a life, such jobs were seen as giving boys (and sometimes girls) independence without discipline and hence, it was feared, the boys slipped easily into unruly behaviour. Worse still, when they reached the age at which they had to be paid an adult wage, they could be dismissed and thrown on to an uncertain labour market with neither skills nor training. This was not merely a concern about youth crime, however; it was symptomatic of a wider concern about the British 'race' which, in the eyes of many, was being undermined by the people of the slums of big cities. The miserable, unskilled, untrained and hence unemployed or underemployed men who had followed the boy labour route, were seen as producing still more weak-kneed, narrow-chested, noisy and volatile slum-dwellers.

While the overall statistics of crime decreased during the First World War, there was alarm about a statistical increase in juvenile offending. This was commonly attributed to special problems caused by the war. Stories of battles were blamed for creating excitement and provoking the mischievous and immoral instincts of children. As ever boys and young men were seen as the principal offenders, but there were concerns that large military camps offered temptations to girls and young women, especially those of a supposedly feeble disposition that were most likely to be free with their sexual favours. The departure of fathers, schoolmasters and many policemen for the front, together with some mothers becoming engaged in war work or standing in for men serving in the trenches, was blamed for creating a breakdown of family discipline. It was noted also that clubs and parks were closed because the war had created a shortage of people to run them. Moreover the wartime restrictions on lighting were seen as reducing the likelihood of offenders being seen and apprehended when stealing from shops or street markets. Many of these causes might be challenged. Most significant in this respect was the fact that the greatest statistical rise in juvenile offending came in the first year of the war when military enlistment was voluntary and largely involved single men from skilled and clerical jobs; in such circumstances the argument about the lack of discipline because fathers were away at the front largely disintegrates. Yet the statistical rise in juvenile offending during the war years was real enough.[7]

The figures for juvenile crime slipped back to their pre-war level in 1920 and continued to decline throughout the decade, but they were rising again in the 1930s and anxieties about juvenile offenders continued throughout the inter-war years. The Second World War brought another upsurge in the statistics. There was a repetition of the concerns that, with fathers out at the front and mothers out at work, children were out of control. But it was also reported that some offending was instigated by parents; the siphoning of paraffin from the hurricane lamps in air-raid shelters was one example.[8] There were renewed worries about girls hanging around military bases, going into pubs and trying to pick up servicemen for sex. And when youths in their mid to late teens found jobs between leaving school and being called up for military service, critics complained that they were paid too much and that this fostered crime since such youths had yet to acquire responsibility, self-control and a recognition of the real value of money.[9] At times during 1940 and 1941 the concern about juvenile offending was such in the Manchester region that there was talk of imposing a night-time curfew on young people; and in 1942 conferences were organised in Stockport to explore the best ways of dealing with 'Dead End Kids' allegedly responsible for thousands of pounds worth of damage.[10]

Wartime brought distinct, sometimes new and always urgent explanations for juvenile offending, but it also revived and refocused traditional concerns. The influential *Our Towns*, published by the Women's Group on Public Welfare in 1943, for example, was based on the experience of housing children evacuated from the big cities because of the danger of enemy bombing. The respectable middle-class women of the English provinces were shocked by the state of many of these children with their filthy clothes, unserviceable footwear, their head lice and problems of bedwetting. The authors feared that little had changed in the big cities since the great sociological surveys of the late nineteenth century. While crime was not central to *Our Towns*, the authors believed that juvenile delinquency was bred in the environment of appalling surroundings, inadequate diet and poor parental care.[11]

There were other explanations that were commonly deployed for juveniles' and young people's offending during the first half of the century. Churchmen in particular, though not alone, lamented a decline in Christian teaching and Christian values. The economic depression left many young men idle and, in 1933, the Chief Constable of Wallasey feared that this was leading youths from respectable working-class families into mischief. He went on to comment adversely on what he saw as

the pernicious and growing habit of youth in using Americanisms with nasal accompaniment to appear, in their own vernacular, 'tough guys.' On one of my officers going to search him a young housebreaker said to him, 'Lay off, cop.' 'Oh yeah?' is a frequent answer to charges, and we are promised 'shoot ups in the burg' and threatened with being 'bumped off' by these would-be racketeers, who are mere boys and who have never been away from their home towns.

The Chief Constable was delighted that several films depicting American gangsters had recently been banned by his Watch Committee. Many more followed his assumptions about the impact of American gangsters in the 'kinema'; and there were those who also found fault in 'cheap trashy literature'.[12]

Yet there was a conflict of opinion over many of these causes. When concerns about juvenile offending reached a peak in 1940 and 1941, a number of letters were published in the correspondence columns of the *Manchester Guardian* arguing both for and against the effects of the cinema, about the supposed lack of Christian teaching and so forth. Moreover, while many people rehearsed their prejudices and fears in assertions about the causes of criminal behaviour by the young, there were also serious attempts to understand and explain the problem of juvenile offending. The most influential here was Cyril Burt's *The Young Delinquent*, first published in 1925. Burt was an applied psychologist working in the

Education Department of the London County Council. He had more than a passing knowledge of the poorer districts of big cities, having worked in a university settlement close to the docks in Liverpool and having undertaken a social study in London's East End. He concluded that criminality did not have a simple, single cause, particularly among the young. But Burt was also a eugenicist and, consequently, while he believed that poor working-class children often existed within a demoralised family, and that they might be adversely affected in body and health by their poor surroundings, he also saw their problems resulting from heritable, biological defects. Burt's conclusions became widely accepted among leading figures within the criminal justice system during the inter-war period. The statistical contrasts revealed in the Judicial Statistics, between juvenile offending in impoverished northern industrial districts as compared with the south, added weight to such perceptions.[13]

At the close of the 1930s, the criminologist Hermann Mannheim, like many others, considered that poverty was a key cause of delinquency, but he found it difficult to pinpoint precisely its impact. 'It may be the ultimate cause of defects and educational backwardness as well as of family quarrels, of the premature death of a parent, of bad housing conditions or unsuitable employment.' But while most offenders came from the working class, in his study of 606 boys sent to Borstal institutions between 1920 and 1934 and 411 girls in the care of the Aylesbury After-Care Association, there was a sprinkling of middle-class offenders who appeared to mix comfortably with their more plebeian fellows. Mannheim's evidence, like that of others, also noted how petty much of the offending was that got young people into trouble. Moreover some of this, while defined as criminal by the law, was often not so defined by the communities in which the young people lived. In particular Mannheim singled out the theft of coal in mining districts and he provided several examples of juvenile offending careers involving such offences.

Boy, born 1910, Welsh. Father War pensioner; twelve children in the family. 'Boy's relations with parents friendly; mother gives him money for cigarettes, and he steals coal for her.'
Work: Colliery helper, 22s[hillings]
Delinquency:
*   1924   Stealing coal, bound over.*
*   1926   Stealing coal, bound over.*
*   (Moreover, six fines for stealing coal)*
*   Stealing coal, three years' B[orstal] I[nstitution].*

Social Worker: 'Parents say he only did what others were doing. Not considered crime to steal coal.'
Medical Officer: 'Comes from a district where stealing coal from pitheads is regarded as fair game. No amount of fines, probation or advice can have any effect. If his mother needed coal, why shouldn't he do as everyone else did?' . . .

Girl, born 1907. Father labourer, out of work; home bad, one brother in Reformatory.
Delinquency:
    1919   *Malicious damage, fined 5 s[hillings]*
    1920   *Stealing coal, fined 2s. 6d.*
    1921   *Stealing coal, fined £1.*
    1923   *Stealing coal, Probation.*
            Stealing boots, Probation, sent to a Home, absconded.
            Breach of Recognizance, three months' imprisonment.
            Stealing boots, fined 10s.
    1924   *Stealing 28lbs of coal, value 5d.; three years' B.I.*
Social Worker: 'Coal lifting in X is a commonplace, everyone more or less does it. Girl is very simple and weak, but morally innocent; feels justified in stealing if family is in need.'
Medical Officer: 'Intelligence below normal though not mentally deficient.'
Chaplain: 'Ought never to have been sent to Aylesbury, but has benefited.'[14]

Stephen Humphries has asserted, that 'the single most important category of juvenile crime' from the late Victorian period to the outbreak of the Second World War, involved 'taking coal from pit heads, chumps of wood from timber yards and taking vegetables from farmer's fields, poaching rabbits and so on'. The assertion may well be correct and Humphries collected a range of oral testimony from people that had grown up in some rough and poverty-stricken areas of England over the period.[15] The press, however, favoured reporting the more sensational crimes such as, for example, a 15-year-old burglar convicted of breaking into the Ladies Army and Navy Club and assaulting a member with intent to rob, or 12 boys being convicted at Bath Juvenile Court of over 100 offences, mainly house-breaking and theft.[16] Few crimes were more sensational than murder and, early in 1922, newspaper columns avidly followed the case of Henry Jacoby, an 18-year-old pantry boy convicted and hanged for the murder of Lady White in the Hotel Spencer. The jury had recommended mercy given Jacoby's youth and there were some concerns about his confession. Requests for a reprieve were rejected by the Home Secretary, and while the stentorian voice of *The Times* insisted that 'as the law provides that one old enough to play a part in the normal affairs of life is also old enough to pay a man's penalty for a crime, that law must be punctiliously upheld by those who are its guardians', others were less sure. The uncertainty was coloured by a case that coincided with that of Jacoby in which the murderer, Ronald True, was a young gentleman and his victim was a prostitute. True was declared insane and sent to Broadmoor Hospital for the criminally insane. The issue of class was not raised overtly, but it appears to have underpinned at least some of the press, and popular outrage.[17]

While the national press favoured the sensational crime story, it also noticed the petty nature of much juvenile offending. 'Stealing Milk from Doorsteps', for example, was the way that the *Manchester Guardian* headlined the trial of a 12-year-old and a 13-year-old at Southport Children's Court in 1927.[18] And a novel or humorous angle could be as appealing to an editor as a sensational story. Early in 1946 four boys appeared at Wolverhampton Juvenile Court accused of breaking into a house to steal oranges and eggs. It was alleged that the boys got the idea from listening to radio broadcasts of the 'Just William' stories of Richmal Crompton. A woman probation officer told the court that some parents had stopped their children from listening to the broadcasts fearing that they might encourage 'wrong notions'. The chair of the bench dismissed the boys with a warning that things did not always go right for Richmal Crompton's naughty schoolboy. The *Daily Mirror* asked the elderly authoress for her opinion; she laughed.[19]

Crompton's 11-year-old schoolboy had a gang of friends known as 'the outlaws'. They were an idealised type of middle-class boy that disliked girls and got into relatively mild scrapes. In the first half of the century particularly there was a branch of thought that revelled in the wildness of boys and their spirit of adventure. Among some influential commentators this spilled over into an admiration for the behaviour of working-class boys who fell foul of the law. Alexander Paterson, a key figure among the Prison Commissioners, saw great potential in the daring raids carried out by young offenders; it was the kind of recklessness that had given England Sir Francis Drake. And Lord Baden-Powell believed that, properly directed, 'the worst hooligan makes the best [Boy] Scout' and thus, potentially, the ideal soldier, useful man and contented citizen.[20]

The period after the Second World War saw no let-up in the concerns about juvenile offending. Initially there were those who regarded the disruption of the war as continuing to affect families in the peace. 'Let no one think that the evil consequences of war conditions have faded happily away with the smoke of the victory bonfires', counselled John Watson of the Metropolitan Juvenile Courts. Unhappy children still passed through the courts never having

known a father's care or the security of a normal home. Some are only half educated through lack of regular schooling. There are girls whose surfeit of premature sexual excitement has made them emotionally unbalanced. Most tragic are the 'misfit' children, who have returned from happy years in their foster-homes to parents who are strangers and homes of their own that are misery and anti-climax.[21]

Watson's explanation appealed to many, and concerns about a lack of morality and the decline of Christian beliefs and values were appended. Even the royal family took up the issue as when, for example, 22-year-old Princess Elizabeth accepted the freedom of Cardiff with a speech lamenting the growth of juvenile crime which she attributed to a decline in the old, fixed standards of morality, 'quarrelling parents, harsh treatment, foolish spoiling . . . the lack of that best of disciplines founded on respect for what is right'.[22]

Leslie Wilkins, an extremely able statistician working in the Home Office, used the figures to explore how far the war had fostered juvenile delinquency. He found that the rate of offending among boys aged between 8 and 17 years had increased by 70 per cent in the years 1938 to 1944; but even more alarming, the rate among girls of the same age had increased by 120 per cent. Wilkins extrapolated from these figures the idea of delinquent cohorts, and he concluded that the most crime-prone generation were those who had experienced the upheaval of war – disrupted schooling, father absent, mother at work – during their fifth year.[23] When his study was published in 1960 his most delinquent cohort was aged between 15 and 20 years, and a key problem with his conclusions about the war were becoming apparent: statistically the generation born after the war appeared even more ready to commit offences.

The growth of a sociologically based, academic criminology after the Second World War led to several serious studies of offending by juveniles and young people, in which researchers observed and interviewed their subjects. Among the first of these was David Downes's study of youths in Stepney, a poor area in which the dock-working community was notorious for its petty theft from the workplace. Downes's youthful offenders had failed at failing schools; they lived for the moment and their delinquency was a way of buying excitement.[24] But, as the statistics of crime rose, there were few prepared to take on the implications of such studies that major educational, economic and social changes might be required to alleviate the problem of juvenile offending. It was easier to believe that children and youths who vandalised property were being violent for gain, or just plain violent. Sensation often drowned out and obscured the realities of petty offending, even among those who had the fine detail at their fingertips. Sir Harold Scott, who had been a career civil servant, principally in the Home Office, and chairman of the Prison Commission before becoming Commissioner of the Metropolitan Police, devoted a chapter of his book *Scotland Yard* (1954) to 'Young men in trouble'. In the first three paragraphs he stressed that young people's crimes were rarely violent and that the 'common denominator' in the lives of many young offenders was a broken home. But the remainder of the chapter focused on the cases of two young murderers – Harry Jenkins and Christopher Craig.[25] Judges might also sound off about such individuals and then be quoted by an approving press. But there was also an increasing recognition that some of the old certainties about the causes of pre-war delinquency were no longer applicable when the decade of post-war austerity gave way to a period of consumerism that spread, in varying degrees, across the social classes.

In the first half of the century social class could play an important part in the way that some youthful horseplay was handled. Young gentlemen at university could be rough and violent in streets and public places, particularly in the celebratory aftermath of games or the bacchanalia of a student rag. Sometimes the young gentlemen appeared in a magistrates' court, but sometimes they, or their university, were simply allowed to pay for the damage and no action was taken. It is difficult to identify precise changes in such attitudes, but in the more egalitarian society that emerged in the aftermath of the Second World War there appears to have been a growing intolerance towards turbulent student behaviour. The London University rag of 1953 is an indicator of the change. The Metropolitan Police withdrew permission for the students' usual bonfire on 5 November on the grounds of potential trouble between the students and the 'local hooligan element'. Outraged by the restriction on their annual night of misrule, the students attacked the police with fireworks, bags of flour, bags of sand and toilet rolls. The following day 189 students appeared before Bow Street magistrates; they were carried on the shoulders of their peers and another rowdy scene developed. There was considerable press comment. Some defended the students, particularly in letter columns. One disgusted resident of Tunbridge Wells demanded to know of *The Times*:

Have we arrived at a time when a boy cannot throw a bag of flour at a policeman's helmet on a night of license . . . without being prosecuted and fined by the law for causing a disturbance of the peace?

But the populist, conservative *Daily Sketch* linked the students' behaviour with that of a stabbing by a group of youths in Liverpool and declared: 'We cannot afford to breed hooligans whether they wear zoot suits or cap and gown.'[26]

The classic zoot suit, with its wide-legged, tight ankle trousers, its long jacket with wide lapels and wide, padded shoulders, had been worn in the urban United States during the early 1940s, primarily by young black and Hispanic working-class men. It was slimmed down for the post-war white working-class and became popular with some young Englishmen. As such it was an early manifestation of the post-war youth culture imported from America. It seemed that every decade in the second half of the century had its own youth groups, stigmatised by much of adult society and the media. In the 1950s it was the Teddy Boys with their sideburns and slicked hair, their bootlace ties, their long, draped jackets with velvet collars and their tight trousers. Some Teddy Boy gangs fought each other; they also became associated with the new rock and roll music and with the disorder in cinemas surrounding the feature film *Rock Around the Clock* (1956). In the early 1960s the Teds had largely disappeared and the so-called Mods became the stigmatised group. They were known for their neat hair, their Italian suits and motor scooters. The media made much of seaside, Bank Holiday confrontations between gangs of Mods and the vestiges of the Teds, the Rockers. By the end of the 1960s yet another group, the Skinheads, had made their first appearance in East London. Again there was a distinct style of appearance: the shaven head, the braces holding up jeans that were short so as to show off the high Dr Martens boots. The Skinheads adopted particularly violent persona based on the aggressive, unskilled, working-class hard man. They were associated with attacks on homosexual men and immigrants – especially those from the Indian sub-continent that they labelled 'Pakis'. They were also linked with increasing violence among football supporters, but, while the football hooligan became a folk devil from the late 1960s to the 1990s, the phenomenon of such violence was not new. Moreover, while it was often associated with poorly educated youths from poor backgrounds as epitomised in *Zigger Zagger*, a play written for the National Youth Theatre in 1967, football violence, by the late 1970s and early 1980s at least, was often organised by groups such as the Inter-City Firm (ICF) or the Gooners which owed allegiance, respectively, to West Ham United and Arsenal. These gangs often contained married men in their twenties with steady jobs and mortgages, and they left calling cards on their battered and bleeding victims: 'Congratulations, you have just met the ICF'.[27]

Immigrant gangs also began to appear, but the Afro-Caribbean 'Rude Boys', who were known for drug-dealing, pimping and gambling, and the religiously inspired Rastafarians, never quite hit the headlines like the 'Skins', except in race confrontations and riots. During the 1970s and 1980s, however, it was not gangs of black youths that were stigmatised, rather it was the individual black youth committing street robbery – the 'mugger' – that became the focus of press panic and police targeting. The numbers of young black muggers was always far fewer than the panic suggested, but that was hardly the point.[28]

Hippies in the 1960s and early 1970s were allegedly peace-loving but, like the Punks of the 1980s who appeared to revel in desecration and nihilism, they rejected existing conventions and norms. All of these youth groups were stigmatised for deviant behaviour. Sometimes this deviance went little further than unconventional hair styles and dress although in other instances, perhaps most noticeably with the use of recreational drugs, it did indeed break the law. But the real problem was these groups' rejection of convention and their refusal to conform to the norms of their elders and, particularly, of established white, essentially middle-class, respectable society. It was the breaking of sexual norms especially that appears to have fostered most of the concerns about delinquency in girls and young women.

The anxiety about girls and young women flocking to the vicinity of military camps during wartime has been noted above. But a war was not essential for girls to gravitate towards military personnel, or for young servicemen to attempt to lure them. In June 1929, for example, a private in the King's Liverpool Regiment was tried for indecently assaulting a 15-year-old girl who had entered his barracks. The judge at the Liverpool Assizes expressed surprise that the girl, apparently one of several, had been able to get in to the barracks; to which an army captain replied, rather lamely: 'They did not get through the gate.' The judge asked a local police inspector 'to put an end to the loitering of girls round the barracks.'[29] But just as it did not take a war for young women to be attracted to soldiers, so it did not take a uniform to bring young people together and to create anxieties about young people's morals.

In the first half of the twentieth century fears of miscegenation prompted investigations into the mixed-race communities of the big seaports such as London, Liverpool and Cardiff. The investigators, commonly drawn from local universities, were inclined to conclude that the girls who 'consorted' with coloured men were generally those working as prostitutes, those that already had an illegitimate child, those that were mentally weak, or those who had become involved through some sense of adventure but could not now break free. The children of such liaisons were also seen as potentially deviant, unable to bridge the gap of the different races from which they had come.[30] Out of a sense of adventure, looking for the opportunity to hear live jazz or simply the opportunity for a relaxed, possibly exotic atmosphere, young white men had often been attracted to the clubs and cafés that were to be found in these ports and that were run by men from overseas. Such attractions became more noticeable and spread beyond the ports during the 1950s and 1960s with the growth of immigration. Clubs frequented by young people, though not necessarily run by immigrants or foreign seamen, became objects of concern.

During the 1960s local government, the local police and the press in Manchester discovered a 'Coffee Club menace'. Even though the Licensing Act of 1961 had led to a relaxation of the licensing laws and had given licensees the opportunity to challenge any refusal to allow them to sell alcohol, these Mancunian clubs did not attempt to sell it. The clubs' concentration on non-alcoholic beverages was one of the problems for the local authorities since it meant that they were, in effect, outside police supervision. It was this independence that contributed to the anxieties. The clubs became notorious for being beyond control, dimly lit and frequented by young women and young men with long hair and dishevelled clothes. The young people, in contrast, saw these clubs as their own space. A few experimented with drugs; a few were found to be on the run from home or approved schools; on occasions some of the clientele brought their own bedrolls, or spent the night on mattresses that were provided by friends or by the proprietors. The Chief Constable's annual report for 1964 included an assessment of the 'Coffee Beat Clubs' prepared by a superintendent on the evidence collected by teenage police cadets. The assessment admitted that 'there was insufficient evidence of misconduct, sexual or disorderly, to justify prosecution of the proprietors for keeping a disorderly house'. But it was highly critical of the physical state of the clubs, of their proprietors and much of the clientele, including the 'sinister' presence of 'men of colour'. There were plenty among the local elite and among the older generations that hoped for greater regulation to restore what was, essentially, an imagined social order of restricted class, gender, racial and moral boundaries. The Manchester Corporation Act of 1965, a private Act of parliament, accordingly provided the police with sweeping powers over the clubs and within a few years most had either closed or changed their form, selling alcohol and catering for a more adult clientele. Yet while the Manchester Police were provided with new powers to guard the morals of the young in relation to coffee houses, they and other police forces, together with other agencies, were beginning to take a less rigorous approach to the enforcing of the law regarding the age of consent, particularly when a girl was nearing her sixteenth birthday, when her boyfriend was of a similar age, and when she did not otherwise appear 'out of control' or 'in moral danger'.[31]

Before the adoption of more liberal public attitudes towards sexual behaviour, something that is generally associated with the 1960s, some young men protested that they were unaware that sexual contact with a girl under 16 was a crime; and perhaps too, they were not aware of the age of the girl involved. In Chelmsford, early in 1935 Malcolm Hilbury, K.C., Commissioner of Assize, bound over an 18-year-old youth who had been charged with an offence against a girl who was under 16 years. The youth declared that he wanted to stand by the girl and marry her. Hilbury protested:

In every town I have before me young men of good character like you who have fallen into this crime, and on most occasions have fallen into it not realizing that it was a crime, however deplorable it may have been from the moral point of view. I believe you when you tell me that you did not realize it was a crime. The sooner it is understood everywhere among young people that this is a crime the better.[32]

The more liberal attitudes of the 1960s, which appear often to have reduced the likelihood of criminal prosecutions in cases such as the above, did not go far enough for some. Law reforms established a gap between the age of consent for consensual heterosexual activity – still 16 years – and that for consensual homosexual activity – 21 years. In the mid-1970s a small group of paedophiles, forming the Paedophile Information Exchange (PIE), publicly campaigned for the complete abolition of the age of consent. They argued that the criminal law should only become involved when consent was not freely given and urged the acceptance of consensual sexual relations between adults and children. A cluster of researchers were interested in the issue, and there was a degree of support from some human rights lobbies. But the acceptance of paedophilia was a step far too far for the majority of those sympathetic to the liberalising of sexual behaviour.

PIE was dissolved following first, the successful prosecution of its chair for conspiracy to corrupt public morals in 1981, and then, three years later, the successful prosecution of other leading figures on charges of circulating child pornography.[33] PIE had successfully raised the profile of paedophiles, but not in the way that its adherents had hoped. By the turn of the century the paedophile had become a major bogeyman in the tabloid press; of particular concern was what to do with such offenders when they had completed a prison sentence.[34]

In the first half of the century particularly, when girls or unmarried young women were sexually assaulted, there was often concern about what to do with them. The suggestion that having an illegitimate child was sufficient to see a young woman incarcerated in a mental institution has probably been overstated. Nevertheless, the law was used more rigorously against young women supposedly unable to control or protect themselves sexually.[35] In 1926 the Plymouth Watch Committee wondered whether, in the case of any girls 'contaminated' by a sexual assault and who might relate their experiences to 'pure-minded girls', it would be a good idea for Local Education Authorities to prevent their return to school. Perhaps, the committee suggested, 'if the case was bad enough' such girls should be sent to a special school or home. The Central Conference of Chief Constables that debated the proposal was sympathetic, but resolved to take no action.[36] Such concerns were not limited to morality-minded town councillors and senior police officers; even children's charities of the period believed that they had to consider the depth of such 'contamination' before agreeing to receive a child into their care.[37]

The year before the chief constables' debate a departmental committee of the Home Office had met to consider sexual offences against children. The committee concluded that the victims of such assaults were 'no more a moral danger' than a girl who had been caught 'pilfering'.[38] The fear that the authorities would remove a child, however, may have been one reason why some parents – mothers especially – refused to let the police proceed with a charge against a suspected paedophile or, in the term more common at the time, a child molester.[39] Equally there was the fear of stigma, concern for a child required to give evidence in court, and concern too about what might happen to the child as a result. While, towards the end of the century, criminologists and those working in child welfare agencies raised major questions about the placing of childhood in the binaries of childhood/adulthood, innocence/corruption, victim/threat, such portrayals had been commonplace and remained popular in the media. An analysis of the increased press reporting of sexual crime during the 1970s noted how the issue of 'consent' was never raised when discussing cases involving heterosexual, underage sex. The girls involved were either virgins – hence innocent victims, or else they were dangerous temptresses – a threat to powerless men.[40] These binaries stretched beyond sex offences to embrace a wide range of crimes involving young people, particularly when parents, guardians and others sought justification for the ill-treatment of, or for inflicting violence upon children and other young people in their care.

It is probably fair to say that some parents and guardians have always ill-treated their children or children in their care; the wicked step-parent has a long tradition in folk tales and popular literature. On occasions the excuse was made that the child was 'wicked' or 'uncontrollable' and that 'chastisement' was inflicted to punish and reform. Corporal punishment, after all, remained a sanction available to the courts until after the Second World War, although there was growing criticism and increasing demands for its abolition during the 1920s and 1930s. A few employers still considered, quite wrongly, that they could punish servants with violence.[41] Teachers, however, and in the case of church schools the local vicar, were permitted to administer corporal punishment until 1982. Such punishment was regulated and monitored more and more before abolition, and brutal treatment could lead to a teacher and even a vicar being prosecuted.[42] Corporal punishment by teachers was accepted by some parents but challenged by others sometimes, it would seem, in areas where the parents believed that it was their priority to exact physical punishment on their offspring.[43] In the same way there could be hostility towards inspectors from the NSPCC. At the beginning of the century the NSPCC inspector was commonly known in working-class districts as 'the cruelty man'. In 1921 the society brought a libel action against Miss Agnes Mott, the secretary of the Mother's Defence League, for a leaflet that urged members of the poor working class not to be afraid of 'the cruelty man', pointing out that he was not a government official and, while he wore a uniform, he did not have the powers of a policeman. But what the society really took exception to was Miss Mott's implication that working-class critics of the society were correct in their beliefs that the inspectors kidnapped children. The case was settled by Miss Mott agreeing to pay costs and not to publish any further such leaflets.[44]

But the need for NSPCC inspectors and for police vigilance remained, as some parents and grandparents could be very violent. At Ratcliffe Police Court in September 1927 a grandmother and her son were found guilty of burning a seven-year old boy with a hot iron to dissuade him from further petty thefts. An eight-year old in London's Lambeth, who burned the little boy next door, was burned in return by his mother.

I burned him deliberately with the curling-tongs as he was a naughty boy . . . The tongs were on the gas fire, and I took them off and burned the boy on the right leg. The burns on his left leg were due to his kicking when I was burning his right leg.

The mother was sentenced to seven weeks' imprisonment with hard labour. But some magistrates could be sympathetic to harsh parental punishment. When another mother appeared at Lambeth Police Court in 1930 after thrashing her 13-year-old son with a dog-lead for cruelty to a dog, the magistrate considered that a boy of such an age who was 'cruel to a dumb animal . . . deserved a thrashing'. The mother was ordered to pay costs and bound over. A Worcestershire mother who beat her daughter was dealt with more severely, but then the girl, accused of being 'very disobedient' by her mother, had to be brought into court in a wheelchair.[45]

Different forms of abuse, violence and neglect were recognised as having an effect on the children that suffered them. At the end of the century especially, it was increasingly noted that those who perpetrated such offences had often been victims themselves. Sometimes the abuse and violence fostered brutal behaviour among victims while they were still children, but what was particularly notable was how, in the concluding years of the century, cruel and violent behaviour by children began to be depicted.

The most extreme form of violent crime is murder and there are very few children that kill others. Between 1946 and 1968, 28 children under the age of 14 were found guilty of killing. This statistic was mentioned when, in December 1968, an 11-year-old girl named Mary Bell was found guilty of manslaughter, through diminished responsibility, for strangling two boys aged 3 years and 4 years. Mary was a damaged girl; her mother was a prostitute and, while it did not come out until years after the trial, Mary herself had been sexually abused by both her mother and her mother's clients. Her offence, nevertheless, was shocking. Those campaigning against violence in films and on television noted that the girl claimed to have watched television detective series and used the case to reinforce their arguments and demands. The prosecuting counsel spoke of plumbing 'unprecedented depths of wickedness' and described the accused as 'a most abnormal child; aggressive, cruel, incapable of remorse . . . [of] unusual intelligence and a degree of cunning that is almost terrifying'. But the general concern in the court, in the Home Office and in the press, was what might be done with her. There were no psychiatric units or hospitals for treating such offenders.[46]

A quarter of a century after the Mary Bell case, another murder by children became a major news story. The victim, two-year-old James Bulger, was lured away from his mother in a Bootle shopping mall by two ten-year-olds, Robert Thompson and Jon Venables, and battered to death. The two killers, like Mary Bell, had experienced a grim and troubled upbringing. Indeed, the serious medical and academic analyses of child killers undertaken at the close of the century suggested a range of causes behind these children's actions, often involving some sort of abuse, serious problems with parents who were themselves sometimes unstable, substance abuse, mental illness; and friendship between two similar children appeared to exacerbate the potential for violence.[47] In the case of Thompson and Venables there were also assertions that they had been encouraged in the murder by watching fictional violence – in this case a horror film, *Child's Play 3*, in which the spirit of a serial killer inhabits a doll called Chucky. The shrill reporting of the murder and the trial demonstrated the changes that had occurred since Mary Bell's prosecution. The Bulger case has already been the subject of comparison with a similar murder in Victorian England, leading to the conclusion that, while people in the late twentieth century may have considered themselves more humane, their aggressive hostility towards Thompson and Venables suggested a disillusion-ment with, and lack of faith in, the criminal justice system quite different from that of their Victorian forbears.[48] The comparison with the Mary Bell case suggests that the change in attitude came principally during the 1970s and 1980s. But it is also notable that the statistics of children being con-victed for murder had not changed during these years: between 1979 and 1984, 12 children under the age of 14 years were convicted of killing – eight for murder and four for manslaughter.[49] The Bulger case came on the eve of, and contributed to the environment that prompted the review of the principle of *doli incapax*. A variety of commentators seized on the case to lament a 'moral vacuum' in the country. James Bulger's parents and *The Sun* newspaper organised a petition to protest that the ten-year sentences handed down to Thompson and Venables were insufficient. Michael Howard, the Home Secretary, increased their sentences to 15 years, but then the Court of Appeal ruled his action to be unlawful.[50]

On the available evidence, and given the shifting degrees of tolerance together with the shifts in the age of criminal responsibility, it would be extremely difficult to prove whether or not children and young people became more or less involved in criminal behaviour during the twentieth century. Efforts were made throughout the century to limit such behaviour; generally the same tropes were employed to explain it, although with varying degrees of emphasis across the period. There was, however, one exception. In the first half of the century there was a greater preparedness by some commentators to attribute even criminal behaviour by young people as 'naughtiness'. This attribution linked with a more optimistic attitude towards solving social problems in general and with a faith in reformative policies for criminal offenders in particular. Criminal 'naughtiness' was the kind of activity that young people could be expected to grow out of with teaching and greater maturity; it was also the kind of behaviour that, if properly harnessed, was seen as something that was good for a boy's character and that could be channelled for the benefit of society as a whole. By the closing decades of the century, with rising crime statistics and a declining faith in the criminal justice system, such optimistic arguments had all but vanished, even among the most liberal observers of juvenile offending.

References and notes

1 Stanley Cohen, *Folk Devils and Moral Panics: the creation of the Mods and Rockers*, London: MacGibbon and Key, 1972.

2 John R. Gillis, 'The evolution of juvenile delinquency in England 1890–1914', *Past and Present*, 67 (1975) pp. 96–126.

3 Andrew Davies, *The Gangs of Manchester: the story of the Scuttlers, Britain's first youth cult*, Preston: Milo Books, 2008.

4 MEPO 2/4256, Prevention of crimes amongst schoolchildren, 1907–1937. Supt Waters's report is dated 5 April 1907. For the Oxford example see Gillis, 'The evolution of juvenile delinquency'.

5 G. Stanley Hall, *Adolescence, Its Psychology and Its Relations to Physiology, Anthropology, Sociology, Sex, Crime, Religion and Education*, 2 vols. New York and London: Appleton, 1904. The British Library catalogue lists subsequent editions in 1908, 1911, 1914, 1916, 1917, 1924 and 1937.

6 *Census Returns for England and Wales, 1911*, London: HMSO, 1917–18, Cd. 8491, p. 164.

7 David Smith, 'Juvenile delinquency in Britain in the First World War', *Criminal Justice History*, 11 (1990) pp. 119–45; Alyson Brown and David Barrett, *Knowledge of Evil: child prostitution and child sexual abuse in twentieth-century England*, Cullompton: Willan, 2002, pp. 67–73.

8 *Daily Herald*, 17 October 1942, p. 3.

9 **Edward Smithies**, *Crime in Wartime: a social history of crime in World War II*, London: George Allen & Unwin, 1982, chap. 10; Brown and Barrett, *Knowledge of Evil*, pp. 116–21.

10 *Manchester Guardian*, 29 May 1940, p. 2, and 30 October 1941, p. 2; *Daily Herald*, 11 July 1942, p. 3.

11 Women's Group on Public Welfare, *Our Towns: a close up*, Oxford: Oxford University Press, 1943. For a useful discussion of the origins and impact of the report see **John Welshman**, 'Evacuation, hygiene and social policy: the *Our Towns* Report of 1943', *Historical Journal*, 42, 3 (1999) pp. 781–807.

12 *Manchester Guardian*, 11 February 1933, p. 6; see also, 3 May 1923, p. 16; 23 April, 1925, p. 18; 10 April 1931, p. 8.

13 *Judicial Statistics of England and Wales for 1929*, 1930–31, Cmd. 3853, p. xxi; *Manchester Guardian*, 18 October 1932, p. 8.

14 **Hermann Mannheim**, *Social Aspects of Crime in England between the Wars*, London: Allen and Unwin, 1940, pp. 261 and 299–300.

15 **Stephen Humphries**, *Hooligans or Rebels? An oral history of working-class childhood and youth, 1889–1939*, Oxford: Basil Blackwell, 1981, p. 151. Humphries admits in a footnote (p. 259) that the Judicial Statistics rarely provide details of goods stolen. He goes on to state that his assertion that food and fuel 'were the two principal items stolen is based on an extensive examination of the literature on juvenile delinquency'.

16 *The Times*, 21 June 1929, p. 5, and 24 February 1939, p. 11.

17 See, for example, *Manchester Guardian*, 29 March 1922, p. 10, and 29 April, p. 13; *The Times*, 8 June 1922, p. 15 and 13 June p. 8.

18 *Manchester Guardian*, 29 September, 1927, p. 3.

19 *Daily Mirror*, 31 January 1946, p. 4.

20 *Manchester Guardian*, 11 October 1916, p. 4, and 17 July 1930, p. 8; *The Times*, 25 May 1933, p. 13; and see also, **Geoffrey Pearson**, *Hooligan: a history of respectable fears*, London: Macmillan, 1983, pp. 34 and 44–5.

21 *The Times*, 5 February 1947, p. 5. For letters supporting and amplifying Watson, see *The Times*, 8 February 1947, p. 5.

22 *Manchester Guardian*, 28 May 1948, p. 3.

23 **Leslie T. Wilkins**, *Delinquent Generations: studies in the causes of delinquency and the treatment of offenders*, London: Home Office, HMSO, 1960.

24 **David Downes**, *The Delinquent Solution: a study in subcultural theory*, London: Routledge and Kegan Paul, 1966.

25 **Sir Harold Scott**, *Scotland Yard*, Harmondsworth: Penguin, 1957, chap. 7. The book was first published by André Deutsch in 1954.

26 **Clive Emsley**, Hard Men: *violence in England since 1750*, London: Hambledon, 2005, pp. 51–4.

27 See, for example, the clutch of press stories surrounding the murder of John Dickinson, a 24-year-old plasterer from Vauxhall in South London. Dickinson, an Arsenal supporter, was killed in a clash with the ICF outside Arsenal's old stadium, Highbury, in May 1982. *The Guardian*, 5 August 1983, p. 1; *The Times*, 6 August 1983, p. 3. See, in general, **Eric Dunning, Patrick Murphy** and **John Williams**, *The Roots of Football Hooliganism: an historical and sociological study*, London: Routledge, 1989.

28 **Stuart Hall, et al.**, *Policing the Crisis: mugging, the state and law and order*, London: Macmillan, 1978.

29 *Manchester Guardian*, 25 June 1929, p. 7.

30 **Pamela Cox**, 'Race, delinquency and difference in twentieth-century Britain', in **Pamela Cox** and **Heather Shore** (eds), *Becoming Delinquent: British and European youth, 1650–1950*, Aldershot: Ashgate, 2002.

31 **Louise A. Jackson**, ' "The Coffee Club menace": policing youth, leisure and sexuality in post-war Manchester', *Cultural and Social History*, 5, 3 (2008) pp. 289–308; see also, **Dick Hobbs, Philip Hadfield, Stuart Lister** and **Simon Winlow**, *Bouncers: violence and governance in the night-time economy*, Oxford: Oxford University Press, 2003, pp. 64–6.

32 *The Times*, 5 February 1935, p. 4.

33 See, *inter alia, The Guardian*, 12 September 1977, p. 9; *The Times*, 14 March 1981, p. 2, and 15 November 1984, p. 3.

34 See, for example, the campaign run in the *News of the World* to name and shame paedophiles, 23 July 2000, p. 1.

35 **Mathew Thomson**, *The Problem of Mental Deficiency: eugenics, democracy, and social policy in Britain, c.1870–1959*, Oxford: Clarendon Press, 1998, pp. 249–52.

36 OUPA, ACPO Bag (32) 65, Central Conference of Chief Constables, 1921–1938, 1 July 1926, p. 6.

37 Brown and Barrett, *Knowledge of Evil*, p. 101.

38 **Louise A. Jackson**, *Child Abuse in Victorian England*, London: Routledge, 2000, p. 152.

39 See, for example, MPHC, Refused Charge Book 'J' Division (Chingford), 8 August, 1907; Refused Charge Book 'K' Division (Isle of Dogs), 20 April,

1926; Refused Charge Book 'Y' Division (Highgate), 26 March, 1912, 16 May 1931 and 21 April 1938; Refused Charge Book 'Y' Division (Southgate), 9 August 1908.

40 **Keith Soothill** and **Sylvia Walby**, *Sex Crime in the News*, London: Routledge, 1991, p. 82.

41 *Manchester Guardian*, 15 June 1929, p. 15.

42 See, for example, *The Times*, 9 July 1930, p. 13 and 27 September 1930, p. 7; Humphries, *Hooligans or Rebels*, p. 129.

43 Humphries, *Hooligans or Rebels*, pp. 49–50, 62 and 78.

44 *Manchester Guardian*, 12 March 1921, p. 11.

45 *Manchester Guardian*, 27 September 1927, p. 12; 27 December 1932, p. 4; 30 August 1930, p. 6; 12 August 1931, p. 7.

46 *The Guardian*, 18 December 1968, p. 10 and 22 December p. 9; *The Times*, 13 December 1968, p. 3 and 18 December, p. 4. For Mary Bell's abuse at the hands of her mother, see **Gitta Sereny**, *Cries Unheard: the story of Mary Bell*, London: Macmillan, 1998.

47 **Paul Cavadino** (ed.), *Children who Kill*, Winchester: Waterside Press, 1996.

48 **Judith Rowbotham**, **Kim Stevenson** and **Samantha Pegg**, 'Children of misfortune: parallels in the cases of child murderers: Thompson and Venables, Barratt and Bradley', *Howard Journal of Criminal Justice*, 42, 2 (2003) pp. 107–22.

49 **Paul Cavadino**, 'A case for change', in Cavadino (ed.), *Children who Kill*, pp. 9–10.

50 See, *inter alia, Daily Mail*, 26 May 1994, p. 30; *The Independent*, 31 July 1996, p. 1; *Daily Mirror*, 31 July 1996, p. 2.

CHAPTER 5

Organised crime: professional criminals

'Organised crime' and 'professional criminal' are slippery terms. The former is generally seen to be the work of the latter but rather than being helpful terms of definition, even as shorthand, they tend to obscure the complexity of both actors and behaviour. 'Organised crime' was a term not much used in England in the first two-thirds of the twentieth century. But from the close of the nineteenth century policemen and others were beginning to speak and to write of the professional criminal. Such comment did not refer to the often pathetic, habitual offenders who spent their lives in and out of prison for petty offences and commonly labelled with some kind of mental defect. Rather the professional criminal was someone of ability who had made a rational choice in his way of life and who skilfully used the expanding opportunities provided by faster communication and new technology.[1]

In the contemporary world the term 'organised crime' has often become interchangeable with 'mafia' and it is employed to conjure an image of hierarchical criminal institutions run along the lines of large corporate bodies, with management teams of criminal masterminds backed by crooked lawyers and crooked financiers. The concept had its origins in the United States where a narrative has been constructed of 'organised crime' originating among late nineteenth- and early twentieth-century immigrants from southern Europe, especially Sicily and Naples. A few of these immigrants did bring the traditions of violent entrepreneurship but, as alien outsiders, Italian immigrants as a whole tended to be stigmatised. American politicians and criminal justice professionals continued to accept the narrative of organised crime as the work of groups of immigrant gangsters throughout the twentieth century. Indeed, so too did many academic criminologists. The American perception was spread through feature films and pulp fiction. In the aftermath of the Cold War, and before the advent of major international terrorism, international criminals – professionals at least by implication – became the new enemy for national and international police organisations; they became the reason for international cooperation and a series of treaties that culminated in the United Nations Convention against Transnational Organised Crime in 2003.

Organised crime can have a profound, destabilising effect on poor, significantly underdeveloped and crisis-prone states or regions. But the impact on developed, essentially pacified states is not as dramatic. Moreover, the popular portrayal of organised crime as the work of demonised outsiders running enterprises parallel to, but outside ordinary civil society in, for example, England ignores the organised lawbreaking of groups firmly situated within state and society. It ignores also the ways in which shifting laws can provide opportunities for entrepreneurs prepared to straddle, or even cross the often hazy line between crime and legality. Finally, it perpetuates the idea that criminals are alien outsiders rather than drawn from ordinary members of society and, more perniciously, it carries the implication that immigrants are criminals. A recent history of organised crime has defined such offending as 'a continuing enterprise, apart from traditional legal and social structures, within which a number of persons work together under their own hierarchy to gain power and profit for their own private gain, through illegal activities.'[2] There is nothing here to suggest that the perpetrators are mainly outsiders and, probably, it is as good a working definition as any; although, as will be suggested below, such offending is often very close to traditional legal and social structures.

The fact that so much organised crime is close to and often embedded within more acceptable areas of society adds further complications to the messy understanding of what constitutes a professional criminal. Towards the end of the twentieth century Dick Hobbs, a highly regarded criminologist who had spent his career studying criminal entrepreneurs and hard men, posed the question of who, legitimately, had a claim to being a professional criminal. Few, he suggested, would query the inclusion of the safe-cracker of the 1950s, the successful armed robbers of the 1960s and early 1970s and the drug-importer of the 1990s. These were actors who had shaped their criminal careers to the opportunities provided by society. But what about

[t]he 14-year-old who commits hundreds of burglaries to support his addiction to video games? The car thief who moves from joy-riding to supplying a team of car-ringers? What about the kid in the mock Armani

*suit with the stolen mobile phone sans batteries; is he a drug-dealer or a
sad bastard with an image problem?*[3]

And, as Hobbs would admit, these vivid suggestions exclude the various businessmen, soldiers and others who will appear in the following paragraphs.

Significantly one of the few mentions of organised crime in the British press during the inter-war period concerned the visit to Europe of New York's Police Commissioner in 1922; he was hoping to forge international links against international criminals and warned that: 'In our country we have an idea that crime is a regular business, highly organised and capitalized by some master mind.' A few weeks earlier the British press had also picked up on the problem of highly organised cocaine trafficking, but while that was on British territory, it was many miles from the metropole, specifically in India.[4] Few of the indigenous peoples of the empire migrated to, and settled in Britain during the late nineteenth and early twentieth centuries. The largest group of migrants in the period from 1880 to 1914 were Jews escaping legal repression, poverty and pogroms on the western fringe of the Russian empire. As a result the Jewish population of London increased during these years from some 20,000 to about 400,000. Fear of the alien foreigner, especially ones who dressed differently, ate differently, and spoke an unknown language, contributed to concern about the alien criminal. Jewish organisations were as active against White Slave trafficking as other voluntary associations in Britain, but for some commentators Jews were seen as the professional offenders masterminding the duping of innocent young white women into filling the brothels on the far side of the world.[5] At the same time popular literature and adventure stories often set British heroes against organised criminal gangs led by criminal masterminds. These masterminds were often foreigners, like the evil Dr Fu Manchu, the archetype of what contemporaries called the 'Yellow Peril' and one manifestation of which was identified as situated in the Chinese-dominated opium dens of seaports. Fu Manchu was always thwarted by Sir Dennis Nayland Smith, originally a colonial police officer but finally commissioner at Scotland Yard.[6] Other popular fictional characters such as Richard Hannay, 'Bulldog' Drummond and Sexton Blake struggled against similar super criminals. The conflict between the boy's own hero and the criminal mastermind declined in both popular literature and feature film in the later years of the century but, at the same time, the power of criminal organisations continued to be evoked by politicians, by some law and order professionals and in the media. At the end of the century such evocations increasingly concentrated on drugs gangs labelled 'mafia', 'triads', 'yardies' and so forth, all indicative of the gangs' foreign origins; and the transnational element continued to be central to the poorly defined concept labelled as organised crime.

But large-scale robberies and fraud also required organisation; so too did much of the other crime that was essentially entrepreneurial activity and might involve only local people in a fairly restricted geographical area. Throughout the century small local groups provided illicit services such as street betting, brothels and prostitutes, drugs, and protection. In wartime they might also supply goods and services that people wanted but that were restricted as a result of the emergency. There were often principal organisers directing these services, but the groupings of offending parties might be loose, with men coming together for particular activities at particular moments and breaking away to pursue other activities at other times.

Legislation can criminalise behaviour that many individuals regard as perfectly acceptable. The Street Betting Act of 1906 was passed on a wave of concern about the working class being corrupted by gambling and especially by the practice of placing bets with the agents of bookmakers in the streets. But the betting man and the betting woman were not to be deterred from their 'bit of a flutter'. Bookmakers continued to receive such bets and a system grew up of runners taking money in the street and running between the punter and the bookie; at the same time stool-pigeons were recruited who, for a few pence or shillings, allowed themselves to be arrested, charged and fined by posing as runners. The police themselves were sometimes involved with the bookies, turning a blind eye to runners proper, but apprehending a stool-pigeon when an arrest was required to demonstrate police activity. Bookies' sweeteners were also paid to the police in the form of cash, Christmas boxes or both. The usual line was that the police were being corrupted by the bookies. Yet the 'corruption' might also be seen often as rather more a form of unofficial negotiation between the police and the bookmakers that enabled the semblance of police control of the streets, given that the legislation that they were required to enforce was unworkable.[7] Betting remained legal on racecourses, but here the bookies confronted each other over pitches, and gangs of strong-arm men were recruited to protect both pitches and bookies. During the interwar period violent clashes between racecourse gangs were luridly reported in the press with, as was noted earlier, particular emphasis on the 'foreigners' involved in the disorders. The main violence occurred between March 1921 and August 1922, with another outbreak in the first half of 1925 that appears to have been provoked by a crackdown on gambling ordered by the prim, evangelical Anglican Home Secretary, William Joynson-Hicks. A decade later Graham Greene chose the turbulent milieu of racecourse gangs for his novel *Brighton Rock*. In the book the central character, the young, violent 'Pinky', aspires to running a major racecourse gang and challenges the successful 'businessman' Mr Colleoni. Greene sketched Colleoni stereotypically; his name seemed Italian, and he was 'a small Jew with a neat round belly . . . [whose] eyes gleamed like raisins'.[8]

Gambling and bookmaking were not confined to horses and grey-hounds. On a more modest level of organisation there were schools of pitch-and-toss generally run on open ground and particularly for male working-class punters. There were several variants of the game, each with its local name: 'Nudges' in Manchester, 'Pitch in the Scrapper' in the north east, 'Shaking in the hat' in the rural East Midlands. In Sheffield the 'towler' or 'toller' collected a toll on the bets and placed his scouts to watch for police interference or other interferences; the chief scout was the 'ponter' or 'pilner'; then came the 'pikers' or 'crows' whose task it was to keep a sharp-eyed lookout as the game progressed. In this variant of the game, three coins were spun from the first two fingers of a hand, and bets were placed on the configuration of heads and tails that resulted as the coins landed on the ground. In Sheffield, during the inter-war period, challenges to pitch-and-toss territory by rival entrepreneurs led to extended, violent gang conflicts.[9]

The Betting and Gaming Act of 1960 legalised off-course betting. Bookies' runners, who had taken street bets, were transformed into clerks in the new betting shops that opened in May 1961. By 1962 there were 13,340 such shops.[10] The betting shops and changes in popular entertainment, most notably the home television set, accelerated the decline of the old forms of street entertainment and gambling. Off-course betting and street gambling had required entrepreneurs to organise things; they had also required a degree of community knowledge and support so that punters knew where to go and who was a bookie's runner. There were other forms of criminality that required organisation, local community acceptance and support; perhaps the best example was theft on the docks.

Theft from the docks took a variety of forms. Often, perhaps most common, the pilferage by an individual was for his own use, or that of his family or friends. The goods appropriated by an individual might be passed on to a small shopkeeper who would pay the docker a small amount and then repackage the purloined sugar, tea or whatever, and sell it on as cheap, legitimate produce to customers. The shipowners who had organised the transportation of the goods lost, but everyone in the local community was a winner: the docker got a few pence for what he had taken; the shopkeeper made a small profit; and the customer purchased goods at less than the market price.[11] Dockers not only lived in tightly knit communities near their place of work but, at least up until the last quarter of the century when containerisation meant the end of the old-style stevedore who unloaded ships by muscle power, they were also often related. Sons were brought into the job by their fathers, and fathers passed the dodges and tricks down to their sons. Moreover, with these close ties of kinship and community, it became very difficult for the authorities to break down the systematic pilferage. A man spotted by a dock policeman carrying something that he had appropriated might rely on the backing of others to escape. In such circumstances it was also possible for the more unscrupulous, some might say the more courageous, to organise theft on a grander scale. In 1926, for example, theft on a large scale was unearthed at the Liverpool Docks involving a superintendent stevedore and a former freight clerk who now described himself as 'a dealer in damaged cargoes'. The director of a large shipping firm was also allegedly involved. In 1949 the Chief Constable of Birkenhead believed that dock theft in his town was becoming much better organised, with dockers developing a range of contacts: some who transported goods and others who marketed them across Cheshire and Lancashire.[12] Yet organised crime at the workplace was not restricted to dock workers. People working in domestic textile production had been involved in fiddles and holding on to perks since at least the eighteenth century. The large textile factories that emerged in the Georgian and Victorian periods found raw materials and useable waste disappearing in pockets and bags, and sometimes just concealed about the persons of their workers; the problem continued in the twentieth century. Some railway workers took goods in transit, and were even known to shunt a train an extra few miles on a branch line to facilitate the theft of goods.[13]

The workplace crimes discussed above generally involved a male workforce; women might be involved as receivers: for example, taking and repackaging for resale goods that had been taken from the docks. The behaviour that most regularly brought women before the courts in the first half of the twentieth century, however, was involvement with prostitution. Prostitution itself was not a criminal offence, but soliciting was and so too was running a brothel. There were accusations that the police organised a rota for arresting individual 'Toms', as they called prostitutes, on the charge of soliciting. In such cases the women appear to have accepted the fine imposed in the Magistrates' Court as a kind of tax on their earnings and as a part of the job. The majority of women workers in the sex industry were British. Some worked for a boy-friend-cum-pimp but, while the popular histories of the London underworld probably overemphasise the importance of gangs in running organised vice rackets, there were also a few bigger entrepreneurs. Here again there were one or two occasions on which a foreigner played a significant role in the way that prostitution was reported. In the inter-war period, and immediately afterwards, it became common for the press and other commentators to emphasise the foreign associations with vice. London's Soho district became an exotic focus for illicit sex provided by 'French' prostitutes who, it was implied, were more prepared than their English sisters to cater for the more rarefied tastes. There was some trafficking in women from overseas, sometimes involving marriages of convenience. The police themselves were prepared to play up to this by making foreign pimps and prostitutes useful scapegoats, especially at times when their own reputation was under scrutiny.[14]

There were a few prominent, well-organised individuals whose activities enabled the press and the police to emphasise the foreign involvement in prostitution, especially in London's Soho. When Metropolitan Police Sergeant George Goddard stood in the dock at the Old Bailey in January 1929, charged with corruptly accepting and obtaining money, an Irish nightclub proprietor, Kate Meyrick, and an Italian restaurateur and nightclub proprietor, Luigi Ribuffini, stood alongside him, charged with giving him the money and with conspiracy to pervert the course of justice. A third defendant who had fled the country, Anna Gadda, was also foreign-born.[15] A few months after Goddard's trial, in April 1929, two French gangsters that had been prominent in some dubious entrepreneurship within cosmopolitan Soho, Juan Antonio Castanar and Casimir Micheletti, were deported. But others remained and the mantle of foreign Soho vice entrepreneurs was passed to the five Messina brothers, born in Malta to a Maltese mother and Sicilian father. The Messinas were probably never quite as powerful as the popular true crime histories would suggest, but their criminal entrepreneurship lasted through the Second World War and into the 1960s. Their careers were punctuated by ferocious violence towards rivals, periodic trials and imprisonment. It appears that they, and other vice entrepreneurs, also tempted police officers and solicitors to join their payroll. The official line on Sergeant Goddard was that he was an isolated rotten apple. The evidence suggests, however, that Goddard was rather the manager of a system of kickbacks and bribes that involved many members of 'C' Division of the Metropolitan Police whose patch included Soho. The conviction of Goddard and, two years later, the dismissal of 27 other men and the transfer to other divisions of 24 more did not prevent the problem from recurring, if not merely continuing. In November 1955, for example, the *Daily Mail* ran a story about bribery and corruption among police officers in London's West End. The authorities denied the allegations, although there appears to have been more than a little truth in the story, and early the following year an inspector was dismissed allegedly for assisting prostitutes.[16]

The Street Offences Act of 1959 aimed to drive prostitutes from the streets by making loitering for the purpose of soliciting a punishable offence. It also increased the penalties for living off immoral earnings, for procuring and for running brothels. But it did not mean an end for the vice entrepreneur, or for the opportunities that such entrepreneurs had for maintaining their positions and their profits by corrupting those responsible for suppressing their activities. Startling revelations began to emerge in the early 1970s about Metropolitan Police detectives and particularly those working in the Obscene Publications Squad. The trade in pornography was booming during these years, partly no doubt because of the more relaxed views that were being adopted towards sexuality and sexual behaviour. The law restricting pornography appeared to many to be behind the times, something that probably contributed to the loss of morale and loss of interest in what they were supposed to be doing among members of the Obscene Publications Squad. By the late 1960s the squad had chosen to work with the entrepreneurs and to act as gatekeepers and regulators of the trade. Acting in this fashion, members of the squad earned considerable sums by arranging permissions and by collecting weekly retainers and Christmas bonuses; some also enjoyed holidays at the expense of their entrepreneurial partners. A few wealthy pornography merchants finally appeared in court, and they were followed by more than a dozen Scotland Yard detectives, most from Obscene Publications, but also including an area CID Commander, Wallace Virgo, and the head of the elite Flying Squad, Kenneth Drury.[17]

Vice was not the only area that provided opportunities for the criminal entrepreneur. Wartime led to shortages and the rationing of many basic items such as food and clothing. This, in turn, provided opportunities for the individuals who were prepared to find, by various means, those things that were either rationed or in short supply and to sell them to those that wanted them. Towards the end of the First World War, so as to avoid the problems arising from a shortage of domestic staff, many wealthy people moved into hotels that could provide them with the lifestyle to which they were accustomed. In order to accommodate the expectations of these long-stay guests, some hotels became involved in the black economy; between

February and June 1918, 15 hotels – including several celebrated West End establishments – were prosecuted for such involvement. Black market activities sometimes involved individuals profiteering from their advantageous position as, for example, a butcher or a grocer who could sell from under the counter either at an inflated price or at the normal price but in contravention of the rationing regulations. During the Second World War and with the continuation of rationing into the early 1950s, the shady individual who could provide a little bit extra of this or that or something for a special occasion or celebration within a family was popularly known as a 'spiv'. He was commonly imagined as an individual with contacts but who largely worked alone; and people buying from the black market did not ask questions. But elements of the black market manifestly involved considerable organisation and regular arrangements, as well as pilferage by dock workers and those involved with road and rail transport. By the end of the 1940s the variety of goods purloined during transportation and storage, and the value of those goods, was enormous (see Table 5.1).[18]

Members of the armed forces also organised themselves to become involved in the black market and other forms of racketeering. They had access to petrol and vehicles, and could find their way into military stores, kitchens and NAAFIs. The opportunities were almost limitless. Some took small amounts: in October 1939, for example, the Judge Advocate General's office advised on the court martial of, among others, a corporal accused of trying to sell petrol to a Yorkshire garage, a service corps private dealing in fraudulent travel warrants and a bombardier accused of taking eight tins of fish and condensed milk from his regimental cookhouse.[19] Two years later 30 soldiers who had been deployed to clear the debris of air raids in London were prosecuted at the Old Bailey for developing a sideline in stealing the lead from the roofs of houses, transporting it in their army lorries to a scrap-metal dealer's yard, selling it on and splitting the profits.[20] This was organised behaviour by a group of workmates not greatly dissimilar to that of the offences committed by dockworkers. Some of the offending by servicemen showed considerable organisational ability. Particularly impressive in scale was the criminal career of 'Turner', as he was identified in John C. Spencer's account of crime in the services. Turner had served in a bomb disposal unit in England and Belgium before deserting. He became involved in black-market activity in Brussels before branching out to work with a group in Paris involved in the theft of army vehicles that were sold on to French dealers. In the immediate post-war period Turner was involved in criminal activity across Europe from Calais to Toulouse and from Graz to The Hague.[21] Turner does not appear to

TABLE 5.1 Metropolitan Police summary showing the value and variety of foodstuffs lost from store and in transit during 1947

Commodities	Ships Side (£-s-d)	Dock Areas (£-s-d)	Road Haulage (£-s-d)	Railways (£-s-d)	Buffer Depots (£-s-d)	Cold Stores (£-s-d)	Miscellaneous (£-s-d)	Totals (£-s-d)
Animal feeding stuffs				1154-10- 8	5-14- 9		2-15-10	1163- 1- 3
Bacon and Ham			1653-14- 0	3555- 7- 2		153- 7- 1		5362- 8- 3
Canned Fish	23044-12- 8	2733- 1- 0	3639-16-11	4941- 8- 3	274- 0- 1		3516-19- 7	38149-18- 6
Canned fruit and vegetables	4892-18- 6	37- 4- 0	970- 7- 9	6703-11- 7	317- 8- 2		649-10- 5	13571- 0- 6
Cereals	210-14- 8	177- 2- 9	1835- 5- 0	9410- 5- 1	136- 4-10		824- 0- 0	12593-12- 4
Cocoa		383-17-11	51-13- 8	226- 3- 2	189- 0- 4		764-19- 6	1615-14- 7
Coffee	2738- 5- 3	17- 2- 2		911-11- 1	32- 4- 5			3699- 2-11
Dehydration				939-12- 0				939-12- 0
Dried Fruit & Nuts	71616-18- 2		13-13- 8	624- 7- 1	2846-10- 4		1294- 1- 1	76395-10- 4
Eggs	6070- 6- 4	3308-15- 2	5527- 5- 1	8793-13- 3	770- 7- 6	11- 5- 0	409- 4- 8	24890-17- 0
Emergency Stores				1-14- 2	27- 0- 9			28-14-11
Fish				860- 9- 8		127- 0- 0		987- 9- 8
Fresh Fruit & Veg, Manufactured food		6913-10- 0		5190- 8- 7	46-11- 0		4-12-11	12155- 2- 6
Meat & livestock	201075-19-11	9807-12-11	961-12- 1	29602- 1- 5	3658- 1-10	33305- 7-11	25702- 0- 1	235578-16- 2
Milk Products	121- 0- 8	395-13- 0	1582-16- 8	15569-16- 3	1620-18- 8	248-10- 0	1599- 8- 9	21138- 4- 0
Oils and Fats	50- 1- 9	36- 0- 2	6-12- 2	8952- 3- 6	208- 4-11		895- 9- 0	10148-11- 6
Overseas gifts				2080- 2- 6				2080- 2- 6
Potatoes & carrots				18693- 7- 0				18693- 7- 0
Preserves & honey			133- 2- 6	344- 1- 1			1223-15- 8	1690-19- 3
Rice			8-13- 9	237-14- 7				246- 8- 4
Salvage	55- 6- 9		386-19- 0	4024-16- 3	1176- 6- 9		45135-14- 1	39492- 5- 4
Starch		1037-13- 8	9-17- 7	266-15- 6	17-19- 0		160-12- 4	1492-18- 1
Sugar				123- 2-11	1049- 5- 7		4805- 2- 7	5977-11- 1
Tea	14311- 0- 0	32848-12- 6	40180- 7- 6	4830-17- 6			5552-10- 0	97723- 7- 6
War Supplies					25-17-11	1069- 0- 7		1094-18- 6
Welfare Foods				1874-18- 4			64755-17-10	66630-16- 2
Saccharin				295- 0- 0			262-16- 2	557-16- 2
TOTALS	324187- 4- 8	57696- 5- 3	55038-13- 2	130197-18- 7	12401-16-10	31696- 5- 3	67288- 2- 5	615113-15- 8

Source: MEPO3/3046

have been alone in large-scale, illicit military entrepreneurship. In July 1945 the *Manchester Guardian* reported 'some evidence of an international organisation which is prepared to buy army stores and vehicles on a large scale and is said to be able to arrange payment in London in any currency.'[22]

Wartime also led to a command economy and a plethora of regulations affecting business and manufacture; this, in turn, provided new opportunities for the entrepreneurs that offered to help firms deal with the restrictions and regulations. Sidney Stanley was one such fixer. Stanley, born Solomon Koshyzchy in Poland in 1899, had come to the East End of London with his family in 1913. He began work in a clothing factory and then became a travelling salesman. In 1933, under the name of Sidney Rechtland, he and his brother were suspected of involvement in fraud, but the police had insufficient evidence to prosecute. Deportation orders were issued but Sidney Stanley/Rechtland disappeared and his brother moved to the United States. When the police caught up with Stanley in 1940, he was given 28 days hard labour for not living at his registered address for the previous seven years but, given the war, he could not be deported and the deportation order was cancelled. In 1940 Stanley was back in the East End garment industry managing a firm's contracts. Two years later he set up his own business as a commission agent, becoming one of the expanding number of intermediaries helping firms to get appropriate allocations of raw materials and government licences. At some point in 1945 his business was successful enough to permit him to move into a flat in London's Park Lane. Three years later, Stanley became a prominent figure in a scandal that threatened to engulf the Labour government. The firm of Sherman Brothers ran a small, legal Football Pools business, but they had exceeded the paper allocation that they were permitted under wartime regulations and the Board of Trade was threatening to prosecute. Stanley offered to help, assuring them of good contacts in the ministry. He had indeed been developing contacts; the scandal led to the resignation of a junior minister and a director of the Bank of England. The opposition press seized the opportunity to condemn 'champagne socialists' – Aneurin Bevan was a popular target for this, though he was never involved with Stanley and those like him. There were also opportunities for the undercurrent of anti-Semitism to break to the surface in the press. But there was no electoral impact. The Labour government, which generally was as upright and moral as it claimed, established a Tribunal of Inquiry under a High Court judge, George Joseph Lynskey, and while there probably was no machiavellian intent, the form of the tribunal meant that both the public and the press lost interest in the complexities of the proceedings.[23]

In the event, there were no criminal prosecutions following the Lynskey Tribunal. Indeed the system of the Tribunal of Inquiry, while it had the advantages of being transparent and requiring witnesses to attend and give evidence under oath, also had the disadvantage that such evidence might preclude a subsequent criminal prosecution by a witness's self-incrimination. Such tribunals had been established in 1921 following an accusation that officials in the Ministry of Munitions had been destroying documentation to avoid scrutiny by the Exchequer and Audit Department. The first tribunal found no corruption, although it did reveal that a superintendent had instructed his subordinates to lose papers so that payments to wartime contractors were speeded up and not delayed by audits. A similar tribunal investigating a budget leak in 1936 did not result in criminal charges, although a minister and an MP had little choice other than to resign.[24] The Poulson affair that broke in the early 1970s, however, did result in criminal prosecutions and exposed a widespread web of bribery involving contractors, civil servants and politicians. Some may question the application of the term 'organised crime' to the affair, yet it contained the kinds of networks and the provision of favours typical of such offending. It is illustrative of the descriptive difficulties discussed at the beginning of this chapter and, in consequence, it underlines once again the problems inherent in defining easily such categories of criminality.

John Poulson was not particularly noteworthy for his architectural abilities. He was allegedly dismissed from his first job as a clerk in an architect's office for poor technical work. He studied, part-time at Leeds College of Art, but never passed a formal exam. Undeterred and having borrowed £50, he set up his own practice in Pontefract in 1932; ten years later he became a licentiate of the Royal Institute of British Architects, a membership rank that was designed for those without qualifications. Poulson's skills lay in developing contacts among potentially useful people, undercutting his competitors and completing work quickly and on time. By the late 1950s his business was highly successful and he increasingly turned his attention towards public sector contracts. During the 1960s, if not before, his cultivation of contacts for the acquisition of contracts involved gifts, holidays, jobs and lavish hospitality. The line at which corporate benefits and hospitality becomes bribery and corruption is often hazy but, as far as those responsible for enforcing the law were concerned, Poulson crossed it. He was, in the words of the satirical magazine *Private Eye* that published the first major exposé of his affairs, 'the Slicker of Wakefield'. Poulson was convicted of bribery in October 1973; George Pottinger, Under-Secretary at the Department of Agriculture in the Scottish

Office and one of the recipients of his largesse, was convicted alongside him. Other figures followed them into the dock, notably Andy Cunningham and T. Dan Smith, two leading figures in the Labour Party's fiefdom of the north-east of England. The network also involved other prominent local politicians, local managers of the railways and various ministries. Three MPs were also named, but not prosecuted: John Cordle, Tory MP for Bournemouth; Albert Roberts, Labour MP for Normanton, and Reginald Maudling who was also Home Secretary in Ted Heath's Conservative government. Cordle resigned as an MP; Maudling was forced to resign from the cabinet, but both he and Roberts clung to their seats even after a Select Committee concluded that their behaviour had not met the standards expected of members of the Commons.[25]

Criminal entrepreneurship and corruption may have been the areas where the biggest money was to be made consistently through illegal activity, but they were not the areas that immediately sprang to mind when people thought of professional criminals and crime during the century. As noted above, the specific term 'organised crime' was not much used until the closing decades, though the press and others spoke of 'professional criminals' and the 'criminal fraternity' as a kind of social grouping functioning outside normal civil society. The metaphor sometimes continued suggesting that this group was 'at war' with society and was made up of individuals separate from normal civil society. As with the various terms applied to young offenders during the century, from time to time particular terms were deployed in the press, and elsewhere, to define more closely the professional criminal.

The inter-war period was the heyday of the 'motor bandit'. The term was commonly applied to criminals who had organised themselves in such a way as to make their getaway in cars. According to some alarm expressed at the Central Conference of Chief Constables, it was also used in a sensational and sometimes fabricated fashion by sections of the press to describe modern highway robbery.[26] For some youths the 'motor bandit' acquired the glamour of the American gangster. Sir Reginald Kennedy-Cox, the Honourable Warden of the Docklands Settlements, was shocked by the 16-year-old youth with an 'anti-social mind' who declared: 'I am fed up with work, and I want to be a motor-bandit.'[27] There were respectable gentlemen, in contrast, who wanted the offenders flogged, and fears were expressed that the motor bandit had 'changed all methods of crime: he can murder, rob, and be in the next county before the police knows anything about it.'[28] But murder was rarely, if ever, on the motor-bandits' agenda; their most popular targets were jeweller's shops and the label attached to their *modus operandi* was 'smash and grab'. The shop window was broken, often with a brick; rings, watches and other items were quickly seized and the gang sped away in what was often a stolen car.[29]

'Motor bandits' also occasionally picked on wages' clerks and on other individuals that were sent out on a regular basis by different businesses to collect considerable sums of money. What is surprising, however, is the relative rarity of such offences, especially given the amount of money that appears to have been carried around the streets by wages' clerks, often young women, and others.[30] Arthur Battle, who left a lively memoir of his time in the police, also described his first job on leaving school. He was employed as the office boy of an estate agents and surveyors in Croydon. Young Battle set off every Monday, dressed in a bowler hat, black jacket and waistcoat, and pinstripe trousers, to collect rents in Croydon, Dulwich, Mitcham, Peckham and Thornton Heath. At the end of the day he had between £60 and £80 in his pockets.

Nobody, myself least of all, ever gave a thought to the possibility of my being held up or robbed of the cash. There was I, a sixteen-year-old boy, walking about some of the toughest districts of London, at a time when real poverty existed, my pockets crammed with cash and calling at the same roads each week as regular as clockwork.[31]

Not everyone was as unconcerned as Battle and his employers. A firm in Hull purchased a system whereby their wages' bag could be padlocked to a belt worn by their female wages' clerk. The gang that targeted her, however, had done their homework. The young woman was bundled into their car and, as it sped off, two of the gang set about her belt with hacksaws before pushing her out of the car some four miles from the city.[32] Rupert Wagner was a brewer's collector in Twickenham. His job was to collect pub takings and he was targeted by a motorised gang in November 1933. In addition to his bag with over £900 in takings, however, Wagner was armed with a semi-automatic pistol and, when the gang seized his bag, Wagner drew the pistol and opened fire. He claimed to have shot at the tyres of the gang's speeding car, but Philip Jaeger, one of the robbers, died from an abdominal wound that had developed into peritonitis. Jaeger's wound deteriorated partly because his family appeared to try to hush his injury up and then came up with the story of him and his brother playing with an old gun. Two other men, known to the police, were tried and convicted of robbing Wagner along with Jaeger. Newspapers expressed concern that Wagner had opened fire in a busy street; and one or two of those who saw the motor bandit as a latter-day Robin Hood, sent letters to the

Commissioner of the Metropolitan Police and to the editor of the *Daily Mirror* threatening to take revenge.[33]

The robbery of individuals carrying large sums for their employers appeared to increase with the overall upswing in the statistics of crime that began during the 1950s. By this time the number of employees collecting large sums of money had significantly reduced and, by the early 1960s, the National Union of Bank Employees was objecting to the fact that many of its members were required to handle money outside bank premises without adequate safety precautions. Increasingly much of this work was taken over by private security firms using heavily protected vehicles and uniformed personnel wearing helmets. In a relatively early use of the term 'organised crime' relating to Britain in 1962 *The Times* lamented the state of society in which 'organised crime should so have stretched the ability of the regular police to meet it, that private and often armed guards' were required to protect cash and valuables in transit.[34] The increasing replacement of the weekly pay packet by payment directly into a bank account reduced the opportunity for the wages snatch. The later introduction of technologies such as bullet-proof screens and the first closed-circuit television cameras, together with the greater recourse of police to firearms, also served to make armed, organised robbery more risky.

The artisanal skills of the safe-cracker, the guts and bloody-mindedness of the armed robber and motor-bandit, and the entrepreneurial enterprises of illicit gambling and protection were staples of those readily accepted as professional criminals during the first two-thirds of the century. Most of these activities required a degree of organisation even if the offenders often worked within a relatively limited geographical area; and while they remained rooted in the area in which they had been born and bred, the ultimate mark of success for the leaders of several such groups was the acquisition of influence in the West End, notably in the clubs of Soho. The arrest, prosecution, conviction and imprisonment of the Richardsons in 1966 and the Krays in 1969 appeared to mark the end of this style of criminality based on local working-class groups, particularly in London. And the fall of the old gangland coincided with the growing use of recreational drugs. Some of the old criminals of the 1960s and 1970s, who had made a bit of money and who were not tied to the old ways saw new opportunities for more, making new money shifting their activity to the drugs market. A few of these were in self-imposed exile in Spain and they noted how easily hashish, for example, might be moved in from Africa, especially as travel was becoming so easy. Charles Wilson, one of the Great Train robbers, was one of these, and was murdered by rivals on the Costa del

Sol in 1990.[35] Others, who remained at home, witnessed the old working-class districts demolished, gentrified or resettled often by immigrants from the Caribbean or the Indian subcontinent. But these also recognised the potential of the new market and the new simplicity of travel; some were also aware of how lorry drivers, increasingly moving their vehicles in and out of an easily accessible Europe, were smuggling tobacco bought cheaply in Belgium or Holland generally for their own use. It required little financial investment, and no great organisational ability once the right contacts were made, to put false compartments into lorries, or to hire trailers, to pay drivers generously and still to make substantial profits.[36] One or two from a younger generation, with entrepreneurial flair and the right breaks, genuinely graduated during the 1980s and 1990s, precisely as the popular trope about criminal careers would have it. Brian Charrington and Curtis 'Cocky' Warren, who came from poor backgrounds in Middlesbrough and Liverpool respectively, went from petty offending as juveniles to organising large-scale drug deals with international connections. Both became millionaires; and in 1997 Warren appeared as a 'property developer' on *The Sunday Times* list of the richest people in Britain.[37]

The growth in the market for drugs coincided with significant changes in old city centres to foster a resurgence in the entrepreneurial crime of protection organised by gangs rooted in poor neighbourhood communities. This resurgence was underpinned by an ostentatious violence that frequently involved firearms. The late 1980s saw a movement to regenerate the centres of cities and big towns; the regeneration was focused on leisure and the belief that popular cultural activities would lead to the restoration and preservation of fine buildings in the old city centres and to significant new employment opportunities. The popular cultural activities that were attracted to the restored and revamped venues, however, were largely directed at young people and the bars, pubs, clubs and music venues, with their extended hours for selling alcohol swamped the local police forces. By the end of the century weekends in the revived centres of Manchester and Nottingham were reported to attract, respectively, 100,000 and 50,000 young people looking for a good time. In the former the police might muster 30–40 officers for late-night weekend duty; in the latter perhaps 20–25. The shortfalls were made up with door staff or, as they had always been popularly known, bouncers. The venues sold alcohol, but the clientele often also sought recreational drugs. The door security staff provided protection for the venue and it rapidly became clear to many involved in the supply of tough men (and over 90 per cent of bouncers were men) for the doors that they might also manage the supply of illicit

drugs inside. Local gangs competed over the market for supplying protection and drugs; they responded to challenges to control of territory or
to 'insults' and 'lack of respect' with the ferocity of the Krays. The gang
members frequently carried knives, machetes and guns as a sign of their
authority and were fully prepared to use them. Indeed in Manchester –
now embarrassed by the various sobriquets 'Madchester', 'Gangchester',
'Gunchester' – one gang leader felt sufficiently secure and sure of himself to
threaten a local councillor that dared to challenge his authority.[38]

While the rampant consumerism of big city night-time economies may
have fostered organised criminal activity and prompted anxieties at home,
Western European consumerism and good wages looked very attractive
to those outside. Some in Africa and Asia already had friends or relatives
in Europe, or at least they had heard the stories of the good life and the
opportunities. They too wanted the chance of a new life in the West, or the
chance to make a nest egg for themselves and their families at home. It was
the same for people in East and Central Europe, particularly after the
collapse of the Soviet Union and its satellite states. Entrepreneurs came
forward to assist the movement of people, for a price. And the new life was
not the one dreamt of. By the mid-1990s the press was beginning to carry
regular stories about 'slave masters' importing girls with the promise of
working as nannies, maids or dancers, and the reality of prostitution. Young
men were smuggled in and worked on building sites, while both men and
women, living in squalid conditions, picked fruit and vegetables over long
hours for little pay. The press made much of the organisation by 'god-
fathers' in the Russian mafia, the Japanese Yakuza, the Chinese Triads,
former members of Soviet and Soviet satellite secret police, as well as by
'criminals' from Africa, Asia and South America involved in the movement
of people, the laundering of money, and the trafficking of drugs and
weaponry.[39] But there were plenty of British gang masters, builders and
farmers prepared to employ the illegal labour, thereby avoiding both tax
and the requirement to pay the minimum wage. It was this confusion of
offending with its transnational links that became subsumed under the
label 'organised crime'. Yet in many ways it was only a more violent – some
would probably say merely more overtly violent – form of entrepreneurial
globalisation than that pursued by banks and other forms of business.

Finally, 'organised crime' is one heading that might subsume the incidence of terrorist attacks. In Britain for much of the century there was a
reluctance to acknowledge both the fact of political crime and the defence
against it, namely the existence of political policing. In 1914, when asked
about 'the special or political branch' of the Metropolitan Police, the

Home Secretary tetchily retorted that there was 'no "political" branch' of the London CID, although there was, he agreed, a Special Branch.[40] The British government never sought to make any sort of legal differentiation between political crime and other forms of crime. The term 'terrorist' was used, but the terrorist's acts were acknowledged as nothing more than crimes. At the beginning of the century the concern centred mainly on anarchists who conducted a wave of assassinations and outrages across Europe and the United States. Anarchism was an international activity. Some adherents were native-born English people, but the most serious threat appeared to come from those with foreign roots, and the Jewish immigrants in London's East End were a particular concern. There was a failed attempt, by a Frenchman, to bomb Greenwich Observatory in 1894, followed by a clutch of trials at the Old Bailey. A decade later there were a few robberies and the shooting of several policemen. In each case the perpetrators appeared to have been born in the Russian Empire; first came the Tottenham Outrage of January 1909, and then a robbery in Houndsditch that became the prelude to the siege of Sidney Street early in 1911. These incidents hardly constituted a wave of terrorism and nor did they indicate a high degree of professionalism and organisation, but they served to fuel the concerns about alien criminality.[41] Much more serious, and much more persistent throughout the century, were the terrorist attacks launched by Irish nationalists.

There were three waves of Irish nationalist attacks in England during the twentieth century. The first began towards the end of the Anglo-Irish War of 1919–20 and spluttered on into 1923. The most notorious incident during this period was the assassination of Field Marshal Sir Henry Wilson, the Chief of the Imperial General Staff and an Ulster Unionist MP who was shot dead in a London street in June 1922. The second wave began in January 1939 and continued to the spring of the following year. The Irish Republican Army (IRA) aimed to hit public services and avoid killing anyone, but the bombings, which began with attacks on electrical installations, left 7 people dead and around 100 injured. The third wave began in the early 1970s; it continued, on and off, until the mid-1990s and was by far the most destructive of lives and property. There were several particularly notorious incidents: an attack on the Parachute Regiment Barracks in Aldershot in February 1972; an attack on two Birmingham pubs in November 1974; an attack on a military parade in Hyde Park in July 1982; the bombing of the Grand Hotel in Brighton while it was hosting the Conservative Party Conference in October 1983; and an attack on Harrods department store shortly before Christmas in 1983. These incidents alone left 42 dead and hundreds injured. During the first wave of terror in the aftermath of the First World War there were reports that the perpetrators of the violence were in league with Bolsheviks and with Egyptian and Indian extremists seeking independence from imperial rule. In the second wave the IRA were said to be receiving aid from Nazi Germany. In the final campaign some of the explosives originated in Soviet satellites, and weapons and explosives were supplied by Libya. However, much of the funding always originated in the United States of America and the police also reported collections for the cause in the Irish districts of British cities. The existence of large numbers of people with Irish ancestry in Britain constituted a major problem for the authorities. While the media and others called for tough and decisive measures, no government in a liberal democracy could openly target an entire ethnic minority even supposing that it felt this necessary. Moreover, following a ruling in the High Court, the expedient of deportation attempted in the 1920s ended with the government having to bring back deportees and pay compensation. Some of the foot soldiers in these campaigns showed rather more enthusiasm than ability, but in the third campaign particularly, tracking down often skilful and well-organised IRA cells without making martyrs and alienating sections of the Irish community was a difficult task for the authorities.[42]

Fiction can, of course, more easily link the terrorist with the professional criminal. In 1907 Joseph Conrad took the anarchist attempt on Greenwich Observatory as the starting point for his novel *The Secret Agent*. Adolf Verloc, Conrad's central character, inhabits a shadowy London underworld and combines the roles of pornographer, police informant and terrorist. In the 1980 gangster film *The Long Good Friday* the well-organised, professional criminal Harold Shand, who is seeking to move into legitimate business with London Docklands development and assistance from New York *mafiosi*, meets his nemesis in the shape of the well-organised professionals of the Provisional IRA. These fictional vignettes herald a switch of focus here to crime as portrayed by the media.

References and notes

1 A good, early example of this is **Sir Robert Anderson**, *Criminals and Crime: some facts and suggestions*, London: Nisbet, 1907. Anderson trained as a barrister; in the Home Office he controlled agents investigating the Fenians; he was secretary to the Prison Commissioners (1887–8) and then Assistant Commissioner of the Metropolitan Police with special responsibility for crime.

2 Mark Galeotti, 'Criminal histories: an introduction', in Mark Galeotti (ed.), *Organised Crime in History*, London: Routledge, 2009, p. 6.

3 Dick Hobbs, *Bad Business: professional crime in modern Britain*, Oxford: Oxford University Press, 1995, p. 1.

4 *The Times*, 12 June 1922, p. 5, and 27 May p. 9.

5 See Paul Knepper, *The Invention of International Crime: a global issue in the making, 1881–1914*, Houndmills, Basingstoke: Palgrave Macmillan, 2009, chapters 3 and 4.

6 Dr Fu Manchu was the creation of the crime novelist Sax Rohmer (Arthur Henry Sarsfield Ward, 1883–1959). He first appeared in a series of short stories in *The Storyteller* on the eve of the First World War; there was a cluster of novels during the 1930s and a few after the Second World War, several of which were written by others after Rohmer's death.

7 David Dixon, *From Prohibition to Regulation: bookmaking, anti-gambling, and the law*, Oxford: Clarendon Press, 1991, especially chap. 7; see also, Mark Clapson, *A Bit of a Flutter: popular gambling and English society, c.1823–1961*, Manchester: Manchester University Press, 1992.

8 Graham Greene, *Brighton Rock*, (first published, 1938) Harmondsworth: Penguin, 1943, p. 63. My thanks to Heather Shore for access to her work on the racecourse gangs.

9 P.P. Bean, *The Sheffield Gang Wars*, Sheffield: D & D Publications, 1981; and for coin-tossing games in general, see Clapson, *A Bit of a Flutter*, pp. 79–84.

10 Clapson, *A Bit of a Flutter*, p. 72.

11 Raphael Samuel, *East End Underworld: chapters in the life of Arthur Harding*, London: Routledge and Kegan Paul, 1981, pp. 16–17.

12 Gerald Mars, *Cheats at Work: an anthology of workplace crime*, London: George Allen and Unwin, 1982, pp. 96–8; *Manchester Guardian*, 25 April 1926, p. 4; 9 November 1926, p. 17 and 19 February 1949. For the Birkenhead Docks see also, Edward Smithies, *The Black Economy in England since 1914*, Dublin: Gill and Macmillan, 1984, pp. 77–9, 105–7 and 114–16.

13 See, for example, *Manchester Guardian*, 15 December 1926, p. 5 and 24 May 1947, p. 6. For a survey of workplace theft before the twentieth century see Clive Emsley, *Crime and Society in England, 1750–1900*, 4th edn, London and Harlow: Longman, 2010, chap. 6.

14 Stefan Slater, 'Pimps, police and *filles de joie*: foreign prostitution in interwar London', *London Journal*, 32, 1 (2007) pp. 53–74.

15 Clive Emsley, 'Sergeant Goddard: the story of a rotten apple, or a diseased orchard?', in Amy Gilman Srebnik and René Lévy (eds), *Crime and Culture:*

an historical perspective, Aldershot: Ashgate, 2005; **Stefan Slater**, 'Prostitutes and popular history: notes on the "underworld", 1918–1939', *CHS*, 13, 1 (2009) pp. 25–48.

16 **James Morton**, *Bent Coppers*, London: Warner Books, 1994, pp. 92–5.

17 **Alan Doig**, *Corruption and Misconduct in Contemporary British Politics*, Harmondsworth: Penguin, 1984, pp. 239–42.

18 See **Edward Smithies**, *Crime in Wartime: a social history of crime in World War II*, London: Allen and Unwin, 1982, chap. 4; *idem, The Black Economy in England since 1914*, Dublin: Gill and Macmillan, 1984, chap. 2; **Mark Roodhouse**, 'Black market activity in Britain, 1939–1955', PhD, Cambridge University, 2003.

19 W.O. 84/53 ff 43, 90–93 and 158.

20 *The Times*, 29 March 1941, p. 2.

21 **John C. Spencer**, *Crime and the Services*, London: Routledge and Kegan Paul, 1954, p. 133.

22 *Manchester Guardian*, 21 July 1945, p. 6.

23 **Mark Roodhouse**, 'The 1948 Belcher Affair and Lynskey Tribunal', *Twentieth-Century British History*, 13, 4 (2002), pp. 384–411.

24 Doig, *Corruption and Misconduct*, pp. 82 and 107–11.

25 Doig, *Corruption and Misconduct*, especially chap. 5.

26 OUPA, ACPO Bag (32) 65, Central Conference of Chief Constables 1921–1938, 13 December 1932, p. 4.

27 *The Times*, 20 October, 1934, p. 9.

28 *The Times*, 20 October, 1931, p. 10, and 6 November, p. 10.

29 See, for example, *Manchester Guardian*, 24 November, 1924, p. 7; 9 March 1925, p. 3; 23 September 1925, p. 9; 24 November 1926, p. 13; 25 August, 1928, p. 13; 16 November 1929, p. 18; 3 December 1929, p. 5; 8 February 1930, p. 17; 23 June 1930, p. 6.

30 See, for example, *Manchester Guardian*, 23 March 1929, p. 11; 3 May 1930, p. 16; 19 June 1930, p. 25; 13 September 1930, p. 20.

31 MPHC, **Arthur Battle**, 'This job's not like it used to be', p. 2.

32 *The Observer*, 7 January 1934, p. 17.

33 MEPO 3/894, Philip Jaeger: sentenced and died in hospital . . . 1933–4.

34 *The Guardian*, 5 January 1961, p. 8; *The Times*, 21 February 1962, p. 11.

35 *The Independent*, 28 April, 1990, p. 31; see also, **Wensley Clarkson**, *Killing Charlie: the bloody, bullet-riddled hunt for the most powerful Great Train Robber of all*, Edinburgh: Mainstream, 2004.

36 Hobbs, *Bad Business*, pp. 65–6.

37 **Tony Barnes, Richard Elias** and **Peter Walsh**, *Cocky: the rise and fall of Curtis Warren, Britain's biggest drugs baron*, Lytham: Milo Books, 2003.

38 See, *inter alia*, **Dick Hobbs, Philip Hadfield, Stuart Lister** and **Simon Winslow**, *Bouncers: violence and governance in the night-time economy*, Oxford: Oxford University Press, 2003, especially chap. 3; **Peter Walsh**, *Gang War: the inside story of the Manchester gangs*, Lytham: Milo Books, 2003. The threat to Councillor Pat Karney is described in the former, p. 96.

39 See, for example, *The Guardian*, 26 August 1995, p. 37; *The Independent*, 11 August 1997, pp. 1 and 4, and 27 November 1997, p. 4; *Newsweek*, 19 December 1993, p. 22; **Liz Felcete** and **Frances Webber**, 'The human trade: smuggling illegal immigrants', *Race and Class*, 39 (1 July 1997) pp. 67–8.

40 *Parl Debs. (Commons)*, 30 April 1914, col. 1874, and see also 5 May, col. 121.

41 See, *inter alia*, Knepper, *The Invention of International Crime*, chap. 5; for the 1894 trials see Oldbaileyonline, t18940430-434 (trial of Giuseppe Farnara and Francis Polti), t18940625-580 (trial of Fritz Brail) and t18940723 (trial of Thomas Cantwell and Charles Thomas Quinn).

42 See, *inter alia*, **Michael E. Hassett**, 'The British government's response to mainland Irish terrorism, c.1867–1979', PhD, Open University, 2007.

CHAPTER 6

Media narratives

While many people experience some kind of petty crime during their lifetime, this is rarely a regular occurrence. Other than criminal justice practitioners or major habitual offenders, however, few experience serious crime and they would be exceptionally unfortunate to suffer it more than once or twice. The principal way that people learn about crime and criminals is through what they read, hear or see in media narratives. The problem has always been that narratives are constructed with a variety of aims – to educate and inform, to excite, to propagandise; and contemporary narratives presented by the news media as well as fictional stories are generally situated in the marketplace. Fictional crime narratives, arguably, have always been designed with some sort of profit in mind; and while this necessity may not appear central to the news media, the latter is required by its managers and owners to make a profit, to maintain audience interest and to entertain, as well as to inform. Crime narratives in the media, as a consequence, tend to focus on the exceptional, the scandalous and the violent, rather than on the everyday, commonplace forms of offending.

The twentieth century witnessed an enormous growth both in media forms and in what was permissible for the media to report, to describe and, in the case of the cinema and television, to show. The portrayal of crime and criminals shifted over the century; particular criminal types – hooligans, motor-bandits, razor-gangs, spivs, cosh-boys, Teddy-boys, muggers, paedophiles (all essentially male[1]) – dominated coverage at particular moments, and sometimes the label in vogue simply described a type of offender that had been previously known under a different name. News, non-fiction presentations and fictional representations of crime and criminal justice are, at least in theory, different things but, particularly towards the end of the twentieth century, the edges between them became considerably blurred. Some people in the media began to describe some of their work with the ugly amalgams of 'faction' and 'infotainment' and actors performed scripts in which events were reordered and reorganised to provide audiences with the spirit of 'actual' incidents and 'real' individuals. It is easy to become snobbish about this and to ignore the fact that, for example, Shakespeare's history plays were also based on reordered and reorganised events. But it is equally important to recognise that by focusing on particular offences and particular kinds of offenders, the different kinds of media constructed images that were at some variance with the reality of crime. Moreover, in so doing, they had an impact on the formation of public and political agendas that tended often to address the media images rather more than the reality of offending.

People read or watch fictional accounts for any number of reasons. The vicarious experience of thrilling or shocking events in a novel, feature film or television movie provides entertainment, an escape, a frisson. There was a vast and expanding range of fictional crime available across the period; moreover fashions changed in the various fictional genres. There was the basic adventure story. Edgar Wallace, who had started a variety of careers before settling down to journalism, became a master of the adventure story in the early years of the century. Many of Wallace's stories involved crimes and police officers; and some of them portrayed central characters who took the law into their own hands, most notably the eponymous four just men of the popular novel that he published in 1905 and, 20 years later, his novels and play about the 'Ringer'.[2] More often, however, crime stories involved a brilliant detective like Sexton Blake or an honest, upright Englishman like 'Bulldog' Drummond and many of Eric Ambler's heroes. In addition there was what might be termed the country-house murder mystery. Here the cerebral detective was central but there were no exciting chases, gun- or fist-fights. The murderer or murderers were revealed on the last page through brilliant deduction that a reader might have hoped to pre-empt while following the clues set out in the story; but he or she was probably unable to match the brilliant intellectual deductions of Hercule Poirot, Miss Marple, Lord Peter Wimsey and their ilk. No one would think of seriously of turning to these stories to find out how murders were solved and how detectives functioned. Yet in the immediate aftermath of the Second World War a fictional character was created who was subsequently to become a benchmark for the English policeman. Police Constable George Dixon was shot dead by a young thug on his first appearance in the film *The Blue Lamp* (1950), but he was resurrected in 1955 as a television character for a series, *Dixon of Dock Green*, that ran for 434 episodes over 21 years.

The Blue Lamp was made with the full cooperation of the Metropolitan Police and was considered by the authorities at Scotland Yard as a potential vehicle for encouraging recruitment. It was well received when it premiered, although *The Times* believed that it showed policemen 'as an indulgent tradition has chosen to think they are' and the *Manchester Guardian* recognised Scotland Yard's interest and felt that it was 'not so much a portrait as an advertising poster'.[3] Nevertheless both the feature film and the television series can be seen as a manifestation of the police procedural novel and broadcast that appeared on both sides of the Atlantic in the years following the Second World War. The 'procedural' put a greater focus on the police officer as investigator or simply as a patrolman; it explored his, and subsequently also her relationship and interaction with the police institution, with various legal and penal bodies and with the public. Another procedural series *The Bill*, which drew its name from the slang word for the police, began in 1984 and ran into the first decade of the next century. It sought to portray a range of officers, both uniformed and detective, serving in the fictional police station of Sun Hill which was situated in the East End of London. It was often criticised for its violence; it upset the Police Federation, particularly for portraying racism among officers; and it was not until it had been running for several years that it began to receive largely unqualified support from the Metropolitan Police.

Unlike most other British police series *The Bill* did not focus on a central character. In the tradition of television 'soaps' there was a wide range of characters with complex, often confused personal lives. Elsewhere, however, fictional media focus was most commonly on the detective, and the British police detective was often quirky and cerebral; the stories involving Inspector Morse in Oxford and Inspector John Rebus in Edinburgh are good examples. The first Morse novel was published in 1975 and the first Rebus novel in 1987, the year that Morse made his first appearance on television. Coincidentally the first Morse novel appeared in the same year as a new kind of television representation of British police detectives. In *The Sweeney* – a title drawn from the cockney-rhyming slang of 'Sweeney Todd' for the Metropolitan Police's elite Flying Squad – DI Jack Regan and DS George Carter were noted for brawn and toughness rather than their brainpower.

The characters of Dixon, Morse and Regan had different appeals to what was essentially the same sort of audience. Dixon provided the comfortable assurance of the ever-present police officer there to solve petty confrontations and minor offences; even in the 1950s, before the statistics of crime had begun their sharp upswing, he reflected a golden age of community. Such a golden age may have been mythical, but this did not affect its appeal and late twentieth-century demands for 'more Bobbies on the beat' resonated with overt references to Dixon. The character of Regan drew on tough, no-nonsense American cops, typified by the 'Dirty Harry' movies, who were present in great numbers on British television and cinema screens.[4] Regan's popularity owed much to the soaring crime rates of the late 1960s and early 1970s and to the fact that he clashed with superiors who wanted to do everything by the rule book. Rule books, in Regan's understanding, meant that criminals got away or got off; again there was a strong resonance with the way in which sections of the press increasingly began to criticise the criminal justice system for focusing on the rights of the offender above the rights of the victim. Morse too, might argue with his superiors – he was noted for being a curmudgeon. But Morse linked the old detective tradition with the police procedural; he was a cerebral detective, and he solved murders committed by cerebral people in a cerebral setting, one of England's great seats of learning, Oxford.

In the first half of the century particularly, popular novelists liked to thrill their readers with criminal masterminds thwarted by heroic, if sometimes unorthodox Englishmen. The criminal masterminds of British popular crime novels were invariably foreigners, planning massive conspiracies. Thus Sherlock Holmes's arch-enemy was the brilliant super-criminal Professor Moriarty. Sexton Blake first appeared in 1893, the year in which Holmes, struggling with Moriarty, disappeared over the Reichenbach Falls. He reached his peak in the inter-war years. Blake, who began life in boys' magazines such as *Union Jack*, *The Boys' Journal* and *The Dreadnought*, acquired sufficient following to have his own *Sexton Blake Library* which ran from 1915 to 1963. In the stories he confronted a series of evil, often foreign masterminds like Prince Wu Ling, Baron Robert de Beauremon and the Council of Eleven, and 'Ace', the criminal King Karl V of Serbovia. Captain Hugh 'Bulldog' Drummond DSO, MC, war hero but, by inclination a simple, relaxed English gentleman, first appeared in a novel in 1920. He was the creation of Lieutenant Colonel Herman Cyril McNeile MC who, as a former member of the Royal Engineers, took the pen-name of 'Sapper'. McNeile followed the lead of John Buchan with his popular Richard Hannay character, but the Drummond stories were more brutal and generally rougher at the edges with overt jingoism, racism and anti-Semitism. Time and again Drummond was called upon to save inter-war Britain from the machinations of the criminal mastermind Carl Peterson, and from coalitions of Jewish financiers and Bolsheviks. Such foreign criminal masterminds continued in the spy novels and movies involving James Bond, but in the last third of the century the gentlemanly English heroes had largely disappeared and the foreign masterminds gave way to the home-grown gang leader modelled on the Krays and the Richardsons. These were epitomised by the character of Harold Shand in the film *The Long Good Friday* (1980) and by Harry Starks, the murderous gangster whose criminal career provides the spine for a trilogy of novels by Jake Arnott published at the turn of the century.[5]

Whereas the crime statistics show that most crime involved some form of non-violent theft, fictional representations were much more interested in the much less common interpersonal violence and, especially, in murder. Research into the most successful crime films in Britain since the Second World War found that murder was the primary offence driving the plot; from the end of the 1960s sex and drugs offences also began to be central features. *Get Carter* (1971), a film far more successful and iconic than the novel on which it was based, provided an early and possibly the best example of the genre. Its central character moved in a world of professional criminals, corrupt businessmen, drugs and vice, and was motivated principally by the desire for vengeance and sexual gratification.[6] The film was also notable for its graphic representation of violence, and in this respect it was symptomatic of an increasing trend that showed victims suffering often extreme forms of brutality or torture. In both *Get Carter* and *The Long Good Friday* the perpetrators of the violence and the killing were gangsters; in other films they were often psychopaths who were complete strangers to their victims. Again, in the case of murder, this contrasted significantly with the evidence of the criminal statistics which suggested that most homicides were the result of brawls between young men or of domestic tensions and arguments.[7]

It is wrong-headed to expect those seeking to produce entertainment and escapism to construct accounts of crime that tallied strictly with the statistics and the evidence of the courts. Since at least the eighteenth century there have been social commentators and criminal justice professionals that have worried that the detailed portrayal of crime, especially violent crime, has encouraged people, particularly young people, to copy the criminal behaviour that they have heard or seen represented. From the beginning of the twentieth century the creation of the cinema provided a new site for these long-standing concerns and prompted the determination to shelter the new mass audience from critical portrayals of any aspect of the criminal justice system. The formation of the British Board of Film

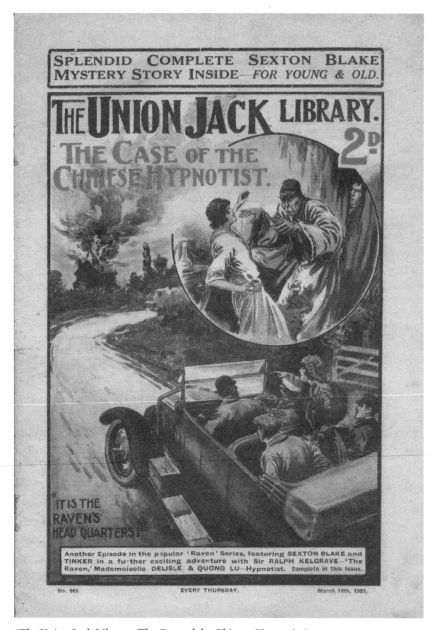

'The Union Jack Library: The Case of the Chinese Hypnotist'

In this edition of the magazine *Union Jack* Sexton Blake and his team grapple with an example of 'the yellow peril' – in this instance a Chinese hypnotist. Note the typical 'damsel in distress'. (*Source*: www.sextonblake.co.uk/IPC Media. © IPC Media)

Censors in 1913 owed much to such concerns. In September 1915 a magistrate at the Juvenile Criminal Court in London's Guildhall lamented the way in which young offenders appeared to get ideas and inspiration from the cinema. Almost exactly a year later the head of the Children's Department at the Home Office declared that he had 'not the least doubt' about the evil effects of the 'cinematograph'. 'Only last week we had a letter from a father stating that he had found his boy trying to throttle his sister, as he had seen a film in which a man throttled a woman.' Early in 1917, at the request of the Cinematograph Trade Council, a commission of inquiry was established by the National Council of Public Morals to investigate the relationship between the cinema and crime and morality. The commission was chaired by the Bishop of Birmingham and included the Chief Scout, Sir Robert Baden-Powell, among its members. The evidence that it heard on the subject of crime and young people was equivocal. For all the critics who fretted over the impact of films, there were those with an alternative view.

Four of the boys who were asked if they would like to do a bit of thieving themselves, replied that they would, but only for the sake of adventure. One boy said he would rather be the detective than the criminal, because the detective always came out on top.[8]

In the same year Frank Fowell, the Secretary and Publicity Director of the Cinematograph Trade Council, published a short pamphlet challenging the idea that the cinema fostered crime. He noted, by way of example, the figures for juvenile offending in Newcastle: there were 400 incidents in 1913 and 575 the following year.

At first glance this looks like a formidable increase in criminality; but a reference to the Chief Constable's report shows that the increase 'is due mainly to an increase of 109 cases of street trading, and of 22 in cases of juvenile gambling'. Well I don't know of any kind of cinematograph film that has ever been accused of producing an increase in street trading offences.

There was a significant upturn in larceny by juveniles in 1915 and Fowell spent the next few pages explaining how the cause of this was most likely the effect of the war.[9] Even so, the fretting about the cinema continued.

During the 1930s American gangster films were cut by the British censors and the practice of submitting British film scripts to the censor before they went into production meant that some films were never made because of the censors' concerns about their content. While thrillers with exciting chases were permitted, there was to be no glamorising of offenders and nothing remotely critical of any aspect of the British system of justice. Thus in 1934 Herbert Wilcox's plan to make *The Hanging Judge* was rejected even though the subject was the seventeenth-century Judge Jeffreys.[10] A cinematic version of Edgar Wallace's novel *When the Gangs came to London* was also rejected. Wallace's book described London's Metropolitan Police having to call on for assistance from American police following the arrival of American gangsters.[11] Yet the evidence suggesting that people learned how to commit crime, or were encouraged to commit crime because of what they saw on the cinema screen was never as strong as the assumptions. Following the publication of the Crime Statistics for 1930, the General Secretary of the Cinematograph Exhibitors' Association of Great Britain could not resist writing to *The Times* to express his satisfaction that

not once in its nearly 200 pages does it mention the cinema. We have become so accustomed to the accusation that the cinema is a cause of crime, particularly of juvenile crime, that it is most refreshing to find here, in a volume compiled by people of knowledge and authority, not a single line of justification for that accusation, not even a word of support for the customary (and generally adult-inspired and unfounded) plea of the juvenile offender, 'I saw it at the pictures.'[12]

The assumption that the fictional media encouraged crime did not go away and in the second half of the century concerns continued to focus on offenders copying particularly such violence as they had witnessed in the cinema or, later, on the television screen. In July 1953, for example, under the heading 'Film-Addict Thief Imprisoned', the *Manchester Guardian* described the trial of an 18-year-old at the Manchester Assizes. The youth allegedly spent most of his spare time in the cinema and one afternoon, a few minutes after watching a film in which a bank was robbed by men wearing handkerchiefs as masks, he tied a handkerchief over his nose and mouth and attempted to rob a jeweller's shop.[13] But some of the most notorious examples of copycat offending arose with Stanley Kubrick's film *A Clockwork Orange*. Even before its British premier the film prompted media outrage over its portrayal of youth violence, involving both murder and rape, in a futuristic Britain. Cinema critics in the United States had acclaimed it as the best film of 1971 when, as it was about to open in London, the British journal *Police* labelled it 'a film of extreme hideousness'. Sections of the press picked up on the story; the Home Secretary,

Reginald Maudling, decided to have a separate showing even before the premier in January 1972, and the rumour spread that several senior police officers had been invited to attend.[14] Some young offenders decided to mimic the dress and behaviour of the film's central character, Alex, and his violent friends, known as the Droogs. In the summer of 1973 trials were heard in Oxford, for murder, and Manchester, for grievous bodily harm, in which the teenage assailants linked themselves with the film. Correspondence columns in the press as well as editorials debated issues about the portrayal of violence in films fostering copycat violence on the streets.[15] Kubrick began to receive what his wife remembered as 'well-researched death threats'. The police advised him and his family to leave the country but Kubrick opted to withdraw the film and the threats ceased.[16]

It is an unsettling paradox that a person or persons who sought to prevent unacceptable depictions of rape and murderous violence on the screen should threaten to murder the individual responsible for such depictions. It is equally unsettling that there may have been individuals prompted to copy the behaviour of fictional characters on a cinema screen, but the considerable academic research conducted in the latter part of the century failed to find the simple cause and effect that critics of media representations of violence insisted were all too obvious. The implication of the research was that while a few people might have been affected, many more were not, and the research tended to highlight the problem of subjectivity in defining what constituted the kind of criminal or violent act that might prompt a copycat response.[17]

The significance of the news media on the popular conception of crime was of at least equal importance to the role of fiction, particularly when the stories were constructed with a convincing mix of stereotypes and statistics. Extreme violence and the use of firearms were popularly considered to be un-English. Throughout the century the press reinforced such beliefs, picking up on the Italians and 'foreign Jews' among racecourse gangs while the populist *John Bull* concluded that the worst vice and violence in London's Soho was the fault of 'the scum of continental gutters'. At the same time *The Observer* contrasted foreign gangsters with 'the average crook in this country [who] does not rely on "firearms". If he or his gang comes up against the police the old English method of a "rough house" is preferred, hitting with fists against fists.'[18]

In March 1951 *Reynolds News* carried an article with the headline: 'Coshes and Knives Out in Thuggery Revival; 8000 will be victims this year'. The journalist responsible, Neville Driver, claimed to have interviewed a professional criminal who was, himself, concerned about 'ignorant young tearaways'. The professional explained that, following a police crackdown on firearms, the young thugs had thrown their 'shooters' in the Thames and had picked up knives and coshes. Driver also quoted café proprietors on the subject of the youth gangs that frequented their premises – 'Them and their Yankee clothes and long hair'. The stereotypes of an almost respectable, non-violent professional criminal and of American-influenced young thugs, were interwoven with what appeared to be unimpeachable statistics: 'to judge from estimated figures so far this year, it is feared that 1951 may see higher figures for crime than ever before. The figure of 8000 compares with 2773 cases in 1938 and over 6000 in 1949.' The Home Secretary was sufficiently concerned by the story to seek an explanation of its veracity from his officials; they passed the matter on to the Metropolitan Police, where there was bewilderment about Driver's figures. They could only assume that he had conflated all offences of violence against the person with all robberies, whether with or without violence.

The figures used in the article for 1938 and 1949 cannot be reproduced exactly but appear to refer to all forms of violence against the person and robbery. The number of such offences in 1950 exceeded 7000 and an upward trend has persisted for four years. Only the January figure is so far available for 1951 and, although this is higher than the corresponding figure for 1950, it is impossible to obtain even an indication of what the year's total may be from one month's figures alone. The estimate of 8000 offences given in the article must therefore be regarded as a guess based on the assumption that the rise over the past few years will continue.[19]

The police response might have been a fair and measured assessment of the situation, but a fair and measured assessment often lacks punch. Driver's article itself was ephemeral, yet it was published at a time when the statistics of crime had been rising, when one or two cases had provided exciting headlines, and in the year following the success of *The Blue Lamp* in which a young thug had murdered a policeman and been caught in part by old-style, professional criminals assisting the police. In 1952 a chief superintendent in the West End expressed his exasperation with 'grossly exaggerated' newspaper articles about vice and the way that one, in particular, drew upon what the superintendent considered the ignorance of a local clergyman.

Firstly, nowhere near 4000 prostitutes are operating in the West End, the number is nearer 800. Generally speaking these women do not molest passers-by and if a man ignores their advances they leave him alone . . . For Archdeacon Lambert to say that it is virtually impossible for decent citizens to venture out alone is just nonsense. Apparently the Archdeacon knows little of what goes on in his own parish and has a vivid imagination, for Soho now is quieter than it has ever been.[20]

But then streets that were thronged with aggressive prostitutes made a good newspaper story, especially when it was supported by a quote from an outraged clergyman.

In addition to the key question about how far the news media's portrayal of crime may have affected people's understanding of crime and the criminal justice system, there is a series of questions which, while they may be largely unanswerable in any precise fashion, at least require some recognition. For what reasons, for example, did people read newspaper reports of crime during the twentieth century? For what reasons did people watch television and other media representations of the news? What did the editors and journalists involved with news media think that they were presenting to their readers and viewers? What prompted their focus on particular stories and the manner in which these stories were presented? How far were readers and viewers aware of the pressures on news editors to maintain their readers and audience? Paradoxically, in spite of the obsessive interest in crime towards the end of the century, the various agencies for providing information were reduced. Local newspapers declined, and so too did their crime reporters. The specialised agencies that reported from the courts also cut back on their coverage; most notable here was the Press Association which drastically reduced its staff at the Central Criminal Court in the last 20 years of the century and had virtually no one to cover the 82 regional Crown Courts, the more than 200 county courts and more than 350 magistrates' courts. As a result crime news was London-focused and picked up major and sensational cases only.[21] It might be presumed that not every reader or watcher of crime news believed that they were getting pure, unmediated 'facts' and a broad perspective of the range of criminal offending. But even then such an assumption was, perhaps, best made only of the more cynical and sophisticated audiences of the last quarter of the century, and it seems unlikely that people regularly asked who was shaping their crime news, in what ways and why.

The popular press often aped the language and tropes of novels and adventure yarns. The drug-related deaths of a young actress, Billie Carlton, and a young dancer, Freda Kempton, shortly after the Great War, gave the press the opportunity to find a reality in, and to play upon the 'Yellow Peril'. Brilliant Chang was a Chinese restaurateur based in London who was involved in supplying cocaine. The press portrayed him as having a magnetic attraction for a few young white women. No charges were brought against him for involvement in the deaths of Carlton and Kempton, but he was sentenced for the illegal possession of cocaine in 1924 and subsequently deported. At roughly the same time Edward Manning, a Jamaican-born jazz drummer, provided the press with a similar bogeyman, but in Manning's case Afro-Caribbean rather than Chinese.[22] The criminal mastermind, whether foreign or British-born, enlivened a story but he was overwhelmingly a figment of the imagination in the ripping yarn and the popular newspaper. In August 1919, for example, the *News of the World* reported a criminal mastermind behind car thefts and robberies in London. Within a week the mastermind's activities had spread to the management of young women thieves wearing the uniform of Queen Mary's Army Auxiliary Corps ingratiating themselves with well-to-do female shoppers, getting invitations back to the shopper's home and then stealing jewels and other property.[23] But the only figures that the paper ever reported as appearing before the courts were Sidney Meredith, the so-called 'prince of motor thieves', and William George Stephenson, a car dealer who allegedly organised the theft of cars to meet orders.[24] Ten years later Edward William Hughes, a 29-year-old dealer, was described by the police as 'the cleverest motor bandit in London and the country'. Hughes's criminal career involved little more than stealing cars to use in wages robberies and handbag snatching. Nevertheless, sentencing Hughes to five years penal servitude, the Recorder at the Old Bailey appears to have regretted receiving a medical report to the effect that he 'was not in a fit state of health to be flogged'.[25]

At the end of the century the press still liked to write about criminal 'masterminds' or 'Mr Big'. Most of those given the title then were involved in paedophilia, organising child pornography on the internet or child sex tours in the Far East, or traffickers planning always to 'flood' British streets with drugs. A foreign origin gave an additional cachet to any story about a drug trafficker, such as René Black, a Peruvian sentenced in December 1989 for cocaine smuggling, or Chanda Keita, allegedly the 'Mr Big' who remained 'at large' following the seizure of a massive consignment of crack cocaine early in 1995.[26] Some such 'masterminds' endeavoured to live up to the media image of the super criminal, though not always successfully. Valerio Viccei had a long criminal record in Italy from whence he had absconded in the mid-1980s while on bail appealing an eight-year prison sentence. He travelled to England where, the police believed, he was involved in at least five bank robberies before being caught after a highly profitable robbery at a safe deposit centre in Knightsbridge. Viccei lived a champagne lifestyle and played up to being the relaxed mastermind. He allegedly told the police: 'The criminal is an erring son of society, but always one of its creatures.' He appeared in court in an Armani suit wearing sunglasses that 'he took off only to grin at the jury as he was pointed out'. Yet the reality of the Knightsbridge raid was rather more mundane than his affected image and some of the press-reporting implied. Viccei's defence counsel pointed out that the robbers were hardly an A team, but more like the replacements for the Z team when it was down with flu. As for the mastermind: 'He leaves his fingerprints and bloodstains all over the doors, flashes around in a Ferrari after the event with £2 million in the boot. Hardly a master criminal is he?' This was probably a ploy to ensure a light sentence; it failed and Viccei got 22 years.[27] 'Mastermind' might have been relevant to some fictional villains. Very occasionally it had a degree of relevance to a flesh and blood offender, but when applied to the leaders of most criminal offences in the police and court records, it was usually flattering.

The press occasionally deployed physical descriptions of offenders and victims that echoed those given in fictional accounts. As has already been described, the press seized the opportunity to emphasis the 'foreign' nature of gangsters who carried guns, engaged in violent affrays with other weapons, or ran vice rackets. In the rose-tinted perception ordinary English criminals simply did not do that sort of thing, at least in the first half of the century. During the First World War army officers tried for serious offences had their gentlemanly appearance and smart military bearing emphasised by a sympathetic press. Thus, when Lieutenant Douglas Malcolm was acquitted of murdering his wife's lover, popular newspapers described his noble impassivity and 'grave demeanour'. His victim, in contrast, was stigmatised as 'an adventurer of Russian-Polish extraction, who had formerly lived with a German woman, since believed to have been executed by the French for espionage'. None of this gave Malcolm any justification for pumping four bullets into his victim at close range while the man lay naked in bed, although the popular press, the jury and even the prosecution appear to have thought rather differently.[28] Similarly with Lieutenant Colonel Norman Rutherford who was accused of shooting a fellow soldier in the mistaken belief that the man was having an affair with his wife. Rutherford's ferocious temper was mentioned, but greater stress was put on his behaviour as an army doctor at the front and on the possibility that he was suffering from shell-shock. According to the *News of the World*, in the dock he 'stood straight and tall, eyes to the front, and his lithe perfect body motionless'.[29] In November 1942 Harry Dobkin was sentenced to death for murdering his wife and hiding her body in a bomb-damaged church to make her look like a victim of the blitz. The *Daily Herald*, which was not one of the more sensational newspapers, noted that Dobkin was 'a Jew, born in Russia', although he had been in Britain since he was two months old. But whereas Malcolm and Rutherford had been portrayed as fine specimens of the English gentleman, the *Herald's* description of Dobkin suggested a criminal type from a popular novel. He was 'a gorilla-like man with wide nostrils, bull neck and short, massive body, with long arms which hung loosely from his shoulders'. The *Daily Express* omitted the description in favour of emphasising the triumph of the forensic evidence. But its account also concluded with echoes of the conclusion to a thriller: 'He was sentenced to death, and he passed from the court with heavy feet. He had not reckoned with science.'[30]

Newspapers jumped on any statement by judges or magistrates that violent attackers were 'cowards', or 'beasts' or 'wild animals' and used such labels in their headlines.[31] Offenders guilty of the most atrocious crimes were stigmatised as 'monsters', or as approaching alien beings quite distinct from ordinary, law-abiding people. In March 1949, shortly after the arrest of John George Haigh 'the acid bath murderer', the *Daily Mirror* ran a series of front-page articles about 'Vampire Horror in Notting Hill'. The paper sought to profit from Haigh's alleged lurid confession of drinking his victims' blood, but sought also to avoid any legal repercussions by not naming Haigh. Even so, the first time the story was reported it was run alongside a photograph with the headline: 'Women struggle to see Haigh charged'. Moreover on the second day of the story the *Mirror* could assure its readers that: 'The Vampire Killer will never strike again. He is safely behind bars, powerless ever again to lure his victims to a hideous death.'[32] After some discussion about the impact on their client's defence, Haigh's lawyers successfully prosecuted a writ for contempt of court against the *Mirror* on the grounds that the story prejudiced his chance of a fair trial. The *Mirror* was fined £10,000 and ordered to pay costs; its editor was sentenced to three months in prison.[33] The sentences passed on the *Mirror* and its editor were exemplary, but they did little to moderate the media's reporting of crime and criminals.

In the early part of the century the police were often suspicious of the press. The Metropolitan Police was cautious in its dealings with it and there was no press bureau in Scotland Yard until the 1920s. Chief constables expressed concern about the way that some journalists followed detectives, buttonholed witnesses – especially witness-victims of sexual assaults – and even, it seemed, fabricated stories for sensation value.[34] Yet senior officers had long recognised that, on occasions, they could use the media to assist in the pursuit of offenders. In 1881, for example, the head of the CID used the press to circulate the physical description and even an artist's impression of a murder suspect. In 1930 the police in Birmingham were keen to use the BBC to circulate the details of two men wanted for the robbery and murder of a bank messenger. Radio was used in this way for the first time three years later, and television for the first time in 1953.[35] In 1962 real crime was given its own five-minute slot by Independent Television. Details of offences were outlined to the public and the presenter urged the audience to be on the watch to assist the police. 'Keep 'em peeled' were his signing-off watchwords. The most successful television programme that brought the police into contact with the public and sought their assistance, however, was the BBC's *Crimewatch*. This began in 1984 and by the turn of the century had spawned a succession of spin-offs that demonstrated police successes as a result of the programme. Alongside the professional presenters of *Crimewatch* there were also serving police officers who gave details of offences and urged the audience to help by telephoning any information that might help lead to arrests. Real, unsolved crimes were presented with the use of actors and, as the technology developed, increasingly with the use of mobile-phone footage. The editors of the series were journalists who insisted that their aim was to help the police, that they were not choosing incidents for their dramatic, entertainment value, and that they agonised over what they could and should show. The lead presenter always concluded the programme by urging the audience to recognise that violent crime was rare and that viewers should sleep well and not have nightmares. Yet the programme also tended to focus on the exceptional and, in consequence, the violent. It also tended to pick offences with a limited range of victims; there was always a disproportionate number of crimes of a sexual nature in which the victims were girls and young women.[36]

In the last third of the twentieth century criminologists and sociologists undertook a series of research projects investigating the way in which the news media reported crime and criminal justice. Some of the most telling research explored the reporting of sexual crimes. There was a statistical increase in the number of such offences recorded by the police, but the increase in newspaper reporting between 1951 and 1985 was proportionately much greater. In addition the reporting became much more explicit; the national press preferred to focus on sensational cases, especially when the perpetrator appeared to be a serial offender. The image of the 'sex beast' was created; and multiple rapes by such an offender became the norm for the stories, whereas, in reality, the serial rapist was the exception. At the same time the press appeared more interested in violent and explicit videos as a cause of rape, rather than any more profound explanation. A follow-up investigation of the way in which newspapers reported sexually motivated murder during 1992 noted how an image was constructed of the perpetrators generally being situated among men who were unemployed and/or from marginalised groups.[37] The broad conclusions of these studies, and others, may not have been particularly surprising, but they were suggestive of the way in which readers might have begun to construct an image of crime in general from news presentations about particular crimes. There was one significant point of agreement between the media represen- tation and the statistics and other information collected by the criminal justice system: criminal behaviour was overwhelmingly the preserve of young males. But if the news media gave an image of the age and gender of offenders that was in line with other evidence, elsewhere there were considerable differences. When it came to discussing victims, the media concentrated particularly on women, children, people with a high social status and celebrities; a celebrity charged with an offence was also given extensive coverage. Statistically people were more likely to be the victims of property crime, often relatively minor, but the news media, like novels and feature films, gave particular emphasis to crimes of violence, especially sexual assaults and murder. Moreover, while the majority of homicides were the result of brawling between young men or domestic disputes, the media tended to pay more attention to murders with a sexual element, or in which motives of financial gain, jealousy or revenge were apparent.[38]

The media appears also to have been tempted to make much of homicides in which the accused was a woman or a child; in such cases the accused appeared to be singularly exceptional and shocking. The twen- tieth century's normative ideals of gender continued to portray women as the weaker sex and a sex that eschewed all forms of violent behaviour. Myra Hindley became the media's most striking twentieth-century repre- sentative of the criminal woman. She was involved with Ian Brady in the sadistic murders of children and teenagers in the mid-1960s. A startling photograph of her face, with bleached-blonde hair and pouting lips, was employed time and again as an iconic image of emotionless evil. She had suffered abuse in her relationship with Brady, and while this in no way condoned her involvement in the appalling murders, she continued to be singled out as an exemplar of 'evil' even after her death in prison in November 2002 some 37 years after her conviction.

In the first half of the century particularly, respectable women were expected to be chaste and sexually passive. Women who broke such expectations, especially in cases of homicide, were often harshly treated in the courts. Such was the case, for example, with Edith Thompson, executed in 1923 with her lover, Freddy Bywaters, for the murder of her husband, and Ruth Ellis, executed in 1955 for shooting dead her abusive lover. But while the media were usually highly critical of the female offender for breaking the norms of femininity, criticism could sometimes be mitigated by the very fact that the accused was a woman, especially where circumstances could feed the assumptions about gender roles and serve to nourish them. During the inter-war period, for example, some newspapers picked up on stories involving women's suffering to attract an increasing female readership: hence the column inches used up on the case of Beatrice Pace, tried and acquitted for the murder of her husband in 1928. The press chose to idealise her as a mother, devoted to her abusive, unfaithful husband and subjected to harsh 'third degree' questioning by the police.[39] Similarly, in a reflective image of the brutalised war veteran, the *World's Pictorial News* chose to portray Margaret Bowman Delvigne as a 'devoted daughter' who gave her mother arsenic so as to prevent her mother's sufferings in her terminal illness. A doctor, who had been summoned to examine the daughter's mental state in 1924, explained that 'she had rendered meritorious services, and had received a decoration for war services in Belgium. He was of opinion that her war services had affected her mentally and bodily'. In the event the jury at the Kent Assizes decided that she was unfit to plead and she was ordered to be detained at His Majesty's pleasure.[40]

The media may have helped create stereotypes of criminal offenders and may also have been guilty of turning some individuals into those stereotypes in its reporting of cases, but sections of the media also played a more honourable, crusading role. In the first half of the century there was something of a gentleman's agreement between the news media and the ruling elite that kept the reporting of any scandal or criticism of any part of the constitutional structure to a minimum. The most notorious example of this was the press's silence about the affair between the Prince of Wales and Wallis Simpson before the abdication crisis of 1936, but it also meant that any criticism of any aspect of the criminal justice system was very low key. In the less deferential world that followed the Second World War and that blossomed during the 1960s criticism of all aspects of the state enjoyed a new freedom. It became less and less easy to assert that Britain had the best police force, the best legal system, the best penal system in the world. Police, the magistracy, the judiciary and the prison system became fair game for the media, and especially for a determined new breed of investigative journalists. Sometimes, as ever, the press were more sanctimonious than accurate; but sometimes journalists' persistence exposed corrupt behaviour and miscarriages of justice. Beginning in 1982 the BBC's occasional television programme *Rough Justice* investigated 32 cases of supposed miscarriages of justice and saw convictions quashed in 15 of them. It was journalists from *The Times* who exposed widespread corruption among the detectives in the Metropolitan Police.[41] Journalists working for the press and in television investigated and reinvestigated the case of the Guildford Four, sentenced for a pub bombing carried out by the Provisional IRA in 1974. Senior judges criticised them. 'Television programmes are designed primarily to entertain', declared Lord Lane. 'Entertainment and justice, or entertainment and truth, are not always compatible.' Lord Denning was even more explicit in criticising the work of journalists whose work served only to undermine 'public confidence in the system'. The extent to which media pressure prompted a new appeal early in 1989 can never be accurately assessed, but constant media nagging had helped to create a powerful phalanx of advocates for an appeal including former home secretaries, senior churchmen and some law lords. The appeal brought to light the kinds of issues that the nagging journalist had suggested: undisclosed papers; major holes in the evidence; seriously misleading evidence from police officers. The Guildford Four were freed immediately; successful appeals followed in other cases; journalists were encouraged to pursue still more. Many of the new appeals were heard before Lord Lane who switched his ire from journalists who mixed entertainment with justice to police officers who fabricated evidence.[42]

It is easy to condemn the media for creating a distorted and sensational image of crime and criminals. Throughout the twentieth century there was evidence available to provide a more nuanced view of the pettiness of most offences and to challenge any assumption that crime was the work of a criminal other, living quite separately from the ordinary law-abiding population and providing for itself by theft, violence, fraud, or drugs and people trafficking. The twentieth-century media portrayal of crime and criminals was not new, though its focus shifted and it became more explicit as the century progressed. There is some justification for arguing that a society gets the media it wants and that, in order to survive, the media is happy to provide that want while, at the same time, pushing back the frontiers of detail and representation to maintain and, where possible, to extend its audience. Perhaps the greatest change in media representation of criminal justice over the century was the manner in which its representation and criticism became less restrained. The film censors and the gentleman's agreement between the news media and the ruling elite stifled serious criticism of the criminal justice system during the first half of the century. The journalists' investigations of the 1970s and 1980s were important and justified for the manner in which they drew attention to a succession of miscarriages of justice and to dubious behaviour by police officers to secure convictions of those that they considered guilty – what some have characterised as 'noble cause corruption'.[43]

The problems for the criminal justice system were compounded when, in the last ten to fifteen years of the century, populist politicians of all major political parties began to take their cues from outrage expressed in the tabloid press. The media, in consequence, enjoyed increasing influence in setting the criminal justice agenda. James Bulger's killers were condemned by the judge that sentenced them of having committed 'an act of unparalleled evil and barbarity'. He declared that they should be held at Her Majesty's pleasure with a recommended tariff of eight years. The Lord Chief Justice felt this insufficient and, initially, increased the tariff to ten years. The *Sun* newspaper promptly organised a petition on behalf of the toddler's parents insisting that the two boys should serve life imprisonment – and life should mean life. The petition attracted over a quarter of a million signatures and the Home Secretary, Michael Howard, responded by raising the sentence to fifteen years. The case was taken to the European Commission on Human Rights whose judges ruled, unanimously, that the courts, not politicians, should set prison sentences. The liberal *Guardian* huffed that 'Britain is probably the only country where the term a prisoner serves can be partly determined by the readers of a tabloid newspaper.'[44]

References and notes

1 The case of a paedophile ring exposed in the summer of 2009, in which two of the three defendants were women – one of whom worked in a day nursery, implied for the first time the scale of child abuse committed by women. See, *inter alia*, *Independent on Sunday*, 13 December 2009, and *The Guardian*, 15 December 2009.

2 **Edgar Wallace**, *The Four Just Men*, London: Tallis Press, 1905; *idem*, *The Ringer*, London: Hodder and Stoughton, 1926, and *The Ringer Returns*, London: Hodder and Stoughton, 1929.

3 *The Times*, 20 January 1950, p. 8; *Manchester Guardian*, 21 January 1950, p. 5. MEPO2/8342, 'The Blue Lamp': Manuscript and correspondence, 1949–1951. In a memo dated 30 September 1948, included in the MEPO file, it was suggested that the film be shot in a new police station rather than in Lenman Street in the East End. It was also suggested that the police inspector in the film be aged 40 to 45 years, rather than 55, on the grounds that a younger man would also aid recruiting. The Home Office was not consulted about the film, and clearly felt that it should have been. A letter to the Commissioner dated 20 January 1949 concluded: 'I hope . . . that you will be able to ensure that we are brought in at an early stage in any future venture of this kind involving official co-operation on your part and the provision of police facilities, so that it can be decided whether any particular project would be best dealt with on a national rather than a purely Metropolitan basis.' MEPO 2/8736, Metropolitan Police cooperation in the making of . . . 'The Long Arm', 1950–1957, reveals the Metropolitan Police communicating with the Home Office from the very beginning when the proposal for a new film was mooted at the end of 1950.

4 Harry Callahan, played by Clint Eastwood, was a detective in the San Francisco Police Force who featured in five films between 1971 and 1988. The first of the films, *Dirty Harry*, was probably the best in the series. Callahan was a tough, street-wise cop who considered overt police power as the best way to deal with vicious criminals irrespective of what the law, police regulations or superiors maintained.

5 **Jake Arnott**, *The Long Firm*, London: Hodder and Stoughton, 1999; *He Kills Coppers*, London: Hodder and Stoughton, 2001; *True Crime*, London: Hodder and Stoughton, 2003.

6 **Ted Lewis**, *Jack's Return Home*, London: Michael Joseph, 1970. The novel itself was based on the murder of Angus Sibbet in County Durham in 1967. Sibbet was involved with night clubs and gambling casinos in Newcastle-upon-Tyne and his killing was commonly referred to as 'the One-Armed Bandit Murder'.

7 For an excellent introduction to this material see **Robert Reiner**, 'Media-made criminality: the representation of crime in the mass media', in **Mike Maguire, Rod Morgan** and **Robert Reiner** (eds), *The Oxford Handbook of Criminology*, 4th edn, Oxford: Oxford University Press, 2007.

8 *The Times*, 4 September 1915, p. 3; 5 October 1916, p. 3; 16 January, pp. 5 and 11, 23 January, p. 5 and 27 March 1917, p. 5.

9 **Frank Fowell**, *The Causes of Juvenile Crime*, London: Cinematograph Trade Council, 1917, p. 9 (copy in OUPA).

10 See, for example, **James Chapman**, 'Celluloid shockers' and **Jeffrey Richards**, 'Tod Slaughter and the cinema of excess', in **Jeffrey Richards** (ed.), *The*

Unknown 1930s: an alternative history of the British cinema, 1929–1939, London: I.B. Taurus, 1998; **Tom Dewe Mathews**, *Censored*, London: Chatto and Windus, 1994, p. 52.

11 **James C. Robertson**, 'The censors and British gangland, 1913–1990', in **Steve Chibnall** and **Robert Murphy** (eds), *British Crime Cinema*, London: Routledge, 1999, p. 16.

12 *The Times*, 9 April 1932, p. 13.

13 *Manchester Guardian*, 7 July 1953, p. 12.

14 OUPA, ACPO Bag (32) 5, General Council, 13 January 1972.

15 *The Times*, 4 July 1973, p. 2 (for the case at Oxford), and 24 July 1973, p. 3 (for the case in Manchester).

16 'The Kubrick Files', Special Supplement, *Sunday Telegraph*, 6 July 2008.

17 Reiner, 'Media-Made Criminality', pp. 318–21.

18 *The Times*, 4 April, 1921, p. 4; *John Bull*, 8 February 1936; *The Observer*, 21 October 1934, p. 15.

19 MEPO2/9071, Crime of Violence, 1951. The file contains the article from *Reynolds News*, 4 March 1951, p. 5.

20 MEPO2/9367, Vice at Piccadilly Circus and surrounding area, 1952. Report from Ch. Supt. Walters, 30 October 1952.

21 **Nick Davies**, *Flat Earth News*, London: Vintage Books, 2009, pp. 77–8 and 82–3.

22 **Marek Kohn**, *Dope Girls: the birth of the British drug underworld*, 2nd edn, London: Granta, 2001.

23 *News of the World*, 24 August, p. 2; 31 August, p. 2, 1919.

24 *News of the World*, 4 September, p. 3, 1919.

25 *The Times*, 1 April 1930, p. 13.

26 See *inter alia*, for example, *Daily Mail*, 27 July 1995; *Sunday Mirror*, 31 December 1995; for Black, *The Times*, 19 December 1989, *The Independent*, 22 December 1989; and for Keita, *The Guardian*, 31 March 1995.

27 *The Independent*, 18 January 1989; *The Guardian*, 31 January, and *The Times*, 31 January 1989.

28 Quote from *Daily Mirror*, 12 September 1917, p. 2; **Clive Emsley**, *Hard Men: violence in England since 1750*, London: Hambledon, 2005, pp. 77–80.

29 *News of the World*, 26 January 1919, p. 3; see also, **Clive Emsley**, 'Violent crime in England in 1919: post-war anxieties and press narratives', *Continuity and Change*, 23, 1 (2008) pp. 173–95.

30 *Daily Herald*, 24 November 1942, p. 3; *Daily Express*, 24 November 1942, p. 3.

31 See, for example, *Manchester Guardian*, 14 May 1949, p. 4; 9 December 1955, p. 5; and 14 July 1956, p. 2.

32 *Daily Mirror*, 3, 4 and 5 March 1949.

33 *Daily Mirror*, 22 March 1949, p. 1 and 26 March 1949, p. 1; *The Times*, 22 March 1949, p. 2 and 26 March p. 3; **Molly Lefebure**, *Murder with a Difference: studies of Haigh and Christie*, London: Heinemann, 1958, chap. 8.

34 OUPA, ACPO Bag (32) 65, Central Conference of Chief Constables 1921–1938: 14 November 1929, pp. 5–6; 13 December 1932, p. 4; 19 October 1938, p. 10.

35 **Alan Moss** and **Keith Skinner**, *The Scotland Yard Files: milestones in criminal detection*, Kew, Richmond: The National Archives, 2006, chap. 5; MEPO3/345, Persons wanted on warrant for robbery with violence . . . 1930.

36 See, for example, **Yvonne Jewkes**, *Media and Crime*, London: Sage, 2004, chap. 6.

37 **Keith Soothill** and **Sylvia Walby**, *Sex Crime in the News*, London: Routledge, 1991; **Chris Grover** and **Keith Soothill**, 'A murderous "underclass"? The press reporting of sexually motivated murder', *Sociological Review*, 44, 3 (1996) pp. 398–415.

38 Reiner, 'Media-made criminality', pp. 312–15.

39 See, for example, **Lucy Bland**, 'The trials and tribulations of Edith Thompson: the capital crime of sexual incitement in 1920s England', *Journal of British Studies*, 47, 3 (2008) pp. 624–48; **Ginger Frost**, ' "She is but a woman": Kitty Byron and the English Edwardian criminal justice system', *Gender and History*, 16, 3 (2004) pp. 538–60; **John Carter Wood**, ' "Those who have had trouble can sympathise with you": press writing, reader response and a murder trial in interwar Britain', *Journal of Social History*, 43, 2 (2009) pp. 439–62.

40 *World's Pictorial News*, 6 November 1927, p. 2; see also, *The Times*, 2 November 1927, p. 9; 7 November, p. 11; 23 November, p. 13; and 25 November, p. 9.

41 **Barry Cox**, **John Shirley** and **Martin Short**, *The Fall of Scotland Yard*, Harmondsworth: Penguin, 1977.

42 **David Rose**, *In the Name of the Law: the collapse of criminal justice*, London: Jonathan Cape, 1996, chap. 1; quotations at p. 4.

43 See below, chap. 8, p. 163.

44 *The Guardian*, 26 July 1994, p. A18. The House of Lords agreed with the European judges, and Lord Chief Justice reaffirmed the eight-year tariff.

CHAPTER 7

Expert narratives

A variety of 'experts' wrote about crime and criminal justice for different audiences across the century. The word 'expert' is used here to mean those that have, or at least claim to have, special knowledge about crime whether gained through different kinds of personal experience or through study. It includes practitioners, such as retired police officers and, less commonly, doctors and pathologists, magistrates and judges, who wrote for popular audiences about their careers, generally following their retirement. An alternative perspective was supplied, often for a similar sort of market, by a few significant 'criminals' who produced autobiographies. Finally there were the various reports and monographs produced by experts involved in, or otherwise seeking to influence policy making and practitioner behaviour. These latter publications might best be linked under the heading 'criminology', but they also serve to demonstrate the range and complexity of the intellectual perspectives that can be encompassed by that title. In Britain, during the first half of the century, criminology followed a course rather different from that in continental Europe; it shied away from theory, preferring to focus on empirical research with practical motives. In the second half of the century British criminology developed in a fashion much closer to that of its overseas neighbours. Increasingly the work began to be situated in universities, funded by various charities, academic research councils and also, significantly, by the Home Office.

Among the first criminal justice experts to burst into print in numbers were police officers. The police autobiography had begun within a generation of the formation of the new police in the second quarter of the nineteenth century. By the beginning of the twentieth century it was a distinct genre. Police officers were, overwhelmingly, working-class men and hence the kind of individual whose life story rarely made it into print. A high percentage of the police memoirs that appeared in the early twentieth century were written by relatively senior detectives.[1] They commonly followed a similar pattern. There was a brief sketch of the author's early life, followed by an equally brief account of joining the police and a year or two patrolling a beat. This, however, was just the prelude. The bulk of these books were concerned with the different cases that the author had been involved in and they were spiced with exotic underworld characters. The detectives rarely portrayed their opponents as the kind of criminal masterminds so popular with detective fiction; rather they were thugs and petty thieves often answering to colourful names. In the introduction to his life in the Metropolitan Police Flying Squad, for example, ex-Chief Inspector F.D. 'Nutty' Sharpe explained that the 'wide 'uns' of the under-world had 'rich', picturesque names, such as 'Cut face Hynie', 'Jimmy the Dip', 'Singing Nell', 'Joe the Waiter', 'Barney the Yank' and 'Tommy the Guesser'. In the next two chapters he plunged his readers into the stories of 'Moisher the Gonnof' a 'wizzer' (pickpocket) and 'Australian Denny . . . undoubtedly the King of the Smash-and-Grab Raiders'.[2] It is unlikely that these nicknames were made up for the books, but the emphasis on them further identified the criminal as alien and distinct from the respectable reader. Criminal argot helped to emphasis this difference. Sharpe included a glossary or, as the sub-heading described it, an 'A.B.C. of the Seamy Side'; Robert Fabian, another senior Metropolitan Police detective who published memoirs in the post-war period, provided 'A Glossary of Thieves' Jargon'.[3] Both glossaries contained a large percentage of cockney rhyming slang, which may have been exotic but it was not a language confined to 'criminals' and, in the early and mid-twentieth century, it was probably little known outside London.

The detectives often recounted incidents employing the forms of the popular novel or boys' adventure stories. John Horwell wrote a chapter

all about pickpockets – or, at least, all about them so far as I am concerned. They gave me some hectic times, for they never 'came quietly'. They always made a fight of it. But I generally won. Not one got away from me.[4]

John Gosling's 'Ghost Squad' was recruited to deal with a rise in the statistics of crime after the Second World War. His recollections were structured in the usual pattern of discreet cases, but with each thrillingly described:

I was in a patrolling Flying Squad car in Wandsworth at half-past three in the morning when the radio spoke: 'Smash and grab raid at jeweller's

shop in Kingston-on-Thames. Motor car number – containing four men
was used.' The message had not finished before the suspect car appeared,
travelling towards us a tremendous speed.[5]

The detectives portrayed themselves as members of a hard-working, dedicated community that prioritised service to the public. Robert Fabian described how his colleagues had to be 'tactful, courageous, painstaking, vigilant'. He dedicated his book to their long-suffering wives 'because they are married to men who, if they are to be any good, have also to be married to their jobs'. The point was re-emphasised by ex-Chief Superintendent Peter Beveridge explaining that the men of the Flying Squad worked an average of 16 hours a day.

They get no extra money, no large expense sheet, but they have the
most fantastic esprit de corps, and are imbued with a spirit of almost
recklessness. They are wildly enthusiastic and entirely dependable. Their
home life is completely neglected because of the demands made of them.
When ordering men to carry on for still more hours of duty I used to feel
that they must have had divine guidance when they chose their long
suffering wives.[6]

The police narratives sometimes reinforced popular concerns about new patterns of crime. The discontented veteran, who had learned the use of guns and violence in the world wars, was a bogeyman of the 1920s and the late 1940s. He was identified as a problem by both Gosling and Horwell, even though he does not appear to have had much grounding in the reality of men brought before the courts, and even though a Commissioner of the Metropolitan Police challenged the very idea of the brutal veteran's existence. Horwell's determination to single out 'brave lads' who had done their bit and who might, after 1945, be encouraged to join the police, led him to stand the bogeyman on his head. In one chapter he suggested that the principal victims of razor gangs in the inter-war period were ex-soldiers; it was their assailants that were cowardly bullies who had 'systematically and successfully avoided military service'.[7] Such narratives often reinforced the image of the criminal as an alien outsider threatening ordinary people. The descriptions of offenders, with their exotic names, rather than providing any clue as to what prompted individuals into crime tended to reinforce stereotypes and this went together with some alarming generalisations that appear to have been based on personal prejudice rather than on the rational consideration of experience. 'Nutty' Sharpe explained that 'women as a rule do not rise high in the scales of crime. Shoplifting and bag-snatching is about as far as they generally get on their own.' Statistically that might have been the case, but Sharpe's tone is more than suggestive of the contemporary assumptions about gender and provided his readers with a reassuring, conventional assumption about women as rather meek and restrained. In contrast Cecil Bishop, another former Metropolitan Police detective, offered an unsettling image of feminism as having released something dangerous on to an unsuspecting society. Bishop argued that the rise in crime following the First World War was primarily the result of female emancipation. If feminists had realised what the outcome would be, he insisted, they would have relinquished their campaign. Bishop's book put considerable emphasis on sexual offences and the book was illustrated with photographs that looked like stills from a particularly salacious *film noir*. 'Crime and sex', he maintained, 'are always closely connected. Criminals are always seeking women in the malleable state of mind resulting from indulgence in erotic emotion.' He was convinced that, because of their different 'functions', men and women could never be truly equal. Women, for example, could not run a business successfully. Yet he appeared to contradict this assertion with another when he declared that 'many efficient gangs, both in London and the Provinces, are led by women, who exploit their sex to maintain control of the men they have gathered around them.'[8] Whatever Bishop's assertions, such female-led gangs do not much figure in other evidence from the period.

The memoirs of other retired police officers reflected contemporary assumptions about national characteristics. Fabian described the men surrounding a French gang leader in London as 'little, loudly dressed braggarts with cold vigilant eyes'. Ex-Detective Inspector Herbert Fitch claimed that prostitutes were the cause of half of the crime committed and that, because it was under the control of 'foreign bullies', prostitution 'in some way or other' was the basic cause of most murders. Fitch's remedy was to 'sweep out and keep out the non-British element of [the] criminal world' and thus lower the taxpayers' burden by one half. At the same time as reflecting some popular beliefs, however, detectives occasionally liked to emphasise their personal expertise by stressing that they knew better than the authors of popular fiction. 'If there is one man the fiction writers have libelled more than any other he is the Chinaman', declared 'Nutty' Sharpe. He continued, somewhat disingenuously: 'Now I'm only a detective and maybe I don't really know what's going on in our dark, sinister-streeted Chinatown.'[9] So much for the fiendish Fu Manchu and the 'Yellow Peril'. Towards the end of the century a greater sensibility towards gender and

ethnicity circumscribed the publication of the more colourful and prejudi-
cial statements in such memoirs. But the broad structure of the retired
detective genre remained much the same.

The detectives dealt with murders and big crimes. Officers who reached
very senior ranks, notably that of commissioner of the Metropolitan Police
or chief constable, wrote in the same style, but they also made much
of their administrative achievements, their clashes with the media and
their relations with politicians. Memoirs of this type were more frequent
towards the end of the century following the success of Sir Robert Mark's
In the Office of Constable; and, rather than addressing thief-taking,
colourful underworld opponents and musings on crime and criminality,
they often opted for a focus on the author's personal struggles within the
institution, on his or her independence and/or controversial behaviour.[10]
The notable exception here was John Alderson who served as Chief
Constable of Devon and Cornwall from 1973 to 1982. Rather than
writing his memoirs, Alderson published a number of books and articles
that drew on his expertise and that advocated a more liberal face for the
police and the development of closer links with the communities in which
they worked.[11] His unashamedly liberal and intellectual approach tended
to make him appear an outsider among most of his contemporary chief
constables.

There was a rather different genre of police memoir written by
those who remained in uniform and did not rise far, if at all, in the police
hierarchy. The memoirs of the uniformed constables who dealt with small,
day-to-day offences rarely made broad generalisations about offenders
or types of offence, and they were rarely involved in dealing with major
crimes. They could be critical of aspects of the police institution but
they preferred to stick to writing about individuals, including petty
offenders, sometimes critically, but sometimes almost affectionately. John
Wainwright described one man who, it appeared, could not help taking
anything that 'wasn't nailed down'. Wainwright thought that 'some-
where between his ears a tiny cog had slipped and he couldn't *not* thieve'.
But after Wainwright did the man a good turn by not humiliating him in
front of his schoolboy son, he became Wainwright's best ever informant.
Harry Cole aimed for the amusing story, larded with homespun philosophy and generalisation. Cole wrote, for example, about one 'problem
family', the O'Sheas who would 'nick anything they could lift and if they
couldn't lift it singly, then they would lift it collectively'. Harry Daley
emphasised the ordinariness of most offenders, several of whom he got to
know well.

Joe Lynch was a likeable villain, much scarred and with a broken nose and cauliflower ears, but a good big mouth and clear humorous eyes twinkling through the wreckage . . . When he was prisoner and I the gaoler, he was pleased to hear that I had often seen him box. 'Come up and see me sometime', he said in effect, and I often visited his dressing room after a show.

The handsome Charlie Fox was a keen winter swimmer who often shared Lime Grove Swimming Baths with Daley on a winter's morning. Fox, according to Daley, 'was a lone wolf and a dreamer, though not completely so, for some of his later crimes had great technical efficiency'.[12] These memoirs suggest a kind of genteel fatalism among many petty offenders when arrested by the police. Perhaps this was because, when writing up their memoirs, these police officers found this one way of emphasising their essential class affinity with most of those brought before the courts. There were violent offenders, but most of those that they arrested had committed only petty offences; they were poor and they accompanied an arresting officer quietly and with resignation.

A similar point was picked up in the memoirs of police court magistrates, unquestionably men from a different social class but men who, after years of working on the bench, appeared to recognise that large numbers of petty offenders were unfortunate rather than wilfully and persistently criminal. Cecil Chapman had served 21 years at the Bar when, in the autumn of 1899, he took up an appointment as a stipendiary magistrate in the London Police Courts. Chapman's memoir, while larded with the usual anecdotes of the early twentieth-century crime expert genre, had a clear liberal agenda. He was a long-time supporter of women's suffrage. He saw the London Police Courts as

pre-eminently the Courts of the Poor, where in all matters affecting life and liberty and all questions affecting the domestic happiness of the working classes, justice is obtainable at a cheaper rate and in a more democratic form than anywhere else.

Chapman argued that 'in so far as there [was] a criminal class . . . it [was] made by society's clumsy and thoughtless method of dealing with those who offend it'. He emphasised that anyone, from any social group, could commit an offence and he stressed the need for less focus on punishment and much more on rehabilitation.[13] J.B. Sandbach was called to the Bar in 1902; after a quarter of a century as a barrister he applied for, and was appointed to the post of stipendiary at Lambeth Police Court. Five years later, at the beginning of 1934, he moved to the court in

Marlborough Street. Sandbach's recollections did not echo Chapman's earnest agenda. He implied that there were indeed identifiable 'criminals' but he exempted from them 'the man or woman who commit[s] an isolated offence under stress of circumstances'. 'Criminals', he maintained, were cruel, hard-hearted and wanton. But for the bulk of his chapter on the subject he focused on characters with 'qualities which are not only good but even loveable'.[14] Like those of Sandbach, Sir Gervais Rentoul's recollections were, as he stated in his title, random. Rentoul was 'quite certain' that there was 'no such thing' as a born criminal and he contrasted the master-criminal of popular fiction with the reality that he had met in the courts. 'Occasionally one meets criminals of real intelligence and capacity, but in my experience the vast majority of them are criminals for one reason only, and that is that they have not the brains or industry to be anything else.' Moreover, most of them were redeemable once an appropriate way was found to communicate with a particular individual.[15]

Like 'Nutty' Sharpe, Chapman, Rentoul and Sandbach all described criminality as gendered. Selling one's body for sex was not a crime; soliciting such a sale was, and it was generally seen as an offence unique to women. Chapman preferred the Victorian epithet of 'the Social Evil' to prostitution; and he was coy in explaining how a young guardsman, who had told a hard luck story to a personal friend, was proposing to extort money and how the friend dared not 'raise the house and cause a scene which must end in a scandal'. Like his 'criminals', Sandbach described prostitutes as possessing many virtues – 'courage, sympathy, kindliness, charity' – even though prostitution was 'a foul thing'.[16] Rentoul, Sandbach and another stipendiary, Henry Cancellor, who had served in the West London Police Court, all also emphasised that shoplifting was a woman's crime. 'I suppose', wrote Sandbach, 'the answer is not that they are more dishonest than men, but that they do the bulk of the shopping.' And Cancellor stressed that, in the big department stores of West London, women from all social classes were culprits, from the wealthy to those 'from a back street in Battersea or Bermondsey, wearing a loose cloak with big pockets for the express purpose of filling them with stolen property'.[17]

As police autobiography had a pattern so too, in many respects, did that of the criminal. Autobiographies written, or ghosted, by former criminals, as well as books based on interviews with offenders, commonly contained the rhetoric of professionalism. In addition, and for obvious reasons, such books concerned only the so-called professionals rather than the often pathetic, persistent and petty offenders. At times they set out to echo the criminals of fiction. Thus, taking a cue from E.W. Hornung's stories about A.J. Raffles, superb gentleman cricketer and daring burglar, George Smithson's autobiography was called *Raffles in Real Life: the confessions of George Smithson, alias 'Gentleman George'*. Raffles only burgled the extremely wealthy, and often titled; thirty years after Smithson's book, Charles John 'Ruby' Sparks published a rather similar autobiography called *Burglar to the Nobility*. Eddie Brown sought to cash in on the inter-war panic about robbers in cars using the subtile *The Confessions of a Motor Bandit*.[18] The criminal autobiography, and biography, commonly described the offender as beginning his criminal career in borstal, which was portrayed as the academy in which they learnt their trade. There were also allusions to a criminal culture and a code by which those who considered themselves to be serious, professional criminals professed to act. It was a tough, heterosexual male world. Billy Hill, a borstal graduate who became styled 'the boss of Britain's underworld', reported that the first man he 'chivved' was a soldier who had taken 'a liberty' with him when he was only 14. There were certain things that members of this fraternity simply did not do: speaking to the police, for example, or insulting another. Breaking the code, or impugning another's honour was the trigger for extreme violence. When Eric Mason, an associate of the Richardsons, insulted Frankie Fraser, an associate of the Krays, Frankie's response was first to pin Mason's hand to his head with an axe, and then to inflict another 30 or so injuries on him. 'Eric wasn't a bad fellow', Fraser recalled, 'but that night he was bang out of order.' The argument was also made that such violence was restricted to the fraternity when the code was broken and that there was no desire to hurt anyone during a robbery and the shotgun was to ensure compliance.[19] Such descriptions fitted with the hard-man tradition of the poor, rough working-class communities from which most of these individuals came. Moreover, wittingly or not, it was also an attempt to promulgate a romantic and probably largely fictional ethical code for the criminal offender. This code enabled the professional criminal to sidestep at least some of the blame for injuring any member of the public who got in the way during a robbery or who, worse still, attempted to play the 'have-a-go-hero'.[20] Part of the fascination of the writing by, and about, these practitioners of crime, and something that they often appear to have played upon in order to enhance their stories for the vicarious delight of their readers, was the description of hard-man culture from which they generally originated and in which they lived their violent lives.

These kinds of offenders were commonly situated within a particular kind of social group, specifically the rougher element of the poorer, urban working class. For generations different kinds of criminal justice experts, journalists and early sociologists had identified offenders as individuals who shied away from honest labour. During the eighteenth century the novelist and magistrate Henry Fielding had written of those who could not work, those that would work had they been able to find it, and those who simply refused to engage in honest labour. Henry Mayhew made a similar differentiation in the mid-nineteenth century. Also during the nineteenth century there was a desire to categorise offenders as a class. Borrowing a term coined in France during the 1840s, commentators wrote of the 'dangerous classes'; by the middle of the century the term 'criminal classes' was being used.[21] At the turn of the century criminal offenders were considered by many to lurk within a social 'residuum', the poorest part of the working class. These concerns coincided with a wave of social investigation, the most notable of which were Charles Booth's monumental survey of the people of London, Seebohm Rowntree' study of York and Arthur Bowley's investigation of the working class in four towns – Northampton, Reading, Stanley and Warrington.[22] These studies provided an enormous amount of data about the economic and social realities of urban living and, within this, about the problems of the urban poor. They did not explain why some of the poorest appeared to slip into crime but, together with the teaching of the moral philosopher, T.H. Green, they inspired committed Christian, liberal young men to do voluntary work in the slums. Among these young men were individuals, most notably Alexander Paterson, who became leading figures in the Prison Service. Through their personality and, to a lesser extent, their writing, they drove the liberal penal policy of the first part of the century. They were convinced that caring and training would rehabilitate young offenders, give their lives purpose and make them good citizens.[23]

Men like Paterson made a practical and optimistic response to the work of the social investigators; at the same time others recycled or reshaped traditional ideas in accordance with their personal perspectives. In *Industrial Democracy* Sidney and Beatrice Webb concluded that there were three varieties of 'unemployables'. First, there were the children, the old and women of child-bearing age; second, was a group composed of individuals who were crippled, sick, mentally ill or morally deficient; and third, were those who appeared fit and able, but who were incapable of applying themselves to the kind of labour required by the 'industrial order'. The Webbs admitted that these differentiations overlapped, but it was within the second group that criminals and the 'incorrigibly idle' were to be found.[24] But even if some appeared 'incorrigible', the Webbs put their faith in a greatly improved social system. So too did contemporaries like Geoffrey Drage, Secretary to the Labour Commission, and Percy Alden, one-time warden of an East End settlement and an active campaigner on behalf of the unemployed. But these men also saw the criminal and the idle and, in Alden's view particularly, 'the vicious vagrant' as lurking among the unemployables.[25] The crucial problem lay in explaining whether the appalling environment of the urban slums and the general demoralisation of their inhabitants created the criminal and his habits, or whether there was something genetic in the offender's nature.

The question of whether 'nature' or 'nurture' was the key cause of criminal behaviour was not new. It had vexed the criminologists or, as they preferred to call themselves, criminal anthropologists, who met in a series of international congresses towards the end of the nineteenth century. The British were not participants in these debates which were dominated by French and Italians. But the British had a long empirical tradition among the doctors and psychiatrists who worked in prisons and who appeared in major trials as expert witnesses. Moreover, as the French and Italian criminal anthropologists furiously debated with each other, motivated as much by national pride as by their assumptions and evidence, a new theoretical perspective was being developed in England that was to have a significant effect on criminological thinking in the early twentieth century. Social theorists had long been concerned about the extent to which the meagre social welfare provisions of the nineteenth century might contribute to the persistence of undesirable elements within the population. In *The Descent of Man* (1871) Charles Darwin wondered whether it might be advantageous to ensure that 'the weak and inferior members of society [did not marry] so freely as the sound'. Darwin did not single out the criminal among his 'inferior members of society' nor, in the event, did he believe that the active interference with reproduction was an acceptable way to proceed. Others, however, readily made the former link and did not share Darwin's objections to the latter.

Sir Francis Galton believed that criminal nature tended to be inherited. In his *Inquiries into Human Faculty and its Development* (1883) he recognised that while criminal women spent many of their child-bearing years in prison,

[t]*he true state of the case appears to be that the criminal population receives steady accessions from those who, without having strongly marked criminal natures, do nevertheless belong to a type of humanity that is exceeding ill suited to play a respectable part in our modern*

*civilization, though it is well suited to flourish under half-savage
conditions, being naturally both healthy and prolific.*

In a footnote to the *Inquiry* Galton referred to the Greek word *eugenes*,
meaning 'good in stock, hereditarily endowed with noble qualities'. From
this root came the word 'eugenics'; it was Galton's hope that eugenics
policies would encourage superior human stock to breed and thus further
the natural course of evolution.[26]

In 1902 Charles Goring, a highly regarded young doctor recently
appointed to the prison medical service, was invited to undertake an
empirical study by the Prison Commissioners to assess the reality behind
the concept of the habitual criminal. Goring declared his aim to be nothing
less than understanding who became a criminal and why, and the ways
and extent to which criminals and non-criminals differed in respect of
physical and mental health. Nearly 4,000 convicts were compared with
schoolboys, university students and teaching staff, and soldiers; 96 different measurements were taken of the subjects and compared. After years of
amassing and processing data *The English Convict* was finally published in
1913. The book was seen by many as demolishing the concept of the born
criminal presented by the influential Italian doctor, Cesare Lombroso, and
his Criminal Anthropologist acolytes. Some Home Office officials were
unimpressed that so much work and so much data had yielded a verdict
to which they already broadly subscribed. But while Goring challenged
the idea of the born criminal, he still concluded that certain 'stocks' were
more prone to criminality than others. Moreover, some among the English
intelligentsia saw Goring's conclusions as adding weight to the ideas of
the eugenicists. Concerns about the 'British race' had been aggravated by
the poor physical state of large numbers of army recruits during the Boer
War, and many were thus encouraged to accept that controlled breeding
might be used to improve the occurrence of desirable heritable characteristics in the population. Goring himself was situated firmly in this camp
and, while he hoped that improving social conditions would alleviate
matters, he also saw merit in restricting the reproduction of those whose
drinking, feeble-mindedness or deficient social instincts, led them into
antisocial activities.[27]

Eugenics continued to be popular in many quarters during the inter-
war period and different kinds of expert and populist thinkers clashed over
the matter, often very publicly. There was, for example, a vigorous debate
in the columns of the *Yorkshire Evening Post* beginning in the late summer
of 1937 when Dr A. Hawkyard, a medical practitioner, barrister, local

magistrate and former Lord Mayor of Leeds, outlined his belief, based on his own experience and the research of others, that there were born criminals. Such criminals, he insisted, had been born without the usual 'inhibitory brain cells'. His principal critic was a local vicar, the Revd. C. Phillips Cape, who had been a missionary in India, had lived with a tribe of 'registered criminals' and written up their jargon for the Royal Asiatic Society. The debate spread beyond those who claimed to speak with confidence about 'the infra-granular layer of the central cortex'. There were those who put their faith in God's ability to change men's hearts and those who pointed to the importance of parental love and care. With characteristic Yorkshire bluntness and common sense, however, 'Man in the Street' proclaimed the theorists' arguments to be 'absurd' and, noting how it was a crime to be a fascist in a communist country and vice versa, he queried whether it was possible to detect from the brain cells of a young German whether he would be a communist or a fascist. He concluded with a flourish: 'There are many ways of parting credulous people from their money which do not bring one within range of the law.'[28]

Alongside such popular debate, the role of the practical expert remained central to what might pass as criminology in Britain. After the publication of *The English Convict* and up until his relatively early death in 1919, Goring served as the Principal Medical Officer of Manchester Prison. The careers of Maurice Hamblin Smith and William Norwood East, both slightly older than Goring, followed similar trajectories. Smith gave a lecture course on the medical aspects of crime and punishment to medical students at the University of Birmingham in the early 1920s; these lectures have some claim to being the first criminology lectures delivered at a British university. East, like Smith, was interested in the psychological approach to crime and, like Goring, was sympathetic to eugenics. He was appointed Medical Inspector of HM Prisons in 1924 and a Commissioner of Prisons and Director of the Convict Prison Medical Service six yeas later. East appeared regularly as an expert witness at the Old Bailey and in the assize courts adjacent to London. But he was not an expert concerned solely with his prison charges and advising courts; he was also interested in researching the psychological behaviour of offenders. During the 1930s he undertook a study of prisoners in Wormwood Scrubs, concluding that most of them were mentally normal, but also that treatment would be of value in certain instances, particularly with reference to sex offenders and arsonists. The *Report on the Psychological Treatment of Crime* that he published with W.H. de B. Hubert in 1939 as a result of the study, recommended the creation of a special institution for research and the treatment of disturbed adult and boy offenders; but it took until 1962 for the recommendation to result in the opening of HMP Grendon in Buckinghamshire. In the same empirical practitioner tradition of these prison medical experts was the work of Cyril Burt.[29]

Unlike the men situated in the prison medical service Burt, as noted in Chapter 4, was an educational psychologist. He was working in this capacity for the London County Council when he published *The Young Delinquent* in 1925. Burt's ideas were imbued with eugenicist perspectives, yet he believed also that the discovery of the psychosocial nature of young offenders could enable reformative treatment. An appendix to *The Young Delinquent* proposed the creation of clinics for this purpose, largely based on those already established in the United States. Philanthropic funding facilitated the establishment of the London Child Guidance Clinic in 1928, within which child psychiatrists and social workers could offer assistance to others and also receive training for themselves. This training led to a system of diagnosis and treatment that explored and sought to take account of the biological history and the emotional and physical traits of the delinquent subject. By the end of the 1930s it had incorporated also the ideas of Freudian psychoanalysis, and it formed the basis of the training for social work practitioners in the criminal justice system, notably probation officers, until the early 1960s.[30]

Freudian ideas became increasingly important in the curriculum for student social workers planning a career in criminal justice during the inter-war period. But it was the political situation in Europe, and particularly in Germany, which ultimately widened the horizons of British criminology. In 1933 both Hermann Mannheim and Max Grünhut fell foul of Nazi racial policy. The former was deprived of his position as a judge in the highest court in Prussia together with his chair of Law at the University of Berlin; the latter lost his chair in criminology at the University of Bonn. Within two years of losing his positions in Germany Mannheim had shifted focus from law to crime and penal policy and was lecturing at the London School of Economics; his position did not become permanent and full-time, however, until 1944. Grünhut found it much more difficult to come to terms with the loss of his position and left Germany only very reluctantly in January 1939. He was given a very junior position at All Souls in Oxford but was not officially appointed to lecture in criminology – the first person to have such a post in Oxford – until 1947.[31] Between the arrivals of Mannheim and Grünhut, a third person with an astonishing breadth of education in the European criminology tradition arrived in England. Leon Radzinowicz was born in Lodz, Poland in 1906. He had begun a law degree in Paris and completed it in Geneva; he had taken a doctorate in Italy which was published in France; he had published a study of the Belgian penal system which earned him a royal decoration; and in 1936, at his own expense but on the recommendation of the Polish Ministry of Justice, he travelled to England to study the borstal system. When Poland fell to the Nazi and Soviet onslaughts, Radzinowicz's return became impossible, but by then he appears to have found life in Cambridge appealing and to have seen great opportunities in remaining.

Shortly after his arrival Radzinowicz began a long a fruitful collaboration with J.W. Cecil Turner, a fellow of Trinity Hall and a member of the Law Faculty in Cambridge. By 1940 Turner had persuaded the Law Faculty to establish a committee to consider the research and teaching of Criminal Science. In the same year Radzinowicz and Turner published an article in the *Cambridge Law Journal* outlining an agenda for the subject. Crime, they argued, had to be studied scientifically with tested facts, controlled experiments and comparative investigations. Criminology, or criminal science, needed to address, with a view to explanation, the causes of crime with reference to the individual offender and to the society in which the offences occurred. Radzinowicz, in particular, believed that he needed also to explore the role of social influences on the criminal law and the machinery of criminal justice. Finally, and most importantly, there was a practical end: all of this research should be deployed in the formation of criminal justice policy.[32] The Cambridge Law Faculty agreed to the creation of a criminology department and Radzinowicz was appointed to it. He spent the remainder of his long life (he died in 1999) progressing this agenda. During the late 1940s through to the 1970s he sat on various Royal Commissions and Home Office committees; he was also involved in criminal justice discussions at the Council of Europe and the United Nations. He urged the British government to establish an interdisciplinary institute for criminology and this was taken up in 1959 as a proposal in a government White Paper.[33] Overtures were made to both London and Cambridge universities. London was lukewarm; Cambridge was not and in 1960 Radzinowicz's department became the first university-based Institute of Criminology in Britain.

From their different university positions in London, Oxford and Cambridge, Mannheim, Grünhut and Radzinowicz each undertook his own research and fostered that of others. It was not that research into crime and criminals had been outside of British universities in the past; the significance of these three was the manner in which they shifted the subject away from medical experts, who often had roles in prisons and who appeared as expert witnesses in the criminal courts, and towards people whose training was most often in the social sciences. As the crime figures increased in the second half of the century, and as the problem of crime moved up the political agenda, so successive governments were increasingly prepared to fund research in the area. The Criminal Justice Act of 1948 authorised the Home Secretary to put money into investigations of the causes of delinquency, the treatment of offenders and related penological matters. In 1957 the Home Office established its own Research Unit to pursue such research on its own account but also to act as a centre for work conducted in universities and by other institutions with an interest in crime and penal matters. Probably no one involved in these developments recognised the potential for tension inherent in bringing new academic experts in criminology together with government.

In the generation after the Second World War most people in government and in those sections of the civil service linked with criminal justice appear to have subscribed to the notion that criminals were different from the rest of society and were possessed of some kind of pathological problem. This positivist perspective was one of the first to be challenged by the new academic experts, many of whom, as well as being brought up in the less deferential environment of the post-war world, were drawn to radical sociology in universities during the 1960s. Positivist criminology, the new academic experts pointed out, failed to explain why the majority of juvenile offenders did not become adult offenders. Similarly, it focused attention on offenders 'mainly drawn from poor, disorganized, lower-class neighbourhoods' and thus concealed the enormous number of crimes committed by corporations and powerful individuals, as well as offending by the police. Indeed, it was argued by some that the entire criminal justice system was structured in such a way as to mystify.[34]

Inevitably, perhaps, government funding and government fora for discussion and the presentation of research that brought together academics and practitioners were never going to foster consensus about the causes of criminal offending and the best methods for prevention or dealing with offenders. Fierce debates developed among the academic experts themselves. There were those that maintained the old liberal, progressive line on the need for rehabilitation, if not reformation in the prison system. Andrew Rutherford's concerns about the efficiency of the criminal justice system and contrasting credos that he found among practitioners was one manifestation of this traditional perspective. Rutherford espoused the caring credo and aspired to seeing it predominant once again.[35] Others adopted criticisms of the system developed from the radical political perspectives of the 1960s. The 'left realists', notably Jock Young, challenged the old discourses of why 'criminals' took to 'crime'. They insisted that crime was behaviour that corresponded with the class and gender relationships within society and that reflected the predominant values of, for example, individualism and masculinity. The left realists also believed that crime had to be taken seriously, and they became the leading figures behind crime surveys and victim studies.[36] A more theoretical branch of critical criminology rejected the left realists' stance on the grounds that they were essentially accepting the definitions of crime and deviance together with the broad policies and practices of the liberal democratic state. This group focused its work on the contexts of exploitation, oppression, power and subordination within social relations.[37] But they also had a practical side and became significant actors in, for example, campaigns for prisoners' rights.

As the crime figures continued to soar throughout the 1970s and 1980s, so the neo-Liberal 'New Right' began to reassert some traditional punitive perspectives based on a positivist outlook but couched in new terms such as Charles Murray's description of the growth of a self-perpetuating criminal 'underclass'. The new right was not much represented within the expanding criminology departments, but once governments, both Conservative and New Labour, began to take up a new punitive stance stemming from the populist appeal of ideas about the underclass and the need to punish with a capital 'P', so problems with academic criminology's dependence on government funding began to appear.

When New Labour came to power in 1997 it had promised to be 'tough on crime and the causes of crime' and also to formulate policy on evidence-based research. But the government's belief that it had to appease the new punitive populism, in the eyes of many academic criminologists, meant that it was drawn further and further away from formulating policy on evidence-based research. By the end of the century the Home Office Research Development and Statistics Directorate was the largest single employer of criminological researchers in the United Kingdom. For some years leading criminologists had been warning about the danger of the commodification of their subject, by which they meant it could become just another service purchased under a restricting contract and by means of competitive tender. At the dawn of the new century some academic experts were gloomily declaring that this state of affairs had arrived, that the government was sitting on results that did not comply with its agenda or simply cherry-picking conclusions that suited existing policies.[38] The further implication here was that government agendas and policies had less to do with the research findings of academic experts and more to do with assuaging populist demands shaped by a sensationalist media.

The rise of the academic expert did not hush the sensational media; neither did it eclipse the expert memoir prepared for the popular market. Indeed the personal memoir, often ghost-written, and the criminal biography still purport to provide accounts of 'true' or 'real' crime. So too does the reality television that emerged in the concluding decades of the twentieth century, much of which was made in the tradition of fly-on-the-wall documentaries, or else, as the technology developed, consisted of compilations of police film and CCTV images. Some fly-on-the-wall documentaries have been scarcely distinguishable from academic studies; one of the most outstanding examples is the BBC television series *Police* transmitted in 1982. An episode from the series, which showed the police response to a rape, is credited with launching a significant change in the manner in which police responded to the offence and to victims; the director of the series, Roger Graef, has held a visiting appointment in the Hermann Mannheim Centre at the London School of Economics. But even the best documentaries are edited to fill a time-slot and to hold their audience.

References and notes

1   Paul Lawrence, ' "Scoundrels and scallywags, and some honest men . . .".
    Memoirs and the self-image of French and English policemen c.1870–1939',
    in **Barry S. Godfrey, Clive Emsley** and **Graeme Dunstall** (eds), *Comparative
    Histories of Crime*, Cullompton: Willan Publishing, 2003; **Haia Shpayer-
    Makov**, 'Explaining the rise and success of detective memoirs in Britain', in
    Clive Emsley and Haia **Shpayer-Makov** (eds), *Police Detectives in History,
    1750–1950*, Aldershot: Ashgate, 2006.

2   **F.D. ('Nutty') Sharpe**, *Sharpe of the Flying Squad*, London: John Long, 1938,
    p. 13 and chapters 2 and 3. See also, **John Gosling**, *The Ghost Squad*, London:
    W.H. Allen, 1959, p. 26.

3   Sharpe, *Sharpe of the Flying Squad*, pp. 329–34; **Robert Fabian**, *Fabian of the
    Yard*, London: Naldrett Press, 1950, pp. 204–8.

4   **John E. Horwell**, *Horwell of the Yard*, London: Andrew Melrose, 1947, p. 61.

5   Gosling, *Ghost Squad*, p. 171.

6   Fabian, *Fabian of the Yard*, p. 21; **Peter Beveridge**, *Inside the C.I.D.*, London:
    Evans Brothers, 1957, p. 72.

7   Gosling, *Ghost Squad*, p. 20; Horwell, *Horwell of the Yard*, pp. 1 and 68.

8   Cecil Bishop, *Women and Crime*, London: Chatto and Windus, 1931, pp. 12 and 13.

9   Sharpe, *Sharpe of the Flying Squad*, p. 150; Fabian, *Fabian of the Yard*, p. 22; H.T. Fitch, *Traitors Within: the adventures of Detective Inspector H.T. Fitch*, London: Hurst and Blackett, 1933, pp. 195 and 228.

10 Robert Mark, *In the Office of Constable*, London: Collins, 1978; David McNee, *McNee's Law*, London: Collins, 1983; Alison Halford, with Trevor Barnes, *No Way Up the Greasy Pole*, London: Constable, 1993; Keith Hellawell, *The Outsider: the autobiography of one of Britain's most controversial policemen*, London: Harper Collins, 2002; Brian MacKenzie, *Two Lives of Brian: from policing to politics*, Spennymoor: Memoir Club, 2004; Brian Paddick, with Kris Hollington, *Line of Fire: the autobiography of Britain's most controversial policeman*, London: Simon and Schuster, 2008.

11 See, for example, John Alderson, *Policing Freedom: a commentary on the dilemmas of policing in Western democracies*, Estover: Macdonald and Evans, 1979; *idem, Law and Disorder*, London: Hamish Hamilton, 1984; *idem, Principled Policing: protecting the public with integrity*, Winchester: Waterside, 1998.

12 John Wainwright, *Wainwright's Beat: one man's journey with a police force*, London: Macmillan, 1987, p. 70; Harry Cole, *Policeman's Progress*, London: Fontana, 1981, p. 218; Harry Daley, *This Small Cloud: a personal memoir*, London: Weidenfeld and Nicolson, 1986, pp. 115–17.

13 Cecil Chapman, *The Poor Man's Court of Justice: twenty-five years as a metropolitan magistrate*, London: Hodder and Stoughton, 1925, quotations at pp. 12 and 275.

14 J.B. Sandbach, *This Old Wig: being some recollections of a former London Metropolitan Police magistrate*, London: Hutchinson, 1950, chap. 12.

15 Sir Gervais Rentoul, *Sometimes I Think: random reflections and recollections*, London: Hodder and Stoughton, 1950, pp. 91 and 217.

16 Chapman, *Poor Man's Court*, chap. 13 and pp. 147–9; Rentoul, *Sometimes I Think*, pp. 151–2, 185–6 recounted a similar story of a youth, with two accomplices, planning to blackmail 'a philanthropic gentleman'; Sandbach, *Old Wig*, chap. 10. In a second book, *From the Bench*, London: Hodder and Stoughton, 1932, Chapman addressed prostitution again, and this time by its name. He also stressed that it was 'not a sexual offence, but an offence against order and decency in our streets, and an offence of loafing to the danger of the public weal'. Hard work was the only real cure (pp. 109–11).

17 Rentoul, *Sometimes I Think* pp. 185–6; Sandbach, *Old Wig*, 84; H.L. Cancellor, *The Life of a London Beak*, London: Hurst and Blackett, 1930, p. 94.

18 George Smithson, *Raffles in Real Life: the confessions of George Smithson, alias 'Gentleman George*, London: Hutchinson, 1930; [Charles John] 'Ruby' Sparks, *Burglar to the Nobility*, London: Barker, 1961; Eddie Brown, *Road Pirate: the confessions of a motor bandit*, London: John Long, 1934.

E.W. Hornung was the brother-in-law of Arthur Conan Doyle, the creator of Sherlock Holmes. Hornung's character Raffles had an assistant, Harry 'Bunny' Manners, akin to Holmes's Dr Watson; indeed, the Raffles adventures are something of an inversion of Holmes. The first book, *The Amateur Cracksman*, was first published in 1899 and was followed by three other books. Raffles was also a popular character on film. The first version of *The Amateur Cracksman* was made in 1905 and there were four Raffles films during the inter-war period.

19 Billy Hill, *Boss of Britain's Underworld*, London: Naldrett Press, 1955, p. 19. See in general, Dick Hobbs, *Bad Business*, Oxford; Oxford University Press, 1995; for the details on the Fraser and Mason confrontation, see p. 109. Among other authors of criminal autobiographies are: John McVicar, *McVicar by Himself*, London: Hutchinson, 1974; Bruce Reynolds, *The Autobiography of a Thief*, London: Bantam, 2005.

Billy Hill began his career as a burglar and armed robber in the inter-war period before moving into protection rackets and mentoring the Krays. McVicar was an armed robber noted for escaping from prison; he eventually did a BA and an MA in Sociology and became a journalist. His autobiography was filmed as *McVicar*, starring the singer Roger Daltry, in 1980. Reynolds was the organiser of the Great Train Robbery.

20 During the early 1990s Martin Gill interviewed 341 armed robbers. He noted how they often sought to excuse any violence committed against bystanders and regarded those that they labelled 'have-a-go-heroes' with resentment and disbelief. Martin Gill, *Commercial Robbery*, London: Blackstone Press, 2000, pp. 80–2.

21 Clive Emsley, *Crime and Society in England, 1750–1900*, 4th edn, London and Harlow: Longman, 2010, chap. 3.

22 Charles Booth (ed.), *Life and Labour of the People in London*, 17 vols. London, 1889–1903; Benjamin Seebohm Rowntree, *Poverty: a study of town life*, London, 1901; A.L. Bowley and A.R. Burnett-Hurst, *Livelihood and Poverty: a study of the economic conditions of working-class households in Northampton, Warrington, Stanley and Reading*, London, 1915.

23 See below, chap. 10. Paterson's papers on prisons and the treatment of offenders were eventually brought together and published in S.K. Ruck (ed.), *Paterson on Prisons*, London: Frederick Muller, 1951; a relatively slender volume of less than 200 pages.

24 Sidney and Beatrice Webb, *Industrial Democracy*, 2nd edn, London, 1902.

25 Geoffrey Drage, *The Unemployed*, London, 1894; **Percy Alden**, *The Unemployed: a national question*, London, 1905. For a useful overview of these debates see, **John Welshman**, *Underclass: a history of the excluded, 1880–2000*, London: Hambledon, 2006, chap. 2.

26 For an excellent introduction see Nicole Rafter (ed.), *The Origins of Criminology: a reader*, Abingdon: Routledge, 2009, especially Part VIII; quotations at pp. 243, 248 and 251.

27 **Charles Goring**, *The English Convict: a statistical study*, London: HMSO, 1913; for a brief introduction see **Leon Radzinowicz** and **Roger Hood**, *The Emergence of Penal Policy in Victorian and Edwardian England*, Oxford: Clarendon Press, 1990, pp. 20–7; see also, **Neil Davie**, *Tracing the Criminal: the rise of scientific criminology in Britain, 1860–1918*, Oxford: Bardwell Press, 2005.

28 See, *inter alia*, *Yorkshire Evening Post*, 24 August 1937, p. 6; 3 September p. 14; 7 September p. 3; 8 September p. 8; 9 September p. 3; 10 September p. 19; 14 September p. 11; 17 September p. 19; 27 September p. 3.

    The 'Registered Criminals' among whom the Revd. Phillips Cape lived were tribes operating on the margins of North Indian society. They were subject to registration under legislation of the 1870s. See, for example, **Mark Brown**, 'Colonial history and theories of the present: some reflections on penal history and theory', in **Barry Godfrey** and **Graeme Dunstall** (eds), *Crime and Empire, 1840–1940: criminal justice in local and global context*, Cullompton: Willan, 2005.

29 See, *inter alia*, **David Garland**, 'Of crime and criminals: the development of criminology in Britain', in **Mike Maguire**, **Rod Morgan** and **Robert Reiner** (eds), *The Oxford Handbook of Criminology*, 3rd edn, Oxford: Oxford University Press, 2002.

30 **Victor Bailey**, *Delinquency and Citizenship: reclaiming the young offender, 1914–1948*, Oxford: Clarendon Press, 1987, pp. 33–4; **Kevin Downing** and **Bill Forsythe**, 'The reform of offenders in England, 1830–1995: a circular debate', in **Louis A. Knafla** (ed.), *Crime, Punishment and Reform in Europe: criminal justice history*, vol. 18 (2003) pp. 145–62; at p. 153.

31 **Roger Hood**, 'Hermann Mannheim and Max Grünhut: criminological pioneers in London and Oxford', *BJC*, 44, 4 (2004) pp. 469–95.

32 **Leon Radzinowicz** and **J.W.C. Turner**, 'The language of criminal science', *Cambridge Law Journal*, 7 (1940) pp. 224–37.

33 *Penal Practice in a Changing Society*, Cmnd. 645, London: HMSO, 1959.

34 See, for example, **Steven Box**, *Power, Crime, and Mystification*, London: Tavistock, 1983; quotation at p. 17.

35 **Andrew Rutherford**, *Criminal Justice and the Pursuit of Decency*, Oxford: Oxford University Press, 1993.

36 The key text outlining the ideas behind the left realists is **John Lea** and **Jock Young**, *What is to be done about Law and Order?*, Harmondsworth: Penguin, 1984.

37 For an essay outlining the position of this group see **Joe Sim, Phil Scraton** and **Paul Gordon**, 'Introduction: crime, the state and critical analysis', in **Phil Scraton** (ed.), *Law, Order and the Authoritarian State*, Milton Keynes: Open University Press, 1987.

38 **A.E. Bottoms**, 'Reflections on the criminological enterprise', *Cambridge Law Journal*, 46 (1987) pp. 240–63; **R.G. Hood**, 'Some reflections on the role of criminology in public policy', *Criminal Law Review*, (1987) pp. 527–38; **Tim Hope** and **Reece Walters**, *Critical Thinking About the Uses of Research*, Centre for Crime and Justice Studies, King's College London, available online only at www.crimeandjustice.org

CHAPTER 8

Police and policing

At the beginning of the twentieth century the police in England and Wales were regarded as a cornerstone of the constitution. They were commonly described as 'the best police in the world'. Unfortunately, aside from reflecting a smug satisfaction with the fact that Britain had avoided revolution during the nineteenth century and assuming that this was because of the superiority of the British constitutional system, what was meant by the adjective 'best' was seldom explained. The description rested primarily on the fact that the Bobby did not, as a rule, carry lethal weapons and therefore, by implication, was not military. It rested also on the further assertion that there was no political police in Britain, although the definition of 'political' was limited. Such assertions continued throughout the century, and were easy to make as Britain faced up to what it defined as Prussian militarism and then to the more overtly and obviously police-dominated regimes of Nazi Germany and the Soviet Union in first hot and then cold wars. As far as the policing of crime went, however, while the Metropolitan Police had taken a lead in the use of fingerprints at the beginning of the century, it lagged behind in technological developments for the next half century and beyond. Indeed, the *modus operandi* of the police, their structure and organisation changed little over the first two-thirds of the century. After that, however, the pace of change became hectic.

In 1900 there were more than 200 separate police forces in England and Wales; by the end of the century the number had been reduced to 43. The reduction in force numbers coincided with the growth of much tighter control and direction from the Home Office. There was also increasing uniformity, partly as a result of this Home Office involvement, but also through the supervisory role of HM Inspectors of Constabulary (HMIC) and, following the Second World War, through development of the Association of Chief Police Officers (ACPO) as both a representative body for senior ranks and an executive arm of government. In addition, there were considerable changes in the practice of policing, with the greatest shifts being from beat policing on foot to motorised patrols and a greater number of specialised departments. Equally important was the first appearance (during the First World War) of women police officers and their slow, often grudging acceptance as equals by male officers. Officers from ethnic minorities, who began to appear in the police in the final third of the century, faced a similar struggle for acceptance.[1]

At the beginning of the twentieth century there were broadly three kinds of police organisation in England and Wales. The largest police institution was the Metropolitan Police of London. This consisted of around 19,000 men, commanded by a commissioner directly responsible to the Home Secretary as the police authority. There had been attempts to bring the force under some local government direction, particularly when the London County Council was created in 1888. But the argument that, given its responsibility for protecting the royal family, senior politicians, government buildings and so forth, the Metropolitan Police was a national, even an imperial force, ensured that local government in London remained formally excluded from the management of the police. The Home Secretary's supervisory role was further ensured by late nineteenth- and early twentieth-century fears of what might happen should the police be under the direction of a London County Council dominated by socialists. The square mile of the City of London itself had its own police force; this was commanded by a commissioner responsible to a committee of the Common Council. Outside London, there were 58 county forces ranging from tiny Rutland, with some 15 men, to the West Riding of Yorkshire with around 1,300 and Lancashire with 1,600. Chief constables, who were often military men, commanded the county forces and they reported to Standing Joint Committees (SJCs) made up of an equal number of magistrates and elected county councillors. The SJCs appear to have conducted business on a relatively informal basis, leaving the chief constable to get on with matters, although it was not unknown for them to be extremely jealous of their authority if they felt that the Home Office was bypassing them by corresponding directly with their chief constable.[2] It was often different in the 130 or so cities and towns that had their own police forces. Again the size of these forces varied greatly; Liverpool and Manchester had forces of 1,500 and 1,250 respectively, while ancient, proud but tiny boroughs, like Penzance, Tiverton and Truro, scarcely mustered a dozen men each. In the cities and towns the chief constable was commonly seen as a servant of the municipality. The direction of the police was in the hands of a watch committee, appointed by the elected town council. These committees had the ultimate authority to appoint, to discipline and dismiss, and to direct police policy. Some watch committees took this authority very seriously and, after years of service on such a committee, some of the members had developed a good understanding of the possibilities and the limitations of policing. But there were other watch committees that seem to have been prepared to leave their senior police officer – often referred to as a head, rather than a chief constable – to make the decisions. This distinction cannot easily be explained by size; in Liverpool, for example, in the last decade of the nineteenth century, a zealous watch committee intent on reforming the city's morals ignored the opinions of the head constable and issued largely unworkable directives about the policing of vice.

Central government had always taken an interest in the provincial police. From the middle of the nineteenth century the Treasury had paid one-quarter of the costs of pay and clothing for all forces deemed efficient during the annual inspections by Her Majesty's Inspectorate of Constabulary. Following the recommendations of the Desborough Committee in 1919, the Treasury increased its subvention to one-half of the total costs of all efficient forces. Since the mid-nineteenth century the Home Office had been unhappy with very small police forces but, at the same time, it shied away from attempts to compel amalgamations. Labour unrest at the turn of the century had led it to urge forces to enter into agreements for mutual aid so that a small force, faced with a strike and potential disorder following the employment of 'blackleg labour', could quickly summon support from its neighbours. But such agreements were slow to be negotiated and, during the industrial unrest on the eve of the First World War, the dynamic young Home Secretary, Winston Churchill, took it upon himself to move Metropolitan Police officers and soldiers into troubled districts.

The exigencies of war fostered new levels of cooperation and a greater measure of central direction. Particularly noteworthy here was the District Conference system established early in 1918 to facilitate the flow of information between police forces and the Home Office. Against a background of concern about public order and the fear of Bolshevism, the country was divided into eight districts in which periodic conferences were held to consider issues of public order. The conferences provided a forum in which county and borough police chiefs could meet formally to discuss matters of common interest. The eight conferences also appointed representatives to a central committee that conferred directly with members of the Home Office.

During the inter-war years a series of decisions drew the police closer to central government. Clashes between chief police officers and their SJC or watch committee tended to be resolved by the Home Office in favour of the police. The notion of the police officer as a servant of a local authority was given a serious blow by Justice McCardie's ruling in 1930 that the police officer was, first and foremost, a servant of the Crown. This ruling suited the ideas voiced by members of the Home Office, but it continued to rankle with, and be challenged by, local authorities and legal experts for the next 30 years and more. Yet whatever the desire of the Home Office to loosen the ties between local government and police forces, no government during the 1930s was prepared to challenge the fierce pride and independence of boroughs that remained determined to maintain their own, often very small police institutions.

The needs of the Second World War encouraged the government to enforce some amalgamations, but these were often in the teeth of local protest. The Chairman of the Civil Defence Committee in Ramsgate, for example, sent a letter to *The Times* at the end of 1942 which reflected the long tradition of local pride and municipal conservatism in matters of policing.

Whitehall officials have never understood civic administration in the provinces. To them a policeman deals with crime only. We know that our Chief Constable and his force are part of the civic life of the town; efficient in the prevention of crime, but ready to assist in any emergency, called into the intimate counsels of the city fathers to help in times of crisis.[3]

Such protests had little impact on post-war policy that saw advantages in fewer, bigger forces and that reached a climax with the Labour government of Harold Wilson in the 1960s. Towards the end of the century was more talk of amalgamations and a further reduction of the 43 independent forces but, in the event, the talk came to nothing.

Watch committees and SJCs disappeared in the wake of the amalgamations which were commenced under the provisions of the 1964 Police Act, and the changes were cemented by reorganisations introduced by the Local Government Act of 1972 which left police authorities with little say in the appointment of chief constables, little supervisory control over them and no say in operational matters. The Police and Magistrates' Courts Act of 1994 made further changes; most importantly it removed police authorities from the structure of local government. The Act reduced the authorities in size from between 30 and 40 members to a uniform 17: nine of the latter were drawn from democratically elected councillors; three were magistrates; and the remaining five, including the chair, were appointed by a complex procedure involving significant input from the Home Office. The Labour government that came to power in the mid-1990s continued the moves to bring uniformity and central direction with one significant exception; with the reorganisation of local government in London in 2000, responsibility for the Metropolitan Police was passed from the Home Secretary to a new Metropolitan Police Authority. Even so, the broad movement of police management and direction over the last 30 years of the century was towards the emasculation of local police authorities by a mixture of direction by central government and professional supervision.

Chief constables had their own associations dating back to the nineteenth century. From the early twentieth century the borough chief constables met for an annual conference that had both a social and a professional side. Leading members of watch committees were also commonly in attendance. In the aftermath of the Second World War this association united with the Chief Constables' Club of county police chiefs to form the Association of Chief Police Officers. The new body was a hybrid. It was a professional association that sought the ear of the Home Office in matters of policing policy, but in some circumstances it could also become an executive arm of government. The most obvious example of the latter was with the creation of the National Reporting Centre in 1972. In an emergency the NRC was responsible for organising the movement of Police Support Units required for dealing with crowds, demonstrations and strikes; the controller of the NRC was the officer then serving as the President of ACPO.

HM Inspectors of Constabulary also dated back to the mid-nineteenth century. Their role was to make annual inspections of every force, except the Metropolitan Police, and to prepare a report of their findings for parliament. Initially the inspections generally involved watching men parade, asking the occasional question and ensuring that police stations were clean. But from early on the inspectors had made occasional, more general comments about, for example, pay and various duties. This continued through the twentieth century but with the reduction of forces during the 1960s and 1970s and increasing government drives for efficiency, effectiveness and economy, the inspectorate changed to reflect the new situation. HM Inspectors were no longer simply given geographical regions, but increasingly they were charged with supervising policing tasks such as crime or traffic. In the last quarter of the century the Inspectorate was also expected to report on the ways in which different forces measured up to national directives. Young chief constables, as well as people from outside the service, began to be seconded to the Inspectorate in an attempt to foster new forms of managerial professionalism.

The *modus operandi* of the police followed a similar trajectory to that of local government involvement with the police: little changed in the first two-thirds of the century, much changed afterwards. Up until the 1960s for most uniformed police officers, the job involved patrolling a beat, usually on foot but sometimes, especially in rural areas, bicycles were permitted. The assumption, established in the Victorian period, was that the patrolling officer prevented crime by his presence but both the route and timing of a beat patrol could be extremely rigid – it was done 'mechanically, like the hands of a clock', to quote one of HM Inspectors of Constabulary. In the early 1930s the same inspector, Lt. Col. W.D. Allan, reported that constables greatly appreciated being given discretion and being allowed to use their initiative in how they worked their beats. He considered also that such a practice would be more beneficial if it was more widely employed, since the element of surprise as to when an officer might appear meant that more crimes would be detected.[4] Officers during these years were almost always male and they were generally recruited from the semi-skilled or unskilled working class. Some chief constables favoured former soldiers because of their discipline and bearing; some favoured men born outside the jurisdiction in which they served so as not to create any difficulties or problems of loyalty when it came to enforcing the law. The prospective officer needed good references and so, when he sought permission to marry, did his wife. As long as the man remained in service he had to maintain a high degree of respectability; and it was expected that he would ensure the same of his wife and children. The police officer's family was required to be a model of the respectable working class. Up until the end of the Second World War some chief constables even prohibited a man's wife from taking paid employment on the grounds that this might compromise his position although, in an isolated police house in a rural area, a wife was often required to act as an auxiliary, answering the phone, taking messages and even feeding prisoners temporarily held in the house.

On the beat an officer was generally on his own. In the populous areas of big cities at the beginning of the century, where beats were relatively close together, he relied on a whistle to call for assistance. A few of the larger forces had begun to introduce police boxes in the cities at the beginning of the century and the number of these boxes increased significantly during the inter-war period. Generally they contained a telephone that enabled the officer to contact, and be contacted by his station. They also provided a place for a sit-down and taking refreshment, though rarely in much comfort.[5] But the police officer was also expected to be tough and, if necessary, to be able to fight his way out of difficulty. He carried a short baton concealed in a trouser pocket for emergencies and, if he was carrying one, he could also use his long, rolled-up wet-weather cape with its lead weights as a weapon. Much patrolling was done at night; the officer looked out for open doors and windows, checked that premises were locked. He also had a relatively free hand in stopping and questioning anyone out late. Whether or not he was allowed to use his initiative in the way that he worked his beat, the officer on the street or in the country lane had considerable discretion when it came to dealing with transgressors. He could make an arrest, give advice or a warning; and few, other than the young offender who felt it, objected when the summary justice of 'a clip round the ear' was administered with hand or glove.[6]

The detective officer, by the very nature of the role, did not patrol a regular beat. An aura of romance surrounded the police detective even if, in the popular literature of the first half of the century, he was often portrayed as plodding and uninspired in comparison with the gifted amateur from a higher social class. Some rural forces did not bother with detectives until at least the late 1930s; the uniformed beat officer was expected to detect and pursue offenders. It was similar in the smaller of the boroughs. Rural or small borough forces called in detectives from the big cities, especially from the Metropolitan Police, when faced with a major inquiry; but calling in men from the big city was often left till days, even weeks after the event and, invariably, little effort had been made to preserve a crime scene or evidence. A few forensic techniques were available from the beginning of the century. The first successful use of fingerprints in a prosecution was in 1902; and three years later fingerprint evidence led to the conviction of Albert and Alfred Stratton for murder.[7] Further advances were made during the inter-war period, usually because of the enthusiasm of a local chief constable keen to emphasise the modernity of his force. A Home Office departmental committee that reported in 1938, after five years' work, was highly critical of the poor quality of detective training in England.[8] Moreover studies undertaken a generation later suggested that, even after improvements in training, detection accounted for little of the crime brought to court. Over 90 per cent of shoplifters taken to court were caught by shop assistants or store detectives; most assailants taken to court were positively identified by their victims; burglaries and robberies that required detection had a clear-up rate of only about 20 per cent.[9] While it is difficult to quantify detective time during the first half of the twentieth century, it would seem that an inordinate amount was spent talking with informants in pubs and that many interrogations were characterised by pressure and bullying.

There were always two sides to the debate about police powers: those that thought the police were too restricted in their ability to pursue and apprehend offenders, and those that thought they had too much power and authority, and that they were inclined to abuse what they had. Occasionally serious concerns were expressed about rough behaviour by individual officers or groups of officers, both uniformed and detectives. Sometimes, evidence supporting these concerns required investigation. Before the First World War, for example, there was an inquiry into violence by Metropolitan Police officers during industrial troubles on the docks and a Royal Commission revealed police officers regularly squaring up to tough working-class figures in the East End.[10] During the inter-war period there were similar incidents. It was generally the left-wing press that criticised police behaviour during strikes and demonstrations although, after its formation in 1934, the National Council for Civil Liberties enlisted a range of MPs and others to raise concerns. The old trope of plain-clothes police acting as spies was revived with the reports of arrests of couples engaged in sexual activity in parks; one newspaper went so far as to label Hyde Park 'Spied Park'. Concerns were expressed about police officers interrogating suspects with violent or oppressive 'third degree' tactics; such behaviour was condemned by press and politicians alike as un-English. A few instances of clumsy, oppressive behaviour towards individuals prompted enquiries that were often critical of the police.[11]

The experienced London magistrate, Cecil Chapman, recorded some high-handed police behaviour including the threatening of respectable people with arrest for being drunk and disorderly when they challenged a constable's authority or queried his behaviour. He also believed that some offenders were beaten in police cells. The recollections of police officers from later in the century testify to this, and also to beatings and the threat of beatings being used routinely to obtain confessions. But Chapman, and probably also the overall perception of the public, still tended to the warm view of the Bobby and put such abuses down to 'Black Sheep'. 'When uncontrolled power is put into the hands of men it is not to be expected that everybody can resist repeated temptation to abuse it.'[12] Another Royal Commission, which convened at the end of the 1920s, broadly shared

Chapman's view. It found problems with one or two particular procedures, criticised some trends and noted individual failings but, overall, it
gave the Metropolitan Police a clean bill of health.[13] Unfortunately, similar
problems with high-handed and rough behaviour arose again in the
generation following the Second World War. In 1959 the Conservative
Home Secretary, R.A. Butler, found himself facing difficult questions in
parliament, and criticism from outside, when men arrested and taken to
Metropolitan Police stations subsequently had to be taken to hospital. At
the end of the year the revelation that the Commissioner had authorised an
out-of-court settlement of £300 to a civil servant, who was suing a police
constable for assault and unlawful imprisonment, prompted a parliamentary
debate. This incident led directly to a new Royal Commission, although
the commission's remit went much further than police accountability and
relations with the public, to assess where control of the police, particularly
the provincial forces, should reside.[14]

In the social environment following the Second World War there
appears to have been less tolerance of police officers meting out summary
punishment to offending juveniles and others. While it is difficult to
estimate the process and speed of such change, it seems also that the use of
threats and the bullying of suspects by police officers became something
of which the public was more aware and which, as a result, became less
acceptable. Some of this may have been because of a greater egalitarianism
engendered by the war and an accompanying forceful articulation of the
notion that rights and duties should be shared equally by all citizens
whatever their social class. The adoption of a common style of dress by
young people regardless of social class made it less easy, from the 1960s,
for police officers to differentiate traditional 'police property' from their
social superiors. Stopping and searching factory workers leaving their
place of employment and young men walking the streets late at night had
long been a way for the police to check for suspected stolen property, for
weaponry or housebreaking implements.[15] But when, from the late 1970s,
stop and search was seen as a tactic employed increasingly and primarily
against Afro-Caribbean youth, its validity was called into question with a
new and sharper urgency.

Abuses by detective officers also continued to be exposed, and in
more serious measure, in the aftermath of the war. The scandal of the
link between pornographers and members of the Metropolitan Police was
mentioned above in Chapter 5. There was also disquiet about the legal and
ethical dilemmas regarding the use of informants. An official reluctance to
authorise detectives to use undercover methods and paid informants had

been overcome, at least to some extent, by concerns about enemy aliens, potential fifth columnists and black marketers during the Second World War. In the immediate aftermath of the war the Metropolitan Police established the Ghost Squad to collect intelligence on a range of criminal suspects and serious offenders. The squad was short-lived, from December 1945 to September 1949, but it encouraged other forces to establish similar plain-clothes units in the provinces. In London its activities were continued on an *ad hoc* basis by members of the elite Flying Squad until a new, intelligence-gathering unit was established in 1960.[16] In the last third of the century such special squads were regularly running paid informants, sometimes successfully, but sometimes with embarrassing results.

Roy Garner, a major London-based offender, helped in the conviction of a string of men involved in robberies. Garner himself avoided arrest time after time and when, in 1988, he appeared on a cocaine charge, the officer who managed him as an informant gave evidence in camera. Garner was sentenced to 16 years; the officer, Detective Chief Superintendent Tony Lundy continued to manage informants and himself came under suspicion. Elsewhere there were one or two instances of major cases collapsing because of the employment of informants. A significant drug trafficking trial in Newcastle, involving Brian Charrington and Curtis Warren, folded in 1993 as a result of Charrington being a police informant. The affair led to questions being asked in parliament, but Charrington, Curtis and their fellow accused all walked free. Eyebrows were raised subsequently when the police officer who had managed Charrington as an informant was reported to have been seen going on holiday driving a £70,000 car owned by Charrington.[17] During the mid-1990s the Metropolitan Police also found themselves in difficulties over the recruitment of informants among the Jamaican Yardie Gangs. One case of armed robbery in Nottingham nearly collapsed since the Nottinghamshire Police knew nothing of the links of one of the robbers, Eaton Green, to the Metropolitan Police. Another informant, Delroy Denton, had a history of appalling sexual violence in Jamaica. He continued this behaviour after his move to London and after being recruited as a police informant; in 1996 he was jailed for life for the rape and murder of 24-year-old Marcia Lewis.[18] Various Codes of Practice and sections of the Regulation of Investigatory Powers Act (2000) sought to establish a tighter framework for the use of what began to be labelled 'covert human intelligence sources' (CHIS).

The clumsiness and lack of awareness on the part of interrogating officers also created concern and miscarriages of justice. Following the

murder of Maxwell Confait, a 26-year-old transvestite, homosexual prostitute, and the burning of his home in South London in 1972, three boys
were arrested and confessed to the crime. One was subsequently found
guilty of murder, one of manslaughter and all three of arson, but three
years later all of the convictions were quashed. An inquiry by Sir Henry
Fisher did not believe that the boys had been subjected to any violence during their interrogation, but he concluded that their personalities
and severe learning difficulties made them very vulnerable and that these
contributed significantly to their confessions.[19] The inquiry with the
incident that prompted a Royal Commission on Criminal Procedure and
its conclusions fed into the Police and Criminal Evidence Act (PACE) of
1984. PACE imposed strict regulations on the holding of suspects and
the conduct of interviews; in future, interviews were normally to be tape-
recorded. The changes probably did result in a reduction in the incidences
of bullying and dubious practice, but occasional scandals continued to
surface. The successful appeals of those convicted of the Provisional IRA
pub bombings in Guildford and Birmingham exposed the ways in which
the police had constructed confessions. Other appeals, in cases not related
to terrorist activities but in which there were questions about police
behaviour in getting evidence, led to the release of three men convicted of
the murder of PC Keith Blakelock during the riot on the Broadwater Farm
Estate in 1985, and to the release of Stefan Kiszko who had spent 16 years
in jail for the sexual assault and murder of an 11-year-old girl.[20] Other
instances were unearthed over the following decade. In August 1989 the
Chief Constable of the West Midlands transferred the 52 members of his
serious crime squad to non-operational duties following allegations of the
fabrication of evidence to ensure the convictions of those that the detectives thought guilty. Three years later the Court of Appeal quashed the
convictions of three men jailed for murdering a prostitute in Cardiff. What
appears to have alarmed the appeal judges most in this instance was the
manner in which the men had been interrogated. One of the interview
tapes revealed a suspect in tears being shouted at and taunted by officers.[21]
Sir John Woodcock, the Chief Inspector of Constabulary, sought to
explain 'malpractice not out of malice or desire for personal gain but
which begins out of good intentions'. Doctoring or constructing evidence
to ensure the conviction of those that they were sure were guilty thus
became what students of police ethics refer to as 'noble cause corruption'.[22] But whatever the attempts to put a gloss on such behaviour, it
remained illegal and it was not always easy to separate malice and desire
for personal gain in the shape of commendations and promotion.

Shifts in cultural and social attitudes towards gender difference also impacted on policing practices. Police matrons, often the wives of station sergeants, had been used to supervise and to search women prisoners from the late Victorian period, and calls for women police officers began to be heard from the feminist movement at the beginning of the century.[23] The First World War provided the opportunity for the first significant experiments with women police who were charged, principally, with watching the behaviour of young women in the vicinity of large army camps and with supervising the women working in munitions factories. At the end of the war most women police, like their sisters who had filled the vacancies left by men recruited into the armed services, were expected to return to their domestic sphere. However, the Metropolitan Police and a few other forces decided to continue with small units of women officers, although sometimes not fully attested as police constables and therefore unable to make arrests in the absence of a full-sworn male officer. Generally these women were recruited from social groups slightly higher than that of the policemen. As a rule their duties were directed towards the policing of women and children, although a few were given the opportunity for plain-clothes work alongside male officers. The Second World War saw a repetition of the demands made upon women in the previous conflict, and for largely the same reasons. But the war also offered women the opportunity for building on such advances as they had made. In February 1941, for example, the *Police Chronicle* reported that five women already serving with the Metropolitan Police CID had been drafted into Special Branch. Several of these women had acted as decoys assisting the Flying Squad with the arrest of bag snatchers and other thieves; and two of them had won promotion after trailing IRA suspects and enemy aliens.[24] In the aftermath of the war the number of women officers remained significantly above that of 1939 and increasingly, and often reluctantly, more and more forces established women's departments. It was not until the gender equality legislation of the early 1970s, however, that women police were fully integrated into the service, and until the end of the century many continued to experience prejudice and sexual harassment from their male colleagues. Indeed, it seems that in some instances the prejudice and harassment increased when the differentiation between male and female officers came to an end, and when women officers were no longer so carefully shielded by the chivalric attitudes that often existed alongside, and indeed as part-and-parcel of the aggressive, working-class male sexuality within the police.

Women officers were not the only individuals that faced difficulties when entering the tough, artisanal culture of the police. There appear to have been one or two black officers scattered in nineteenth- and early twentieth-century police forces. When, however, in the aftermath of the Second World War labour shortages prompted immigrants from the West Indies and subsequently from the Indian subcontinent, the police stead-fastly resisted the recruitment of black and Asian officers. Afro-Caribbean immigrants found employment in many public sector jobs, notably in transport and in the National Health Service, but the argument generally presented by senior police officers was that such migrants would not be able to develop the rapport with the British public that was expected of police constables. It was not until 20 years after the first migrant ship arrived from the West Indies that the first three officers, born to immigrant parents, were appointed – two in the Midlands and one in London. The few officers from minority ethnic groups that served during the 1970s and 1980s appear generally to have had a hard time. Sometimes the prejudice was overt from their fellow police officers, and sometimes also from their communities where many saw them as traitors who had turned against their own kind. By the end of the century some black and Asian officers, like some women officers, were clawing their way to the higher ranks. Yet prejudice remained and was highlighted first in Lord Scarman's investigation of the inner-city rioting of 1981 and then in Sir William Macpherson's inquiry into the murder of the black teenager, Stephen Lawrence, which famously concluded that the Metropolitan Police was 'institutionally racist'.[25]

Changes in the recruitment pool for personnel were matched by changes in the environment within which police officers did their job. The financial retrenchment of the inter-war period ensured that police numbers would not be increased, yet the suburbs expanded considerably. At the end of the First World War, for example, Major General Sir Wyndham Childs was brought to Scotland Yard to supervise the CID. He was shocked by old equipment, such as cheap microscopes for detective work that could not be replaced without the permission of the Receiver of Police, and his inability to get more men 'because of the sacred word "economy" '. He expressed his frustration in his memoirs:

London grows at the rate of about 100 houses a day and several miles of street a week. Traffic control absorbs something like 1400 men every day and conditions are getting worse as the streets become more congested. Every new house is a potential for burglary. New legislation to suit the fancy of the Government of the day is introduced every session, legislation frequently containing penal clauses which require to be enforced by the police.

But the limits on police numbers remained, and the problems continued to mount. The Commissioner of the Metropolitan Police echoed Childs in his annual report for 1937. In the previous seven years, he explained, streets in just one police division had increased by 226 miles, and the number of houses had grown by 53,000.[26] The Chief Constable of Sheffield made the same point. His uniformed officers were so stretched that they were insufficient 'to give the supervision one would desire on some of the new housing estates'. He had been forced to have one constable working two beats 'with the consequent loss of close observation of premises on those beats'. He hoped that 'in the near future the provision of small motor cars for mobile supervision' would help. In 1937 the Sheffield force purchased six Morris Eight cars for this purpose.[27]

The growth of motor traffic itself brought the police more problems. Ensuring the free flow of traffic and dealing with individuals not in any fit state to be in charge of a vehicle, driving too fast or driving poorly were tasks that pre-dated the modern police. But the speed of motor vehicles and their increasing availability as a means of private transport aggravated the dangers on the roads. Moreover, since the first people to be able to afford private cars came from the respectable middle class, for the first time in their history the police began to find themselves in confrontation with members of that class. The problem became increasingly apparent during the inter-war years, and it was encapsulated in a scene in *The Blue Lamp* made shortly after the Second World War. PC Andy Mitchell had been mentored by PC George Dixon. Shortly after being present when the news of Dixon's murder had been told to Dixon's wife, Mitchell has occasion to stop and speak to a wealthy woman who has nearly knocked down a man on a pedestrian crossing. 'Haven't you anything better to do?' asks the woman in her cut-glass accent. 'One of your own men shot down in cold blood and all you do is pester the life out of innocent and respectable people. I'm not surprised all these murderers get away with it.' It was clear where the cinema audience's sympathy was supposed to be; but it could so easily be very different on the road.

During the 1960s the shortages of manpower and the enthusiasm for technological solutions combined to develop the system known as Unit Beat Policing. Town centres continued to be policed in traditional ways but in the Unit Beat system the districts beyond the centre were divided into areas that became the 24-hour responsibility of an individual officer who patrolled as and when he saw fit. Two of these areas were covered by a police car, again on duty throughout the 24 hours; there were further links to detective officers who received and collated material. The most celebrated trials of the system were made in Kirby, a desolate new town, lacking in amenities that had been established on the fringe of Liverpool. Critics argued that Unit Beat Policing reduced the links between the police and the community; but for the earnest advocates, which included the Home Secretary Roy Jenkins, members of the Home Office and senior police officers, the system was good for morale and demonstrated how technology could aid the fight against crime. By the end of 1968 it was estimated that 60 per cent of the population were covered by the system.[28]

Other advances in technology were seen as offering assistance to a variety of policing duties. Radios had been introduced into police cars and on to motor cycles during the inter-war period, and there were a few experiments with pocket sets for officers on foot patrol. But the beat officer remained dependent on his whistle and his physical prowess for a generation after 1945. Personal radios were successfully introduced for operational policing only in 1966. While these radios were not universally available for beat officers for several more years, the introduction of this new means of communication meant that an officer had instant contact with his base for advice or back-up; and, the radios were, of course, central to Unit Beat Policing.[29]

In 1964 it was stated that while, with its computer system, the New York Police Department could compare 100,000 fingerprints in three hours, there were no computers in the British Police. It could take 10 of the 134 employees in the Fingerprint Department at Scotland Yard six weeks to find a print.[30] The statement about New York was erroneous; it was impossible to compare fingerprints by computer during the 1960s, but what people believe to be the case is often more important than the reality. The same year saw a study initiated to consider building a Police National Computer, but it was another five years before the Labour government announced plans for the go-ahead and a further four before it was ready for use and linked up to a terminal in every police force in England and Wales. Initially the computer held details of cars and their owners taken from the Driver and Vehicle Licensing Computer in Swansea; these were followed by indices for criminal records and fingerprints. The hope that it would be possible to categorise the *modus operandi* of known offenders into computer-readable form and thus to identify a perpetrator from infor- mation at a crime scene, was never realised. But, at the end of the century the police also had access to a database, created by the Forensic Science Service, of DNA taken from convicted offenders. DNA was first used in a criminal case towards the end of 1986. The database was established in 1995 and, four years later, it was claimed that there were about 500 matches made each week between traces found at scenes of crime and suspects.[31]

Few doubted that the police could benefit from the storage and speedy retrieval of information on computers, but almost immediately after the first Police National Computer had linked up with forces across the country, anxiety was expressed that the system could be abused and contribute to the creation of a surveillance state. The concerns focused particularly on the collection of intelligence, at least some of which appeared to be based on gossip and assumption. The Committee on Data Protection chaired by Sir Norman Lindop recognised the value of computers for the police, but the police were not particularly forthcoming in their evidence to the committee. The committee, in turn, expressed concerns about collecting and collating intelligence that was 'speculative, suppositional, hearsay and unverified' and suggested that the police be subject to its proposal for a Data Protection Agency. The concerns came to the fore again at the end of the 1970s when jurors for cases involving politics, official secrets and terrorism were being vetted by the police and, specifically, Special Branch.[32] An article in *The Guardian* in September the following year, one of a series reflecting doubts about the increasing use of computers in society, gave voice to the fears about the police collection and use of computerised intelligence.

The police view is that if an individual has done nothing wrong, he or she has nothing to fear from their computers. Yet who would agree with a definition of potential subversion that apparently includes going on a march against cuts in the education budget? And how far do we trust the police? As they are the people feeding the information to the computers and handling it to catch suspects, this is a vital question. The opportunities for misuse of the information are obvious.[33]

There had been concerns about the militarisation of the police on their creation in the early nineteenth century and, on and off, throughout the Victorian period. They had been revived during the inter-war period: for example, by the men dismissed following the police strike of 1919. Concern about political partiality and violence towards demonstrators by the police followed a similar trajectory and contributed to the launch of the National Council for Civil Liberties in 1934. These concerns were revived during a variety of political demonstrations in the 1960s against nuclear weapons, against apartheid in South Africa, and against the war in Vietnam. They spread with the industrial disorders of the 1970s when the police, according to some critics, acquired an increasingly paramilitary image during demonstrations. The most striking representations of this image appeared during the 1980s when the police confronted inner-city riots and, above all, the picket lines of the year-long miners' strike of 1984 to 1985. When Margaret Thatcher's government came to power in 1979 it immediately implemented in full a massive pay rise for the police; the Labour government had held back half of the award for reasons of public expenditure control. The Tory generosity, and the subsequent deployment of the police against the miners, led to the police becoming closely identified with the government. Some police officers had few qualms about this, and one or two senior officers appear positively to have relished open clashes with their local police authorities when concerns were expressed that marching police officers off to supervise picket lines reduced the number of men available for the prevention and detection of crime. Other officers, from all ranks, were uncomfortable with the way in which the situation evolved. 'No question, we were "Maggie's boys" ', recalled one, 'I hated that.'[34]

The Thatcher government may have been initially sympathetic to the police but it also believed that the police, like every other public body, needed to recognise that it must provide 'value for money' in the fight against crime and for the maintenance of order. Indeed, the failure of the police to reduce the rising crime statistics in spite of the money directed towards law and order by the government strengthened the demands. Home Office circulars called for improved financial management (circular 114/83 in 1983) and general management improvement (circular 106/88 in 1988). The PACE legislation of 1984 has already been touched upon with reference to the way that it sought to reduce the abuse of police interviews. The Act also gave the Home Secretary powers to set national police objectives supported by performance indicators. In addition it sought to limit the friction between young blacks and the police by insisting that an officer must have 'reasonable suspicion' to justify the stop and search of an individual; moreover the suspicion was not to be grounded in the social or racial characteristics of the person stopped. The simultaneous creation of the Crown Prosecution Service removed final decisions about proceeding with a criminal prosecution from the police as well as removing the role of prosecutor from police officers in the lower courts. Ten years after PACE, as well as reorganising the police authorities, the Police and Magistrates' Courts Act entrenched the new emphases on financial accountability and targets for policing and also sought to legislate for better links between the police and the communities in which they served.

By the last 10 or 15 years of the century senior police officers were realising that, for all their expertise, they were not as well integrated with their local communities as the traditional rhetoric of 'the best police in the world' implied. This may have been partly because from the 1960s the police increasingly, as well as a large proportion of the population, had begun to drive round in cars and consequently day-to-day contact between a local police officer and the population on his beat had been lost. But it was also becoming much more apparent, and much less acceptable, that police officers had often treated some members of the public as second-class citizens. Following Lord Scarman's report on the Brixton riots of 1981, the Home Office urged the police to establish consultative committees with local communities to improve the links between local police commanders and the people within their area. The committees became a statutory requirement under PACE, although the evidence suggests that the committees, as constituted, were unrepresentative of local communities and had little input into policing.[35] At the same time, members of ACPO began to think about re-emphasising the police role as that of a 'service' rather than a 'force'.

'The prevention of crime' had been central to the instructions given to the Metropolitan Police constables when they had first taken to the streets in 1829. But the crime prevention officers developed with specialist prevention units from the mid-1960s were generally looked down upon by those officers who revelled in the masculinity of the job and the notion of 'crime-fighting'. In the new context of targets, value for money and reconnecting with communities, police spokesmen began to argue that the police could not be expected to prevent crime unaided. These comments were in tune with the thinking that emerged within the Home Office and that were set out most clearly in the 1991 report of the Standing Conference on Crime Prevention, generally known as the Morgan Report. As a result of this new thinking, increasing emphasis was put on concepts such as community policing and then multi-agency policing, but it was not until New Labour's Crime and Disorder Act of 1998 that this kind of activity was given a statutory requirement. The Act required the creation of Crime and Disorder Reduction Partnerships in England and Community Safety Partnerships in Wales. It identified local authorities, local health authorities, police authorities, fire and rescue authorities and the police themselves as 'responsible authorities' and directed them to work together in partnerships. They were to bring together a range of other public, private and voluntary bodies to devise and implement strategies for dealing with crime, disorder and drug misuse. In addition the partnerships were to make triennial audits on the scale of these local problems.

The attempts to reconnect with local communities coincided with another development that had a significant impact on the vestiges of the beat officer's *modus operandi*, specifically the growth of risk assessment and health and safety regulations. The police were exempt from the 1974 Health and Safety at Work Act, which imposed legal duties on employers in respect of their employees. The employment status of police officers fell outside of the Act's definition of employment. This was largely the result of the legal ruling that persons holding the office of constable were not employees, but were appointed as members of a police force and attested as officers of the Crown. Police forces made varying attempts to apply the spirit of the 1974 Act on a voluntary basis, but with little consistency or uniformity. With the exception of breakdowns in public order, such as the disturbances at the Notting Hill Carnival from 1976, and the 1981 disturbances at Brixton and elsewhere, that necessitated the introduction of specialist tactics and personal protective equipment, the impact of the 1974 Act upon everyday policing was small. Increasing levels of sickness and injuries on duty during the 1980s and 1990s, however, prompted the police service to look at ways of improving officer safety. In 1997 the government took the decision to bring the police service into line when it enacted the Police (Health and Safety) Act. Pressure for the Act's introduction had come principally from two directions. First, the police service itself – in particular the Police Federation – wanted officers' health and safety to be covered on a statutory basis. Secondly, the new Act enabled the government to implement more fully a series of European Union directives on health and safety, which were applicable to all workers. Support also came from ACPO, which was concerned by the drain on force budgets from sickness and early retirements due to accidents and assaults.[36]

The legislation may have made officers more aware of the risks that they faced in their job and the need for risk assessment before acting, but there remained instances where police officers had to make on-the-spot decisions that put their lives in danger. In addition, an analysis of Officer Safety Training Programmes in a rural force at the turn of the millennium concluded that, while such training had provided significant improvements to the occupational welfare of front-line officers, it was structured in a way that appeared to encourage the use of force against citizens by those officers.[37]

Force is central to the police; indeed, it has been argued that the ability to use force is the element that distinguishes the police officer from other state agents responsible for seeing that laws are obeyed.[38] In England, however, social commentators, traditional police historians and the police themselves have always been keen to stress that they only use force limited by the needs of the incident. There has been similar stress on the fact that the police work with the consent of their fellow citizens. Just about everyone might agree that they were opposed to crime and wanted the police to deal with it; even so the level and scale of consent has never been constant and has depended on a variety of factors in addition to public awareness of police high-handedness or violence. In the first half of the century officers were known to strike offending juveniles. They were known to be rough in some instances of disorder and they were occasionally criticised for bullying suspects. During the inter-war period also, they were increasingly in verbal confrontations with middle-class car drivers. Yet the overall image of the police was generally good. Many citizens subscribed wholeheartedly to the notion of the best police in the world; and linked with this there appears to have been a largely accepted narrative that they were reasonably successful in controlling crime. The society that emerged in the wake of the Second World War was less deferential and more ready to question authority and the assertions of authority about its functionaries and its way of governing. At the same time rising crime rates, increasingly the subject of political debate, challenged the assertions about the crime-fighting abilities of the police. It is always difficult to assess convincingly the standing of an institution. Occasionally during the century the reputation of the police in England and Wales took serious knocks. Periodically polls demonstrated a decline in respect for the police; yet respect remained, and sometimes, perhaps, even affection.[39] The police were still hailed as a 'thin blue line' protecting society, and in popular representations in film and literature, tough, maverick policemen who sometimes bent and broke the rules to get the villains continued to be satisfying and popular.[40]

References and notes

1 Except where stated, the discussion of the interrelationship between police, local government and central government draws largely on **Clive Emsley**, 'The police', in Vernon Bogdanor (ed.), *The British Constitution in the Twentieth Century*, Oxford: Oxford University Press, 2003.

2 See, for example, the complaints of the Bucks SJC; Bucks CRO, Standing Joint Committee Minutes, 3 (April 1910–March 1917) fol. 97 (17 October 1911) and fol. 191 (15 April 1913).

3 *The Times*, 12 December 1942, p. 5.

4 *Report of H.M. Inspectors of Constabulary for 1932*, p. 11; and see also, *Report of H.M. Inspectors of Constabulary for 1933*, p. 9.

5 **John Bunker**, *From Rattle to Radio*, Studley, Warks: Brewin Books, 1988, chap. 4.

6 The problem is always to know just how common such behaviour was. Stephen Humphries quotes oral testimony of victims; **Stephen Humphries**, *Hooligans or Rebels? An oral history of working-class childhood and youth 1889–1939*, Oxford: Basil Blackwell, 1981, p. 147. Mike Brodgen quotes oral testimony of perpetrators; **Mike Brogden**, *On the Mersey Beat: policing Liverpool between the wars*, Oxford: Oxford University Press, 1991, p. 101. C.H. Rolph, a former police officer, writer on police affairs, but by no means apologist for the police, was rather more sceptical about its scale and incidence. **C.H. Rolph**, 'What does it all amount to?', in **C.H. Rolph** (ed.), *The Police and the Public: an enquiry*, London: Heinemann, 1962, pp. 187–9.

7 Oldbaileyonline, t19020909-686 (trial of Harry Jackson), t19050502-415 (trial of the Strattons); and for a general introduction see, **Bob Morris**, 'History of criminal investigation', in **Tim Newburn**, **Tom Williamson** and **Alan Wright** (eds), *Handbook of Criminal Investigation*, Cullompton: Willan, 2007.

8 *Report of the Departmental Committee on Detective Work and Procedure*, 5 vols. London: HMSO, 1938.

9 **R.G.V. Clarke** and **J.M. Hough** (eds), *The Effectiveness of Policing*, Farnborough, Hants.: Gower, 1980; **David Steer**, *Uncovering Crime: the police role*, London: HMSO, 1980.

10 *Report of the Royal Commission upon the Duties of the Metropolitan Police*, Cmd 4185, London: HMSO, 1908, p. 66; *Report on Disturbances at Rotherhithe on June 11 1912, and Complaints against the Conduct of the Police in connection therewith*, Cd. 6367, London: HMSO, 1912.

11 **Janet Clark**, ' "Striving to preserve the peace!" The National Council for Civil Liberties, the Metropolitan Police and the dynamics of disorder in interwar Britain', PhD, Open University, 2008; *World's Pictorial News*, 13 May 1928, p. 4; **Clive Emsley**, *The English Police: a political and social history*, 2nd edn, London: Longman, 1996, p. 144.

12 **Cecil Chapman**, *The Poor Man's Court of Justice: twenty-five years as a metropolitan magistrate*, London: Hodder and Stoughton, 1925, pp. 146–61; quotation at p. 154. For police beatings, and threats of beatings during the period after the Second World War, see **Keith Hellawell**, *The Outsider: the autobiography of one of Britain's most controversial policemen*, London: Harper Collins, 2002, pp. 40 and 51–2; and **Clive Emsley**, *The Great British*

Bobby: a history of British policing from the 18th century to the present, revised edn, London: Quercus, 2010, pp. 251–3.

13 *Report of the Royal Commission on Police Powers and Procedure*, Cmd. 3297, London: HMSO, 1929.

14 **Clive Emsley**, *Hard Men: violence in England since 1750*, London: Hambledon, 2005, p. 144; *Final Report of the Royal Commission on the Police*, Cmd. 1782, London: HMSO, 1962.

15 For a response to criticism of the Lancashire Police stopping and searching men leaving factories in the early 1960s see OUPA ERICSJ/1/4/1/229, Eric St Johnston to Frank Allaun, MP, 19 May 1961.

16 **Mark Roodhouse**, 'The "Ghost Squad": undercover policing in London, 1945–49', in **Gerard Oram** (ed.), *Conflict and Legality: policing mid-twentieth-century Europe*, London: Francis Boutle, 2003.

17 **David Rose**, *In the Name of the Law: the collapse of criminal justice*, London: Jonathan Cape, 1996, pp. 174–88; *Parl. Debs. (Commons)*, 21 January 1994, col. 846 and 24 January 1994, col. 321.

  A BBC TV programme, *Supergrass*, transmitted on BBC 2, 13 May 2007, generated a series of complaints from Lundy, retired and living in Spain. His complaint regarding a factual error was upheld; it was agreed that he should have been told that a journalist who had been critical of his behaviour would be appearing in the programme; however, it was considered that the programme gave a fair representation of the later stages of his career. The programme 'said that he had been cleared of all wrongdoing, despite being "the most investigated police officer in British History", and promoted to Detective Chief Superintendent, but also that he nevertheless remained the subject of suspicion at a high level in the Metropolitan Police'. See, www.bbc.co.uk/complaints/pdf/ecu_octdec07.pdf

18 **Philip Etienne** and **Martin Maynard**, with **Tony Thompson**, *The Infiltrators*, London: Michael Joseph, 2000; *The Guardian*, 16 February 1999, p. 6 and 16 July, p. 4; *Daily Mirror*, 14 August 1999, pp. 24–5.

19 **Sir Henry Fisher**, *The Confait Case: report*, London: HMSO, 1977.

20 Rose, *In the Name of the* Law, pp. 46–7 and 298–305.

21 See, for example, *The Guardian*, 16 August 1989, p. 2 and 11 December 1992, p. 2; *The Independent*, 12 August 1991, p. 4.

22 See, for example, *The Guardian*, 14 October 1992, pp. 18–20; **Michael A. Caldero** and **John P. Crank**, *Police Ethics: the corruption of noble cause*, 2nd edn, Cincinnati, OH: Anderson, 2004.

23 Unless otherwise stated, the information deployed in this paragraph is drawn from **Louise A. Jackson**, *Women Police: gender, welfare and surveillance in the twentieth century*, Manchester University Press, 2006.

24 *Police Chronicle*, 14 February 1941, p. 5.

25 **James Whitfield**, *Unhappy Dialogue: the Metropolitan Police and black Londoners in post-war Britain*, Cullompton: Willan Publishing, 2004.

26 **Major General Sir Wyndham Childs**, *Episodes and Reflections*, London: Cassell and Co. 1930, p. 195; *Annual Report of the Commissioner of the Metropolitan Police for 1937*, p. 7.

27 *Annual Report of the City of Sheffield Police and Auxiliary Services*, 1936, pp. 4–5, and 1937, p. 5.

28 **T.A. Critchley**, *A History of Police in England and Wales*, Revised edn, London: Constable, 1978, pp. 307–8. Secretary to the Royal Commission on Police (1960–62) and a senior figure in the Police Department at the Home Office until 1971, Tom Critchley was a keen supporter of police modernisation.

29 Bunker, *From Rattle to Radio*, pp. 175–216.

30 **Ben Whitaker**, *The Police*, Harmondsworth: Penguin, 1964, p. 53.

31 **Sarah Manwaring-White**, *The Policing Revolution: police technology, democracy and liberty in Britain*, Brighton: Harvester, 1983, chap. 3; **Chris A. Williams**, 'The origins of the UK's Police National Computer 1958–77', paper presented to the Twentieth Colloquium for Police History held at the German Historical Institute, London, 9–11 July 2009; **Alan Moss** and **Keith Skinner**, *The Scotland Yard Files: milestones in criminal detection*, London: The National Archives, 2006, pp. 51–6.

32 *Report of the Committee on Data Protection* (Lindop Committee), London: HMSO, 1978, Cmnd 7341; **John Hostetter**, *The Criminal Jury Old and New: jury power from early times to the present day*, Winchester: Waterside Press, 2004, p. 129; *The Times*, 31 October 1978, p. 3; *The Guardian*, 15 August 1979, p. 24.

33 *The Guardian*, 22 September 1980, p. 17.

34 **Roger Graef**, *Talking Blues: the police in their own words*, London; Collins Harvill, 1989, p. 74. Some of the most notable clashes occurred on Merseyside where the friction between the Chief Constable, Sir Kenneth Oxford, and the chair of his local police committee, the veteran Labour activist Margaret Simey, went back many years. See **Margaret Simey**, *Democracy Rediscovered: a study in police accountability*, London: Pluto Press, 1988.

35 **Rod Morgan**, 'Talking about policing', in **David Downes** (ed.), *Unravelling Criminal Justice*, London: Macmillan, 1992.

36 *Parl. Debs. (Lords)*, Vol. 578, col. 1435, 28 February 1997.

37 **John W. Buttle**, 'A constructive critique of the Officer Safety Programme used in England and Wales', *Policing and Society*, 17, 2 (2007) pp. 164–81.

38 See, *inter alia*, **David H. Bayley**, *Patterns of Policing: a comparative international analysis*, New Brunswick, NJ: Rutgers University Press, 1985, pp. 12–13.

39 See, for example, *The Police and the Public in England and Wales*, Home Office Research Report 117, London: HMSO, 1990, for evidence that the public were losing faith in the police.

40 *Sunday Mirror*, 15 March 1987, pp. 1–11 for a special report on 'The thin blue line'.

CHAPTER 9

The courts

Just as the police institution was allowed to jog along fairly comfortably until the last third of the twentieth century, the court system also continued with only a modicum of tinkering until the last years of the century. Again, like the police, the courts and their personnel had to come to terms, often reluctantly and grudgingly, with changing attitudes towards gender and race.

At the beginning of the century there were three kinds of court at which criminal offences might be tried. At the lowest level were the courts of summary jurisdiction presided over by two or three local justices of the peace or magistrates. These courts were sometimes known as petty sessions or, in the big cities, as police courts, although the police had no special powers or authority within them. There had been a significant growth in these courts particularly from the mid-nineteenth century as legislation allowed more and more of the less serious offences, particularly those relating to juvenile offenders, to be brought before them. The magistrates in these courts might have an initial hearing to decide on whether or not a case was serious enough to be passed to a higher court where the decision on guilt was made by a jury; and in some instances a defendant had the option for selecting to be tried in the higher court by a jury. The second kind of court was that of quarter sessions, also presided over by magistrates. These courts were so called because they met four times a year, assembling every three months. They had once been the centre of local government for the incorporated boroughs and the counties but with the creation of, first, elected borough councils (1835) and then county councils (1888), their responsibilities were increasingly reduced to those of a criminal court. And this responsibility also declined with the growing authority of the summary courts. The most serious criminal cases were heard before judges at the assizes which met three or four times a year; and in London such cases went before the Central Criminal Court, popularly known as the Old Bailey, which usually had 12 sessions a year. For first two-thirds of the century this three-tier system of courts was maintained with relatively limited tinkering at the edges.

The statistical increase in crime from the 1950s put enormous pressures on the courts and this, together with its enthusiasm to modernise institutions, led the Labour government of Harold Wilson to appoint a Royal Commission to investigate the courts in 1966. The Commission, chaired by Lord Beeching, published its report in 1969 and it was left to a Conservative government to implement changes based on its recommendations. Thus, in the early 1970s a two-tier system of criminal courts was established. The quarter sessions were abolished; Magistrates' Courts, presided over by a bench of three lay justices or, where the burden of work was too heavy, by a district judge with a legal background, decided on lesser offences; Crown Courts, presided over by judges, heard the more serious cases, and here juries continued to determine the verdicts. At the end of the century there were 328 Petty Sessional areas and 78 Crown Courts; there were also proposals under discussion for a unified court system.[1]

Until the end of the First World War the personnel of the courts was entirely male. At the top of the legal hierarchy were the judges that heard the cases at assizes and the Old Bailey. These men were largely the products of public schools and Oxbridge. They had begun their careers by being admitted to one of the Inns of Court; they had then been called to the Bar, had acted as barristers for at least ten years and had progressed to the senior rank of King's or Queen's Counsel – the term was dependent upon whether there was a male or female monarch. Barristers were also appointed to officiate as recorders in the busiest magistrates' courts of the largest cities and boroughs and as stipendiary magistrates in the London police courts. Occasionally a man with legal training might chair a county court of quarter sessions but most magistrates were without any formal legal training and they relied, for advice, on a clerk who was so trained. At the beginning of the century magistrates were drawn from the local elites of town or county.

There was some extension to the magistracy in 1906 when the abolition of the property qualification for the post allowed the appointment of working-class men, and a Royal Commission that reported four years later recommended that working men, with personal experience of the living conditions of their class, should be selected to serve. But hardly any working-class men could afford to take time off their work in order to act as justices. In addition, those responsible for recommending individuals to the Lord Chancellor for appointment to the magistracy had little opportunity for knowing where to find competent working men with time to spare, and in consequence very few working-class men made it into the post until some years after the Second World War.

A real change in the magistracy, and in the legal profession itself, was heralded by the Sex Disqualification (Removal) Act of 1919. Admission to every kind of public office and profession had been a central demand of feminists and suffragettes and the 1919 Act, together with the extension of the franchise, was an important step towards the equality that they sought. As a result of the Act women could apply to become members of the Inns of Court and hence be called to the Bar. But those who took this route faced considerable prejudice from the male hierarchy and, in consequence, experienced difficulties entering and working their way up through the system; by the early 1930s women made up less than one per cent of those holding certificates permitting them to practise at the Bar. Helena Normanton was the first woman to practise as a barrister; she was an extremely able advocate who achieved a series of firsts in her career: the first female counsel to appear in a High Court of Justice, specifically the Old Bailey in 1924; the first woman to lead in a prosecution for murder, in 1948; one of the first two women to be appointed a King's Counsel, in 1949. But she was never fully accepted by many of the profession; indeed, the general progress of women at the Bar remained slow throughout the century. In 1983, out of a total of 77 High Court Judges, only three were women. At the close of the century, even though women formed more than half of those newly admitted as barristers and solicitors, there were still only seven women acting as judges in the High Court. In addition, out of 547 circuit court judges only 30 were women; and out of 91 stipendiaries and 337 district court judges, the number of women was, respectively, 14 and 31.[2]

Legal practice required extensive training and hence it was some time before women could acquire the necessary qualifications to act as solicitors, barristers or judges. But with the exception of the stipendiaries, who served in the big towns and who were drawn from members of the legal profession, the magistracy was made up of laymen with no legal training. Hence a woman only needed the appropriate nomination to be able to serve immediately. The Sex Disqualification (Removal) Act became law in mid-December 1919 and the first women magistrates were appointed on Christmas Eve.

The first women magistrates were rather like the majority of their male equivalents in class and social background. But whereas the men commonly had a business or professional background, the first women magistrates generally came with a background in women's political activism or volunteer philanthropic work. The career opportunities for these women were restricted; the position of magistrate enabled them to play a significant and officially sanctioned public role. For most of the century women remained a minority on the bench but the growth of the proportion of women justices was faster than that of women in the legal profession. Women made up around 10 per cent of the magistracy during the 1930s; their numbers grew steadily, especially after the Second World War, and reached about 40 per cent at the beginning of the 1980s. In the early years particularly, their impact was out of proportion to their numbers. Women magistrates were the most active and vocal in organising training for the position during the 1920s and 1930s. They played a major role in the development of the Magistrates' Association that was intended to advise on duties and best practice. Summer Schools organised by, and primarily for women magistrates began in the 1920s; more general training was introduced after the Second World War, but was not made compulsory until the 1966. Up until then magistrates, particularly the male magistrates, relied on their 'common sense' and, if they were bothered, on their reading of *Stone's Justices' Manual* and the weekly *Justice of the Peace*.[3]

At the end of the century, as women clawed their way to parity in numbers with men as magistrates, so attempts were made to bring ethnic minorities on to the bench. The first black justice of the peace, E.G. Irons, was appointed to the Nottinghamshire Bench in April 1962. Fifteen years later people from the African, Afro-Caribbean and Asian communities made up just under 5 per cent of the magistracy.[4]

The theory on which much of the criminal justice system was based had evolved slowly and haphazardly over time. It was rooted in the idea that the impartial presentation of evidence before lay people led to the right decision being made on guilt and innocence. The lay element of the magistracy was paralleled in the higher courts by the system of juries composed of ordinary people. At the beginning of the century, trials at quarter sessions, assizes and at the Old Bailey were heard before juries. The jury held a hallowed place in the English criminal justice system, yet the growth of the summary courts since the mid-eighteenth century meant that fewer and fewer cases were heard before juries. By the beginning of the twentieth century, as many as 98 per cent of criminal cases were heard in the petty sessions courts that met without jurors, and the percentage was much the same a hundred years later.[5]

At the beginning of the century jurors, like all other individuals with an official position in the courts, were male. They were selected according to various local property qualifications, something that annoyed the leaders of trade unions especially when working men were prosecuted for an offence involving industrial activity. A few working men had made it on to juries before the beginning of the century, but there was a draw-back to jury service for the less well-to-do in that, until the Juries Act of 1949, there was no provision to recompense jurors for loss of pay. The Sex Disqualification (Removal) Act enabled the relatively small number of women with the appropriate property qualifications to be selected as jurors. But judges had the facility for ordering juries to be composed of just one gender and, at the beginning, some judges and barristers were reluctant to have women exposed to what they considered to be the sordid and potentially corrupting nature of evidence presented in trials for sexual offences. One barrister wrote to *The Times* that he

should shudder even at the thought of having to discuss such evidence with my wife, who is now . . . by law liable to be called upon at any moment to consider 'filth' in all its details, and, worse still, discuss it in a public Court with men and women who are comparative strangers to her.[6]

Some women accepted the misogynist line: 'I am so awfully nervous', declared one, 'I don't think I am suitable.' But, like many men, women also had responsibilities for which jury service made no provision: caring for children and elderly relatives, for example, or looking after small busi-nesses.[7] The property qualification did not mean that an individual, male or female, had leisure and financial independence and the 1949 legislation provided assistance to women jurors as much as to men. Yet the property qualification did mean that there was often a significant social difference between jurors and the accused. As one celebrated judge and strong sup-porter of the jury system put it in 1956, the juries were 'predominantly male, middle-aged, middle-minded and middle-class'. In 1965 a committee appointed to investigate jury service recommended that the criterion for appointment should be citizenship as evidenced by inclusion on the electoral register; the recommendation was implemented by the Jury Act of 1974.[8]

The courts employed an adversarial system by which the evidence for and against the defendant was presented by separate advocates. At the Old

'When we get women on juries'

The cartoonist W.K. Haselden's comment on women jurors, published in the *Daily Mirror*, 18 March 1920. (*Source*: British Cartoon Archive, University of Kent/Mirrorpix)

Bailey, the assizes and later the Crown Courts, these advocates were barristers, bewigged and begowned like the judges that some of them were to become. Trevor Grove, a journalist who served on an Old Bailey jury towards the end of the 1990s, recorded that he had never felt more class-conscious in his life than when at the court. 'Crudely speaking, judges and barristers are toffs, whereas almost everyone else is a prole.' He was annoyed by the monotonous regularity with which jurors were required to leave the court while matters of law were discussed. He became aware of the impact of barristers' presentation and performance.

I have no doubt that Mr Gale is a very able barrister. His oratory was remarkable. For one thing, when it wasn't targeted witheringly at George Fraghistas [a kidnap victim and prosecution witness], it seemed to be addressed over the heads of us rude mechanicals in the jury box to some invisible audience of impressionable law students. For another, it demonstrated those perhaps rather neglected, old-fashioned skills, the sustained sneer and the condescending put-down . . .

One had to hand it to Mr Curran. He was singing for his supper. He quoted Dickens (Bleak House), the Bible . . . the Duke of Wellington . . . and Lewis Carroll's Humpty Dumpty ('When I use a word, it means just what I choose it to mean – neither more nor less'). Some of these allusions, I fear, may not have hit their target, given the state of English education.

Nevertheless, Grove's experiences led him to become a staunch supporter of the jury system. He recorded how seriously he and his fellow jurors – a cross-section of society from cleaners to a retired schools' inspector with a PhD, and from postal workers to a supermarket checkout lady – took their duty, listening to the evidence and the closing speeches of the barristers, and then thinking hard and working over the evidence to reach their verdict.[9] Jurors were banned from reporting on how they had reached their verdicts, but there is no reason to doubt that most probably took their responsibilities as seriously as Grove maintained.

Advocates were not much in evidence on the part of defendants in the summary courts at the beginning of the century but, with the growth in legal aid, so the opportunities grew for representation in these courts, but by solicitors rather than by barristers.[10] Occasionally defendants chose to act on their own account before magistrates and even sometimes in the higher courts. Such behaviour might be done with malicious intent, and then the judge had to tread a difficult line to ensure that silencing a line of questioning did not provide grounds for an appeal.[11] Until 1986 when the

Crown Prosecution Service became operational, police officers, rather than solicitors, often prosecuted cases before magistrates. At the turn of the century this had been criticised by members of the legal profession who labelled the police 'amateur advocates'. Later the criticism followed two lines of attack: first, that police officers acting as advocates might imply too close a link between the police and the courts; and second, that the untrained police officer was at a serious disadvantage before the trained lawyer. Both might have had an element of truth; both might also have been a cover for maintaining the exclusivity of the legal profession. John Wainwright recalled an Inspector Tosh, one of his superiors in the West Riding Police, 'who knew more ploys of "unofficial" court-room antics' than any barrister or solicitor. Among these ploys:

Previous convictions are not of course given until the accused has been found guilty of whatever offence he's charged with. A prior knowledge that the guy in the dock was a regular visitor to criminal courts might sway the magistrates in their decision. But, needless to say, Tosh had all the papers relating to the offence there in front of him, including the Previous Conviction Card. And all the papers were white, except the Previous Conviction Card which was an eye-catching yellow. We all knew this. Certainly the bench knew it; they'd seen similar cards scores of times when in the past 'previous cons' had been read out.

Once the Prosecution had had its say, that yellow card took pride of place on top of all Tosh's other papers. Indeed, he was given to playing with it idly, vaguely lifting it up and down . . . just to make sure everybody saw it. If the poor guy had previous convictions, that at least was not left in doubt.[12]

No doubt Inspector Tosh deployed his courtroom antics because he considered that the police *knew* the defendant to be guilty and that therefore it was permissible to ensure that everything was done to ensure that the magistrates came to the *right* verdict. He was another example of an officer engaged in that dubious bypassing of police ethics known as 'noble cause corruption'. And there was the added problem here that magistrates were commonly suspected of accepting a police officer's word simply because he was a police officer, and this belief was not one shared merely among defendants.[13]

Like the popular press, a good advocate could play upon the prejudices of the jurors. Thus, at the trial of Lieutenant Malcolm for murder in 1917, defence counsel played upon the fact that the accused, and his brother, were serving heroically on the Western Front, while the murder victim was an illegitimate Jew from Eastern Europe with a phoney title, who had cavorted with a woman allegedly shot by the French as a spy, and who had set out to seduce Malcolm's wife. A few year's later when Marie Marguerite Fahmy was tried for murdering her Egyptian husband, defence counsel played upon ethnic prejudices by emphasising

the Eastern feeling of possession of the woman, the Turk in his Harem, the man who is entitled to have four wives if he liked for chattels . . . which to we Western people with our ideas of woman is almost unintelligible.

Both Lieutenant Malcolm and Madame Fahmy were acquitted against the evidence.[14]

Instances such as these occasionally raised disquiet and, like others, were raised more publicly at the end of the century when society was less deferential towards the legal system and more responsive to critical questioning. Even the system's defenders might acknowledge the problem. In the mid-1990s Ron Thwaites QC, a successful criminal barrister, explained to an investigating journalist:

Defendants don't ask for your judgement on them but your advocacy. There is no such thing as a hopeless case, only a hopeless barrister. If there are more acquittals than there used to be, that reflects the commitment and the skill of counsel. Am I supposed to do my job half-heartedly? Am I supposed to ignore my best point?

In such circumstances acting in a criminal case was a job, just like any other, and Thwaites was quite open about how witnesses could be grilled and how innocent mistakes by police officers could be converted into 'sinister lies' by a good advocate.[15]

In addition to the varying abilities of those presenting the evidence respectively for the prosecution and the defence, there were also differing abilities and degrees of confidence among witnesses. A barrister writing on the eve of the Second World War considered that the cross-examination of witnesses could be 'extremely dangerous' and a 'weapon of abuse'.

When a witness is honest and not frightened by his unaccustomed surroundings, cross-examination will merely bring out the fact that he is honest. But it is very common for an honest witness to feel so strange in his new surroundings, and to be so little accustomed to thinking quickly while standing up, that he begins to hesitate and doubt under the mildest cross-examination, and all but the most experienced will get the totally erroneous impression that he is not telling the truth.[16]

On occasions some of the witnesses called were experts in particular fields, such as the forensic pathologist, Bernard Spilsbury, who made his name when he appeared to give evidence for the prosecution for murder of Dr Crippen at the Old Bailey in 1910. Spilsbury was young and relatively inexperienced, but he spoke with clarity and confidence. The prosecution counsel, Richard Muir, manipulated him at the expense of Dr. G.M. Turnbull, the director of the London Hospital of Pathology who, although far more experienced than Spilsbury, was hesitant and easily bullied in the witness box.[17] Spilsbury developed a formidable reputation as an expert witness. Time after time he was summoned to appear and he was known always to give his evidence with assurance and confidence. But his notoriety, and the enthusiasm with which the press greeted the announcement that he was to be a witness, did not make him popular with some members of the legal profession. 'It will be a very sorry day for the administration of justice in this land', complained one distinguished counsel, 'if we are to be thrust into a position that, because Sir Bernard Spilsbury expressed an opinion, it is of such weight that it is impossible to question it.'[18] And if Spilsbury's reputation was formidable, there were other experts that did not always find a welcome and who were made to feel uncomfortable as witnesses. Sir Travers Humphreys had been called to the Bar in 1889; he served as a junior counsel in the prosecution of both Oscar Wilde and Dr Crippen, and by the inter-war period was recognised as one of the leading counsel acting in criminal cases. He was generally noted as fair-minded and his wife was one of the first women justices in Middlesex. But according to one of Spilsbury's colleagues, Keith Simpson, when Sir Travers subsequently became a judge he was noted for his 'inhospitality to any psychiatrist who ventured to appear as an expert witness in his court'.[19]

Many fretted about class bias and out-of-date attitudes among judges, barristers and magistrates. The left-wing Barrister writing at the close of the 1930s pointed out that these people often did not speak the same language as many of those that were brought before them.

The judge asked a workman: 'When did this happen?' and received the answer: 'In the dinner-hour.' He could not understand the laughter that followed when he replied: 'Can't you make it more definite? "Dinner-hour" may mean anything between seven and nine.'

Moreover, while he believed that many judges and chairmen of quarter sessions were humane, he doubted that they had much understanding of the day-to-day realities of working-class life.[20] At the beginning of the century the cartoonist W.K. Haselden contrasted judges and magistrates

'One law for rich and one for poor'
W.K. Haselden's comment on class justice in 1905, published in the *Daily Mirror*, 28 October 1905.
(*Source*: British Cartoon Archive, University of Kent/Mirrorpix)

grimly dealing out prison sentences to the poor for petty theft, and apologising for having to impose a small fine as punishment on smirking toffs or the hard-faced wealthy. David Low took a similar line; reflecting on recent varied verdicts for drunk driving, he proposed a schedule of penalties to help magistrates, ranging from 'Unshaven common working person driving home-made mustard tin. Penalty – Death' to 'Extremely wealthy titled person driving very costly car. Expenses paid from the Poor Box.'[21] The contrasting sentences handed down to the hotel boy Henry Jacoby and the well-to-do Ronald True may have been justified as the law stood, but they smacked of class bias to critics.[22] Nearly 40 years later, in 1960, when Penguin Books were prosecuted for obscenity after publishing *Lady Chatterley's Lover*, Mervyn Griffith-Jones, who led for the prosecution, fuelled allegations that the legal profession was class-bound and behind the times when he asked jurors, male and female, if the book was the kind

'Cheap cruelty: a comment and criticism'

W.K. Haselden's comment on class justice in 1923, published in the *Daily Mirror*, 16 March 1923. (*Source*: British Cartoon Archive, University of Kent/Mirrorpix)

that they would wish their wives and servants to read.[23] Early in 1982 there were demands for the dismissal of Judge Bertrand Richards when he sentenced a rapist to a £2,000 fine commenting: 'I am not saying a girl hitching home late at night should not be protected by the law, but she was guilty of a great deal of contributory negligence.'[24] Suspicions that judges were out of touch also arose when they set out to defend the criminal justice system from criticism and, in so doing, appeared to defend the indefensible. Lord Lane's and Lord Denning's responses to appeals on behalf of those convicted for IRA bombings are prime examples.

There were fears too that jurors might be biased. The defence had the opportunity of challenging potential jurors in order to construct what was seen as a more sympathetic jury. The numbers of jurors that might be challenged in this way was reduced as the century progressed, from 25 to 12 in 1925, to seven in 1949, to three in 1977; and the peremptory challenge was abolished entirely in 1988. As noted above it was possible for judges to select all-male or all-female juries if they so wished; the only all-female jury, however, appears to have been selected in 1969 for trial of a woman for the manslaughter of her niece. After that the facility for selection by gender was removed. In 1977, during the trial of 17 black defendants on a charge of conspiracy, the defence requested a jury with six black members; the request was denied, but challenges resulted in a jury with five black members. In 1989 the Court of Appeal ruled that there was no principle that any jury should be racially balanced.[25]

But the problem was that across the court system there were ways in which broad social attitudes towards class, race and gender, together with perceptions of offenders and victims, especially as played upon by prosecution and defence, could influence outcomes. Recent research has demonstrated convincingly how court proceedings and gender perceptions were stacked against women victims of rape, and particularly those whose sexual experience transgressed strict codes of morality largely formulated on a Victorian ideal. But by the 1970s women activists were stressing how cross-examination in court could resemble a second assault for the victim and that a woman's previous sexual conduct should have no bearing on her claim to have been raped. An official inquiry was launched into the law of rape resulting in the Sexual Offences (Amendment) Act of 1976 which prohibited any reference by the defence to a woman's previous behaviour and which sought to give guidance when an accused claimed that he thought a woman had given consent.[26]

Anette Ballinger has argued that the 12 women who were hanged, out of the 130 convicted of murder in England and Wales between 1900 and

1955, were singled out for execution because they failed to conform to the expectations of femininity in terms of their domestic and sexual behaviour, and their respectability.[27] But there is also evidence to suggest that a woman could play, or see her defenders play the gender card to her advantage. Marie Marguerite Fahmy, whose acquittal on a charge of shooting dead her Egyptian husband was noted above, was a beneficiary first, of a general fear of miscegenation, and second of assumptions about her 'oriental' husband's violence and sexual perversions.[28] A few years later Beatrice Pace was accused of poisoning her brutal and philandering husband. During her trial her loyalty to, and care for her husband were emphasised. She won over the press, the public and, ultimately, the judge who directed the jury to return a not guilty verdict without even the necessity for Pace's counsel to present a defence. Following her acquittal in 1929 she cashed in on a mixture of celebrity and victimhood to become a national figure, writing her autobiography for a newspaper, receiving letters from fans across the English-speaking world and advising women in difficulties.[29]

Class and gender attitudes also infused the magistrates' courts, particularly in the early part of the century. This was nowhere more in evidence than in the juvenile courts that were first mooted in 1904 and finally established four years later. The aim was to keep juveniles out of the formal criminal justice system and treat them as vulnerable and impressionable. Initially the magistrates that presided in these courts, as elsewhere, were men, but in 1910, as a member of the Royal Commission on the Selection of Justices of the Peace, the Labour MP Arthur Henderson, raised the idea of women on the bench to hear 'certain cases'; and the cases that he had in mind appear to have been those involving juveniles. When it came, the appointment of women magistrates became closely linked with the idea that they might deal with young offenders in the juvenile courts. Middle-class women had been involved in volunteer social work with children in the courts long before they were appointed as magistrates. While sometimes active feminists, they still brought with them to the bench a part of the ideological baggage of separate spheres and they played an important role in bringing a caring ethos to the juvenile court. Moreover, once they were allowed on the bench, the juvenile courts were seen as able to act in the form of the idealised, patriarchal family. The woman magistrate was to be the understanding mother while her potential for manifesting the female traits of being 'soppy and sentimental' in dealing with naughty children was checked by the understanding, fatherly male magistrate. There was some nervousness, not least in the Home Office, about giving women too much authority in the courts, and especially about letting them be considered as the virtual equal of the legally trained stipendiaries in London. But during the first 50 years that women served as magistrates, they first acquired and then exercised considerable authority in the juvenile courts.[30]

The juvenile courts became arenas in which traditional notions of childhood and family were central to decision making. The accused in these courts were divided along gender lines like those in other courts; fewer girls than boys appeared before them. This may have been because girls committed fewer offences than boys. It may also have been because police officers felt that arresting and charging girls, especially with any kind of violent offence, in some way undermined their masculinity and that it was preferable to treat such offenders as an amusing irritant that was to be warned, rather than apprehended. The implication of an arrest was, after all, that they were a serious threat worthy of the majesty of the law. Most of the girls that appeared before the juvenile courts did so in the cities and big towns; this appears to have encouraged ideas among magistrates that those appearing in the courts outside the larger urban centres were exceptional and hence very bad. In addition, magistrates drew distinctions between juveniles that appeared to be genuinely and seriously delinquent and those that appeared, primarily, to be vulnerable. Generally speaking all children needed protection, but such protection was also based on a young person's behaviour and the extent to which this behaviour demonstrated an awareness of proper boyhood, proper girl-hood and of appropriate sexual relations.[31] Towards the end of the century academic observers in the courts noted how magistrates made careful assessments of families and the offending juvenile before reaching their verdict and recommendation. And several magistrates were happy to com-ment to researchers on the way that their observation of court demeanour by both parents and the accused could shape their attitude: 'I like to see both parents in court, not just the mother. That is an influence in itself'; 'You can tell a lot from [the defendant's] demeanour, really, whether they are really hardened or whether they are frightened.'[32]

The law and the courts spoke of equality, and the research into sentenc-ing patterns conducted towards the end of the century suggested that when men and women stood before the courts in similar circumstances, with similar records and charged with similar offences, they received similar treatment. But these studies also often went on to stress that society was divided by class, gender and race. These divisions often meant inequality in circumstances and what the courts did was make decisions that served to maintain the divisions. While, for example, the number of married women in waged labour increased during the century, and while political parties spoke of dealing with social inequality and social exclusion, the broad assumption appeared to remain that, ideally, a family unit consisted of a male breadwinner who provided for his wife and children, and of a wife who fulfilled a traditional domestic role. This meant that when help was offered to a woman by a court, it was often because of her perceived family role rather than because of her needs as an individual or as a woman. There were also assumptions that offences were committed because of abnormal circumstances and that problems would be solved when the individual's circumstances were normal.[33] Recognising and understanding this situation is important; yet from the point of view of the historian it is fruitless to criticise or condemn courts in the past for acting in this fashion and mistaken to assume that minor organs of the state, such as the magistrates' courts, were the kind of instruments that might have consistently challenged the *status quo* with contemporary perspectives.

Judges and magistrates may have passed sentences that served to enforce the *status quo* and they may have acted within a broadly conservative perspective, but their behaviour did not always coincide with what legislators intended, nor was this necessarily to the disadvantage of the defendant. At the beginning of the century, for example, judges and magistrates saw off a series of new proposals that were formulated as law by enthusiasts at the Home Office. Judges resisted imposing long, indeterminate sentences of preventive detention as authorised under the 1908 Prevention of Crime Act. In 1910 they even found backing from the new, progressive Home Secretary, Winston Churchill, who considered the indeterminate sentence for a pathetic, if persistent petty offender to be a backward step. In the same period both judges and magistrates resisted sentencing those committed for offences related to drunkenness to lengthy terms in inebriate reformatories; they either refused to use the specified sentences, or simply sentenced as they had done previously. There seems to be every reason to believe that the penal labour colonies, devised for vagrants, collapsed for a similar reason; those responsible for passing sentence considered the punishment to be too draconian.[34] At the end of the century the New Labour government introduced measures requiring mandatory sentences for those convicted of burglary for the third time and for repeat offences of a sexual nature or of violence. Judges were unhappy about the government limiting their discretion for making decisions on the basis of the evidence before them about the offender. Generally speaking they appear to have followed the new guidelines regarding those guilty of repeated sexual and violent offences, but in the first year of the new policy no burglar found guilty of a third offence was given the mandatory three-year sentence. The judges employed an earlier legislative clause allowing them to pass sentence according to their reading of the circumstances. The retributive tabloids relegated the information on the sexual and violent offenders to their small print and chose to criticise the Home Secretary, for not imposing his will, and the judges for flouting what the public – in the eyes of the tabloids – wanted. A headline in the *Daily Mirror* caught the tone: 'Judges in snub over crime blitz'.[35]

Equally important, in matters of sentencing, judges and magistrates neither thought, nor acted with uniformity. They were human actors and, as such, they made their own assessments of the individuals who stood before them in the dock. Such assessments were made, in part, from prejudice and assumptions based on the accused's behaviour in court. But they were also made with advice and information about previous behaviour and, as the century progressed, such advice was increasingly provided by different kinds of medical expert and social worker. Judges and magistrates also had their own ideas about what worked best in terms of punishment and what might be best for a particular individual. Corporal punishment was ended before compulsory training was introduced for magistrates, but the differences in attitude towards sentences of corporal punishment illustrate particularly sharply how different attitudes shaped the use of a sentence. Most of the magistrates active in the juvenile courts who appeared before the 1938 Departmental Committee on Corporal Punishment were opposed to the use of the birch and did not pass birching sentences. Thus, in 1935, there were no sentences of corporal punishment ordered by the juvenile courts of, among other cities and big towns, London, Birmingham, Leeds, Liverpool, Newcastle-upon-Tyne, Nottingham and Sheffield. In several rather smaller towns, in contrast, a significant percentage of juvenile offenders were ordered to be birched: in Wallasey the number was 14 out of 110 such offenders, in Accrington two out of 23, in Warrington six out of 55 and in Windsor seven out of 35.[36]

A sociological study of sentencing patterns in magistrates' courts during the 1950s suggested that the social and economic aspects of the area in which magistrates worked, together with the social class perspectives and the cohesiveness of a group working regularly together, all had an influence on sentencing. Interestingly, there appeared to be no consistent connection between the level of recorded crime and the level of sentencing. And generally magistrates tended to be more severe on those guilty of indecent assault than on those guilty of larceny.[37]

The London Police Court magistrates who wrote their recollections in the first part of the century all stressed that their courts were what Cecil Chapman called 'a poor man's court of justice'. Sir Charles Biron, who had been appointed to the Old Street Police Court in the East End in 1906, believed that it was his 'bounden duty to see [that the poor] were not unduly harassed by school inspectors, landlords and authorities in general'.[38] '[W]eek in and week out' explained Sir Gervais Rentoul,

[these courts] quietly carry on their work of humanity and mercy. Open every day of the year except Sundays, Christmas Day and Good Friday, to them any poor person can repair for advice and assistance in any legal domestic difficulty. When, therefore, one hears complaints regarding the law's delays, the excessive lengths of legal vacations and so forth, it is well to remember that there are some Courts which never close and where justice does not sleep.[39]

Poor people went to these courts for advice on 'hire-purchase agreements, loan and benefit clubs, the technicalities of the law between land lord and tenant, the riddles of the Rent Restriction Act, the relations between husband and wife or parent and child'. 'It is good', claimed H.T. Waddy, 'that it should be known that every metropolitan magistrate sits as a "poor-man's lawyer".' If nothing else it helped to demonstrate the falseness of the belief that 'the magistrate is the creature of the police'.[40] This role as a provider of free legal advice was something that gradually declined as the century progressed, and especially after the Second World War.[41]

For much of the century many judges and magistrates appear to have acted with a caring credo, believing that a Whig notion of progress was pervading the criminal justice system; as Rentoul put it in 1940:

Judges and Magistrates are now animated by a more humane spirit, and an ever-increasing leniency is the key-note of criminal administration.

This does not mean that crime is regarded with any less disapproval and detestation, but merely that we have come to realize that the old savage punishments were dictated by a feeling of blind revenge and often defeated their own ends.[42]

Yet there were also others whose sentencing practices appeared to possess a little less emphasis on humanity and more on the belief that punishment was the best deterrent.

The complexities inherent in evaluating the attitudes of magistrates become visible in considering the career of the first woman stipendiary, Sybil Campbell. She was appointed to the Tower Bridge Police Court in 1945 in what appears to have been an act of positive discrimination by the then Home Secretary, Herbert Morrison. Sybil Campbell had enjoyed a long career in public service, first enforcing the minimum wage in 'sweated trades' and then enforcing the food controls imposed during the latter stages of the First World War. She had enrolled at the Middle Temple at the beginning of 1920 and was one of the first women to be called to the Bar in 1922 but, given the shortage of work for women barristers, she spent the inter-war years working as an inspector of workers' conditions and determining their wages. During the Second World War she returned to the enforcement of food regulations and, described in the press as 'Britain's number one food detective', she set about pursuing, with considerable vigour, black marketeers and those profiteering from food shortages. Her wartime experiences appear to have given her a loathing of those who avoided the rationing regulations, and she began her term as a London stipendiary by passing some extremely heavy sentences. These excited much critical comment from the press, from local Labour groups and from dock workers who disliked the manner in which she came down on their perks. Yet her assault on the black marketeers and the perks was tempered by a sympathy towards those who appeared nervous and had difficulty expressing themselves in court; in addition, her experience in investigating the sweated trades and workers' conditions had strengthened a humanitarian streak that led to her making visits to borstals, probation hostels and prisons – a practice that was then extremely rare among judges and magistrates.[43] Human actors always tend to be far more complex than the simple labels that are often attached to different jobs and roles suggest.

The progressive perspective inherent in the Whig view meant that judges and magistrates were generally prepared to go along with the policy of trying to keep people out of prison and, generally speaking, the prison sentences were much shorter in the early part of the century than in the concluding decade. At the end of the Second World War more than 95 per cent of offenders sentenced to immediate imprisonment were given less than 18 months, and life sentences were almost unknown. By the turn of the millennium around one-fifth of offenders were sentenced to imprisonment for 18 months or more, and around one in ten of the prison population was serving a determinate sentence of ten years or more, or life. Between 1991 and 2000 the number of short sentences of less than one year increased by 142 per cent; the number of middle-range sentences,

from one to four years, increased by 14 per cent; and the number of long
sentences, of four years to life, increased by 49 per cent. It is difficult to be
precise about the reasons for this. There was a more punitive legislative
structure, and more punitive guidelines were issued by governments. There
was a more punitive climate of opinion, at least expressed in the tabloid
press. There were probably some changes in the patterns of offending. And
all of these had some impact on those responsible for passing sentences in
the courts.[44]

References and notes

1 *Report of the Royal Commission on Assizes and Quarter Sessions*,
  Cmnd. 4153, London: HMSO, 1969; **Robin C.A. White**, 'The structure
  and organisation of criminal justice in England and Wales: an overview', in
  Mike McConville and **Geoffrey Wilson** (eds), *The Handbook of Criminal
  Justice Process*, Oxford: Oxford University Press, 2002, p. 11.

2 **Clare McGlynn**, 'Appointing women judges', *New Law Journal*, 148
  (24 April 1998) p. 597.

3 **Anne Logan**, 'Professionalism and the impact of England's first women
  justices, 1920–1950', *Historical Journal*, 49, 3 (2006) pp. 833–50.

4 **Sir Thomas Skyrme**, *History of the Justices of the Peace*, 3 vols. Chichester:
  Barry Rose and the Justice of the Peace, 1991, ii, pp. 292–93.

5 **G.G. Alexander**, *The Administration of Criminal Justice*, Cambridge:
  Cambridge University Press, 1915, pp. 202–3; White, 'The structure and
  organisation of criminal justice', p. 11.

6 See, for example, *The Times*, 2 February, 1921, p. 6; see also 28 January,
  p. 10.

7 *The Times*, 12 January 1921, p. 7.

8 **John Hostettler**, *The Criminal Jury Old and New: jury power from early times
  to the present day*, Winchester: Waterside Press, 2004, p. 126.

9 **Trevor Grove**, *The Juryman's Tale*, London: Bloomsbury, 1998, pp. 59, 154
  and 167.

10 The key legislation was the Poor Prisoners Defence Acts of 1906 and 1930,
   and the Legal Aid and Advice Act of 1949.

11 One of the most notorious instances of this occurred in the summer of 1996
   when Ralston Edwards, charged with rape, insisted on conducting his own
   defence and, wearing the same clothes that he had worn during the assault, he
   proceeded to question, intimately, his victim. The judge, Ann Goddard QC,

felt that she had no alternative but to let him continue for fear that attempting to limit his questions would give him grounds for appeal. (See, *inter alia*, *Evening Standard*, 22 August 1982, p. 6, and *The Guardian*, 23 August 1996, p. 2.) The Youth Justice and Criminal Evidence Act of 1999 prevented this from happening in future.

12 **John Wainwright**, *Wainwright's Beat: one man's journey with a police force*, London: Macmillan, 1987, pp. 40–1; see also, **Clive Emsley**, *The English Police: a political and social history*, 2nd edn, London: Longman, 1996, p. 235.

13 **A Barrister**, *Justice in England*, London: Victor Gollancz, 1938, pp. 275–8; **David Rose**, *In the Name of the Law: the collapse of criminal justice*, London: Jonathan Cape, 1996, p. 38.

14 **Clive Emsley**, *Hard Men: violence in England since 1750*, London: Hambledon, 2005, pp. 78–9; **Lucy Bland**, 'The trial of Madame Fahmy: orientalism, violence, sexual perversity and the fear of miscegenation', in **Shani D'Cruze** (ed.), *Everyday Violence in Britain, 1850–1950; gender and class*, Harlow: Longman, 2000, pp. 188–9.

15 Rose, *In the Name of the Law*, p. 311.

16 Barrister, *Justice in England*, pp. 102–03.

17 **Jenny Ward**, *Crime Busting: breakthroughs in forensic science*, London: Blandford Press, 1998, pp. 102–3; Oldbaileyonline t19101011-74 (trial of Crippen).

18 **Keith Simpson**, *Forty Years of Murder: an autobiography*, London: Harrap and Co., 1978, p. 30.

19 Simpson, *Forty Years of Murder*, p. 200.

20 Barrister, *Justice in England*, pp. 27 and 123.

21 'One law for the rich and one for the poor', *Daily Mirror*, 28 October 1905; 'Cheap cruelty: a comment and criticism', *Daily Mirror*, 16 March 1923; 'The high cost of flivving', *The Star*, 23 August 1924.

22 See above, chap. 4 pp. 70–1.

23 **C.H. Rolph**, *The Trial of Lady Chatterley*, Harmondsworth: Penguin, 1961.

24 *The Guardian*, 6 January 1982, p. 3 and 8 January, p. 4.

25 Hostettler, *The Criminal Jury*, pp. 126 and 129.

26 *Report of the Advisory Group on the Law of Rape*, Cmnd. 6352, London: HMSO, 1975.

27 **Anette Ballinger**, *Dead Woman Walking: executed women in England and Wales 1900–1955*, Aldershot: Ashgate, 2000.

28 Bland, 'The trial of Madame Fahmy'.

29 My thanks to John Carter Wood for sharing with me his work on the affair
    of Mrs Pace; and see, **John Carter Wood**, ' "Mrs. Pace" and the ambiguous
    language of victimisation', in **Lisa Dresdner** and **Laurel Peterson** (eds),
    (Re)Interpretations: the shapes of justice in women's experience, Newcastle:
    Cambridge Scholars Publishing, 2009; *idem*, ' "Those who have had trouble
    can sympathise with you": press writing, reader responses and a murder trial
    in interwar Britain', *Journal of Social History* 43, 2 (2009) pp. 439–62.

30 *Report of the Royal Commission on the Selection of Justices of the Peace,
    Evidence, Appendices and Index*, Cd. 5358, London: HMSO, 1910,
    pp. 1196–98; and see in general, **Anne Logan**, ' "A suitable person for
    suitable cases": the gendering of juvenile courts in England, c.1910–39',
    Twentieth-Century British History, 16, 2 (2005) pp. 129–45; *idem,
    Feminism and Criminal Justice: a historical perspective*, Houndmills
    Basingstoke: Palgrave Macmillan, 2008, chap. 2.

31 **Pamela Cox**, *Gender, Justice and Welfare: bad girls in Britain 1900–1950*,
    London: Palgrave, 2003, especially chap. 2.

32 **Sheila Brown**, *Magistrates at Work*, Milton Keynes: Open University Press,
    1991, p. 74.

33 **Pat Carlen**, *Magistrate's Justice*, Oxford: Martin Robertson, 1976; **David P.
    Farrington** and **Allison M. Morris**, 'Sex, sentencing and reconviction', *BJC*,
    23, 3 (1983) pp. 229–48; **Mary Eaton**, *Justice for Women? Family court and
    social control*, Milton Keynes: Open University Press, 1986.

34 **Leon Radzinowicz** and **Roger Hood**, *The Emergence of Penal Policy in
    Victorian and Edwardian England*, Oxford: Clarendon Press, 1990,
    pp. 271–87 and 307–15; **Victor Bailey**, 'English prisons, penal culture and
    the abatement of imprisonment, 1895–1922', *Journal of British Studies*, 36, 3
    (1997) pp. 304–5.

35 *Daily Mirror*, 27 December 2000, p. 22; and see also, among others,
    The Independent, 27 December 2000, p. 3; *Daily Mail*, 28 December 2000,
    pp. 1 and 12.

36 **Victor Bailey**, *Delinquency and Citizenship: reclaiming the young offender
    1914–1948*, Oxford: Clarendon Press, 1987, p. 134; **George Ryley Scott**,
    The History of Corporal Punishment, 10th impression, London: Torchstream
    Books, 1954, pp. 62–5.

37 **Roger Hood**, *Sentencing in Magistrates' Courts: a Study in variations of
    policy*, London: Stevens and Sons, 1962.

38 *The Times*, 21 March 1939, p. 56.

39 **Sir Gervais Rentoul**, *Sometimes I Think: random reflections and recollections*,
    London: Hodder and Stoughton, 1940, p. 87; see also, **Cecil Chapman**, *The*

Poor Man's Court of Justice: twenty-five years as a metropolitan magistrate, London: Hodder and Stoughton, 1925; **H.L. Cancellor**, *The Life of a London Beak*, London: Hurst and Blackett, 1930, p. 35 and Part II, chap. 1.

40 **H.T. Waddy**, *The Police Court and its Work*, London: Butterworth and Co. 1925, pp. 6–7 and 56.

41 A solicitor and district court judge described to me how this use of the magistrates' court was still present during the 1970s when he began to practise. It rapidly declined thereafter.

42 Rentoul, *Sometimes I Think*, p. 202. See also, Waddy, *The Police Court*, p. 108.

43 **Patrick Polden**, 'The Lady of Tower Bridge: Sybil Campbell, England's first woman judge', *Women's History Review*, 8, 3 (1999) pp. 505–26.

44 For a discussion of the developments during the 1990s see, **Andrew Millie, Jessica Jackson** and **Michael Hough**, 'Understanding the growth in the prison population in England and Wales', in **Clive Emsley** (ed.), *The Persistent Prison: problems, images, alternatives*, London: Francis Boutle, 2005.

CHAPTER 10

Penal policy and penal experience

In 1898 the plot of land on which Newgate Prison stood was sold to the Corporation of the City of London to provide space for an extension to the Central Criminal Court. The prison's inmates were transferred to the penitentiaries of Holloway and Pentonville and, on 15 August 1902, workmen began demolition. A prison had stood on the site of Newgate since the twelfth century. It was associated with the Bloody Code of the eighteenth century and with public executions that had taken place just outside its walls from 1783 to 1868. Its grim notoriety had been portrayed in a succession of 'Newgate novels', most notably by Charles Dickens. Its destruction appeared to symbolise a new age of liberal penal policies.[1]

Until roughly the late 1970s the usual narrative of penal history in England was one of progress inspired by liberal and humanitarian ideals. Such a narrative could begin with the torture and mutilations inflicted on transgressors in the medieval period, and move on to the Bloody Code under which there were over 200 capital offences (although not, it must be stressed, over 200 different and distinct capital crimes).[2] From the Bloody Code the narrative focus then shifted to a succession of humanitarian reformers who gradually demolished the system in which execution was the principal punishment for felony and, in its place, built a new order in which the prison, significantly a setting for both punishment and reformation, was the central feature. This narrative informed the thinking of many of those involved with penal policy, from the members of the Gladstone Committee, whose report of 1895 did so much to crystallise liberal penal thinking, to members of the Prison Commission that administered the system until superseded by the Prison Department of the Home Office in 1963, and indeed beyond.

For liberal, humanitarian penal reformers the continued existence of corporal and capital punishments at the beginning of the century was the last vestiges of a barbaric legal code. Corporal punishment was only meted out to male offenders. Boys between the ages of 8 and 14 years could be sentenced to six strokes of the rod for any felony, except murder; youths aged 14 to 16 years could be beaten for a variety of specified offences under the terms of various statutes. The beating was administered on bare buttocks with a birch rod, usually by a police officer but occasionally a magistrates' court authorised the boy's father to give the beating in the presence of a police officer. The flogging of adult males had been given a new lease of life in 1863 when new legislation mandated the sentence for garrotters, as street robbers of the period were known. At the close of the nineteenth century the punishment had been extended first to 'incorrigible rogues' and then to those found guilty of White Slave trafficking, male solicitation and indecent exposure. Corporal punishment for adults was administered to the victim's bare back by prison officers using a 'cat' with nine tails of whipcord. The victim had his head screened so that he could not see the officer wielding the cat; his kidneys and neck were protected by leather bands. Capital punishment was inflicted only for murder and high treason. Eleven of the thirteen men executed for treason and spying during the First World War were shot by military firing squads in the Tower of London; only one man was shot for similar offences during the Second World War, and 15 others were hanged. All of the other individuals executed in England and Wales between 1900 and 1964 were hanged using a system by which, with a noose round their necks, they were dropped through a trap door on the gallows. The drop was sufficient distance to break the neck and prevent the slow strangulation that had been common in earlier periods. A misjudgement on the part of the hangman about the condemned's weight and the necessary length of rope, however, could result either in strangulation or decapitation.

The campaign for the abolition of capital punishment was relatively muted at the beginning of the century and arguments about corporal punishment did not divide neatly between those who favoured tough, retributive policies and those of a more liberal and humanitarian persuasion. There were, for example, reformers who believed that a beating was a better way of dealing with some young offenders than a lengthy period of detention in some form of approved school – those found guilty of cruelty to animals, for example. The beating of young offenders increased during the First World War over and above the recorded increase in juvenile offending. In 1913 a little over 2,000 such offenders were sentenced to be beaten, some

16 per cent of those found guilty; four years later nearly 5,000 juveniles received such a sentence, 21.5 per cent of those found guilty. By the late 1920s, however, the number so sentenced had fallen to less than 200, which was under 2 per cent of those found guilty; the numbers continued to fall throughout the following decade and this seems indicative of a growing assumption among magistrates that the sanction simply did not work as a deterrent. By the 1930s, moreover, the debate on the flogging of juveniles polarised increasingly between the conservatives and the liberal reformers who now, virtually to a man, opposed the punishment. The debate about flogging adult males polarised similarly but, while the number of men flogged with the cat had always been far fewer than the number of boys that were birched, the number and proportion of offenders sentenced to the cat increased. Between 1904 and 1913 out of 1,414 men convicted of robbery with violence, 61 had been sentenced to be flogged by Assize Courts and Quarter Sessions. Between 1926 and 1935, in contrast, out of 656 convictions, 235 men were sentenced to be flogged.[3]

Proposals for the abolition of corporal punishment were put before parliament at the beginning of the 1930s, but were not supported by the Labour government. In 1931, however, the same government included in its Children's Bill a clause repealing the power of summary courts to order the birching of children under the age of 14 years. The clause fell before an onslaught from the House of Lords where a majority shared Lord Danesfort's opinion critical of 'this effeminate, over-humanitarian, ultra-sentimental view that to correct a child by reasonable correction is something which is out of date'.[4] But this defeat did not dissuade the abolitionists whose numbers included magistrates and both medical officers and psychiatrists with long experience of working in prisons. The Home Office sought to maintain a neutral position in individual cases, although it also sought to discourage sentences of corporal punishment, particularly where juveniles were involved. In March 1937, with the aim of acquiring a balanced assessment of the effects, and particularly of the deterrent impact of corporal punishment, Sir John Simon, the Home Secretary, appointed a departmental committee to investigate. The chair of the committee was Sir Edward Cadogan, a former MP, a barrister, a magistrate and a member of the Borstal Association. There were three other magistrates, as well as a doctor, on the committee of ten. None of its members had been involved with the movement for the abolition of corporal punishment, but the evidence presented was overwhelmingly abolitionist. Unsurprisingly the committee concluded that there was no evidence to suggest that flogging acted as any form of deterrent. Nor did it think that there was any evidence that it reformed anyone; on the contrary, it feared that it some instances it might make offenders worse. The committee's main recommendation was that corporal punishment should be retained only in prisons where it might serve as the ultimate weapon to use against those responsible for fomenting serious disorder or violently assaulting prison staff.[5]

The recommendations of the Cadogan Committee were incorporated into a Criminal Justice Bill that had first been presented to parliament early in 1938. The bill was generally well received both in parliament and by the press, although there were criticisms not least from those who stood by their understanding of the preventive and reformative virtues of flogging. Discussions about criminal justice reform dragged on into the following year and then, with the deteriorating international situation, it was agreed to shelve the bill until a more settled time. The wartime increase in the statistics of juvenile offending prompted an increase in sentences of birching in 1940 and 1941, but in June 1941 a Memorandum on Juvenile Offenders reminded magistrates of the conclusions of the Cadogan Committee and advised that 'corporal punishment is not a suitable or effective remedy for dealing with young offenders'.[6] An incident at the Hereford Juvenile Court at the beginning of 1943 highlighted one of the problems with the sentence. The general assumption was that, for maximum impact, any birching had to be carried out quickly after the sentence was pronounced. But parents had the right of appeal and when an 11-year-old and a 13-year-old were sentenced for malicious damage by the Hereford Court, their parents appealed. Appeals took time; the court instructed the police to proceed with the sentence and in the ensuing outrage the Home Secretary ordered a Tribunal of Inquiry. The tribunal absolved both the court and the police; nevertheless concerns remained and the incident probably contributed to a decline in such sentences which, by 1945, were below pre-war levels.[7]

Two years after the end of the war a new Criminal Justice Bill was introduced; it passed in 1948. Like its predecessor ten years before, it incorporated the recommendations of the Cadogan Committee. As a result of the new Act the sanction of corporal punishment was restricted to violent and recalcitrant prisoners; this clause remained on the statute book until 1967, but no such sentence was confirmed after 1962. Supporters of corporal punishment remained vocal, even in parliament, and a string of myths were perpetuated to emphasise its effectiveness. In 1958, for example, at the height of a panic over Teddy Boys, advocates of corporal punishment in Manchester insisted that it was flogging that had curbed the violence of the youths involved in the Scuttler gangs of the late Victorian and Edwardian years. In reality, however, the birch was never used against Scuttlers;[8] and in the wake of the 1948 abolition governments of all political hues remained deaf to those who urged the restoration of corporal punishment.

Corporal punishment aroused passion among those who argued for its abolition and those who argued for its retention. But these arguments were as nothing compared with those aroused by the death penalty. There were some minor changes to the capital sanction during the first third of the twentieth century but new legislation largely reflected existing practice. The Royal Prerogative of Mercy, which was essentially in the hands of the Home Secretary, had meant that virtually no one under the age of 18 years had been executed since 1887; the Children Act of 1908 and the Children and Young Persons Act of 1922 formally abolished the death penalty for those under 16 years and under 18 years respectively. No mother had been executed for killing her baby since 1849; legislation of 1922 and 1938 confirmed that such a mother would only be tried for manslaughter.

In spite of the wider moves for penal reform, campaigning for the abolition of capital punishment was relatively dormant at the beginning of the twentieth century.[9] It revived during the 1920s. The execution of Edith Thompson early in 1923 raised particular disquiet. Thompson had been convicted of assisting her lover, Frederick Bywaters, in the murder of her husband. Bywaters had always insisted that Thompson played no part in the killing and the feeling grew that she had been targeted for her adulterous behaviour. In addition the governor of Holloway Prison, the chaplain, various other members of the prison staff and even the executioner were all deeply distressed by events on the scaffold. The execution prompted the formation of the National Council for the Abolition of the Death Penalty, renamed the National Council for the Abolition of Capital Punishment (NCACP) two years later and which was to work closely over the coming years with the new Howard League for Penal Reform.[10] Also in 1923 the Labour Party Conference passed a motion in favour of abolition. Labour MPs, many of whom had fought in the trenches during the First World War, played a central role in the successful campaign to limit the army's use of the death penalty, and a parliamentary debate on abolition of the civilian penalty in 1929 led to the appointment of a select committee. Evidence amassed by this committee showed that there had been no adverse effects in those countries that had already taken the abolitionist road. But the committee divided on party lines, with the Conservatives favouring retention and the Labour majority recommending abolition for a trial period of five years. The division on the committee undermined the force of the recommendations, as many in the press and elsewhere were quick to point out, and the Labour government allowed no time for discussion of the report before its disintegration towards the end of 1931.

Arguments for and against retention continued through the 1930s. A majority within the country appears to have remained retentionist; nevertheless the minority favouring abolition seems to have gained increasing support. Sir Samuel Hoare, as Home Secretary, was wary of inserting an abolition clause in the Criminal Justice Bill of 1938; an amendment clause introduced during debate, proposing abolition for a five-year trial period, was lost. Abolitionists had great hopes of the Labour government elected in 1945, but the government dithered about whether to include a clause in the bill of 1948. In spite of their impressive majority, ministers were worried that any such clause would be rejected by the House of Lords where there was a Conservative majority in favour of retention, and where both the Law Lords and the bishops were primarily of a retentionist persuasion. Moreover the attitude in the Lords seemed more in keeping with the sentiment outside Westminster. The increasing sympathy for abolition during the 1930s appeared to have swung into reverse, possibly because of the war which had, after all, ended with the trial and execution of Nazi and Japanese 'war criminals'; possibly also because of the concerns about a violent crime wave that followed the war. The bill introduced by the government had no clause relating to capital punishment, and ministers were embarrassed when a Labour MP, Sydney Silverman, introduced such a clause as an amendment. In a free vote Silverman's clause passed with most of the support coming from the Labour benches. The House of Lords, as was expected, rejected the clause and, after an attempt at compromise, in preference to confrontation the government decided to drop any reference to capital punishment and to address the matter by means of a Royal Commission.

The Royal Commission reported in 1953, when a Conservative government was back in power. It concluded that there was no way in which the law might be modified to distinguish between particularly heinous murders and other forms – such a distinction had formed the basis for the compromise clause in 1948. The commission also concluded that there was no evidence to prove that capital punishment was an effective deterrent. The government did its best to marginalise the commission's report, but the indefatigable Silverman kept up his campaign within parliament, the Howard League and the NCACP continued to be active outside, and a series of executions, while not creating an abolitionist majority, created serious disquiet. In 1953 19-year-old Derek Bentley was executed as an accessory to murder even though he had been in police custody at the moment when his 16-year-old companion shot and killed a police officer; Christopher Craig, the boy who shot the officer, was too young to face the hangman. In the same year John Christie confessed to, and was executed for murders for which Timothy Evans had been executed three years earlier. Both Bentley and Evans were inarticulate and had learning difficulties. In 1955 Ruth Ellis, a divorced mother of two, shot and killed one of her lovers, a man who, three days before she shot him, had assaulted her so violently as to bring about a miscarriage. Ellis was executed in spite of a wave of sympathy and a large petition to the Home Secretary for clemency. As in the case of Edith Thompson, there was the suspicion that her sexual behaviour had sealed her fate.

Rising support for abolition in the Commons, not least among a group of progressive young Conservative MPs who took their seats following the election of 1955, prompted the government to try to seize the initiative and reform the death penalty, without abolishing it. But the only reform that ministers could come up with was that of two distinct classes of murder, already rejected by the Royal Commission. The government's Homicide Bill was denied a free vote. Predictably it was passed and became law in March 1957; predictably also, as the Royal Commission had warned, the differentiation between kinds of murder was unworkable. By the early 1960s a Conservative Home Secretary, Henry Brooke, was privately confiding that the death penalty would have to be abolished. In the event abolition came in 1965, but under a Labour government. The abolition was to be for a trial period of five years. It appears that parliamentary leaders were not keen to see capital punishment become an issue in the general election scheduled for 1970 and, though the Conservatives protested when Labour brought the vote forward to the end of 1969, on a free vote both houses voted in favour of abolition. Significantly the leaders of the major parties all voted in favour. As with corporal punishment, the years up to the end of the century saw calls for the reintroduction of the death penalty from both inside and outside parliament, particularly with reference to terrorist offences. But again, as with corporal punishment, the ears of parliament were deaf; motions were introduced, Prime Minister Margaret Thatcher herself favoured the reintroduction of the death penalty, but each time that the matter came before parliament it was decided on a free vote and those in favour of restoration were in a significant minority.[11]

The end of punishments directed against the body of the convicted offender fitted well with the narrative of progress and civilisation popular with Whig historians and, perhaps more importantly, with the aspirations of many of those involved in the abolitionist campaigns. The end of capital punishment also came during a decade of legislative liberalisation affecting the laws on abortion, gambling, homosexuality, prostitution and suicide. This liberalisation of the 'permissive' 1960s in turn fostered a new and alternative narrative of decline; this decline was seen as the direct result of the abandonment of old mores and a general relaxation of rules. These world-views – an optimistic faith in civilisation and progress, and a gloomy assumption of a society and a world sliding beyond control – cannot be proven in any historical sense, yet their recognition is important to under-standing people's behaviour and perceptions of events. The abolition of capital punishment, however, stands as the climax of the optimistic view. It shows a governing elite in a democracy prepared to take a lead and to change a highly contentious matter of domestic policy in a way that ran counter to the sentiments of a majority of the electorate. As such it was a high-profile manifestation of the modernist, rehabilitative policies, driven by expert thinking that characterised penal development for much of the century. Capital punishment, however, was a dramatic and exceptional punishment. The number of executions in England and Wales between 1900 and 1964 rarely rose above a dozen or so in each year; for most serious offenders, even for most murderers, conviction generally meant a prison sentence.

It was during the Victorian period that the prison became the principal site where offenders might be punished, for what was seen as their moral culpability, but also where they might be encouraged to mend their ways. Generally speaking the prison regime was tough. Prison buildings were solid and imposing; they were designed to deter as well as to punish and reform. In 1877, with the aim of ensuring a centrally directed penal policy, uniformly implemented across the whole country, the local prisons under the management of boroughs or counties were brought together with the state's convict prisons into a centralised system administered by a Prison Commission accountable to the Home Secretary. The division continued, however, with local prisons holding those people on remand, those serving short sentences and, in separate cellular confinement, those serving the first nine months of a sentence of penal servitude. The convict prisons held those sentenced to penal servitude; the aim was that these convicts should be required to labour on some form of public works. In the mid-1890s the system, and its chief administrator Major-General Sir Edmund Du Cane, came under intense scrutiny and were severely criticised. A departmental committee under Herbert Gladstone, then under-secretary at the Home Office, was set up to investigate the working of the prison system. The resulting Gladstone Report of 1895 has often been seen as a key moment in heralding a change to a more liberal penal system, specifically a system that was more informed by the ideas of the emergent positivist criminology and which elevated the reformation of the prisoner to a central aim of imprisonment. In keeping with the times, the report reflected the Philosophical Idealism of T.H. Green who, up to his early death some ten years before, had been Professor of Moral Philosophy at Oxford.[12] Green argued that the ideal citizen should seek to achieve the best in himself through his pursuit of the common good. He argued also that the state had a duty to ensure a condition of life that enabled morality in the widest sense. Thus, as the Gladstone Committee deliberated, well-to-do young men inspired by Green saw it as their calling to do voluntary work in the urban slums and, at the same time, legislators were fostering both social regulation at the workplace and new policies designed to improve the situation and to reform the behaviour of those that they considered to be misfits and unfortunates.

The authoritarian, no-nonsense old soldier Du Cane did not fit into this intellectual world and retired shortly after the publication of the Gladstone Report. He was replaced by Evelyn Ruggles-Brise, a career civil servant who had joined the Home Office in 1880, who had served as principal private secretary to four Home Secretaries and who had worked alongside Du Cane on the Prison Commission. Like many of his generation active in public policy, Ruggles-Brise was a devotee of T.H. Green and he used his new position to moderate harsh practices and to develop reforming projects. Thus he employed the freedom given him under the 1898 Prison Act to abolish the exhausting and pointless labour of the treadmill and the crank. He followed the Gladstone Report's recommendation regarding the importance of education and training in forms of industrial work for young offenders by encouraging the creation of a penal reformatory institution designed for offenders in their late teens. This institution was mid-way between the old reformatory school and the prison. It began with an experiment at Bedford Prison in 1900 which was developed further in the following year at a largely empty convict prison at Borstal, near Rochester, in Kent. Within a few years Borstal had given its name to the whole system of young offenders' institutions. Equally progressive, over the quarter century of Ruggles-Brise's stewardship, the number of floggings in prisons decreased, the prison diet was improved, male prisoners were no longer required to submit to the very short convict crop of their hair and were permitted to wear moustaches and beards. But for all that his ideas were liberal and reformist, Ruggles-Brise did not subscribe unreservedly to the ideas being broached on continental Europe in the new science of criminal anthropology. He had little time for Lombroso and had encouraged Goring's study of English convicts as a critique of the Italian. Criminal behaviour, for Ruggles-Brise, might perhaps have been something influenced by heredity or environment, but it remained, above all, a matter of individual choice.

The Prison Commission had five members at any one time; working to them were the prison inspectors whose task was to ensure that policy was being implemented on the ground. During Ruggles-Brise's tenure, both the commissioners and the inspectors began to acquire special responsibilities, and then to be appointed because of their particular specialisms. Thus one commissioner was medically qualified to keep his fellows in touch with medical-criminological theory and to handle questions and pressure from medical organisations. There was a chaplain inspector and a Controller of Industries whose task was to develop work in prisons and to move away from the often pointless labour of the Victorian period, epitomised by crank turning, treadmill stepping and oakum picking. In 1908 the first woman commissioner was appointed: Dr Mary Gordon, a Harley Street physician. This was not a happy appointment. Ruggles-Brise did not want it; Dr Gordon felt that she was a token and a 'sop to feminism'. Matters probably reached their lowest point in 1914 when Gordon's secret correspondence with the suffragette Emmeline Pethick-Lawrence was discovered during a police raid. Gordon went to serve in a military hospital overseas; she returned at the end of the war and was reappointed to the commission. But the tensions remained, and not just for Gordon. The employment of professional women in the prison service proceeded at a snail's pace throughout the first half of the century.[13]

Home secretaries followed each other rapidly in the two decades between the Gladstone Report and the outbreak of war. Several of these, most notably Herbert Gladstone himself (1905–10) and Winston Churchill (1910–11), were as committed to penal reorganisation as Ruggles-Brise. In consequence, there was a wave of penal legislation which, together with the Gladstone Report, has been interpreted as both heralding the beginning of the modern penal complex and the 'decentring' of the prison in the system of judicial punishments. The new legislation provided alternatives to incarceration and set up special institutions where particular kinds of offender might be segregated or given extended training. The Probation of Offenders Act of 1907 established a formal system whereby a convicted offender might be kept out of prison in order that, under supervision, he could demonstrate his intention of living an honest and orderly life in future. Petty Sessions divisions were empowered to appoint probation officers; in most instances it seems that police court missionaries from the Church of England Temperance Society, who had been performing a similar sort of role for some 30 years, were selected. The Criminal Justice Administration Act of 1914 included another measure that reduced prison receptions: magistrates were now required to give individuals time to pay fines thus significantly reducing the number of imprisoned defaulters. The Inebriates Act of 1898 and the Mental Deficiency Act of 1913 also reduced prison receptions by permitting magistrates to send drunkards and offenders diagnosed with mental illness to institutions that were specifically designed for treating those with such problems. The Children Act of 1908, that forbade the imprisonment of those under 16 years of age, also had some impact on prison receptions. At the beginning of the century annual prison receptions were running at close to 200,000 with the average daily prison population being around 20,000; in 1914 the figures stood at roughly 150,000 and 18,000 respectively; and in 1918 at 30,000 and under 9,000. Thereafter the 1914 figures were not reached again until after the Second World War. On the eve of the latter war politicians from across the spectrum acknowledged that improvements might still be made in, for example, accommodation, diet and the facility for exercise. But they also congratulated themselves on what they perceived as a more liberal and less punitive penal system.[14] What the politicians, the liberal reformers in the Prison Commission and their like-minded administrators and governors invariably missed was the power relationship that existed within the prisons and the impact that prison officer discretion might have regardless of liberal changes decreed from above.

Where early twentieth-century governors and deputy governors subscribed to new ideas about alleviating the harshness of prison conditions, the prison officers, who worked daily in face-to-face contact with prisoners, sometimes felt that their authority and their personal safety were being undermined. An inquiry into a disturbance at Wormwood Scrubs Prison in 1907 concluded that the governor's leniency towards prisoners had led to him failing in the duty that he owed towards his staff. The officers themselves tended to respond to prisoners that they considered to be difficult with their own forms of rough justice.[15] At the conclusion of his career the system managed by Ruggles-Brise was subjected to sharp criticism, in particular by a report prepared by the Labour Research Committee and edited by two men, A. Fenner Brockway and Stephen Hobhouse, who had been imprisoned during the war as conscientious objectors.[16] Conscientious objectors, like the suffragettes imprisoned a few years earlier, were not typical of the people incarcerated in the prison system in the first two decades of the twentieth century. Many of them came from a different social class and were able, and keen, to stress that a principled stand, rather than a common crime, had led to their imprisonment. But they were also able to articulate the grim nature of the system for their peers in the way that others often could not. Apart from their personal experience, Hobhouse and Brockway's book also drew evidence from some more ordinary prisoners. It made the point that things had changed, generally for the better since the days of Du Cane. Even so, *English Prisons Today* emphasised the difference between Ruggles-Brise's aspirations and the harsh realities experienced by those within the prison system.

The potential for division between the liberal aspirations of the men responsible for the administration of the penal system, and the discretionary practices of the prison officers continued through the inter-war years. Eighteen local prisons were closed during this period and the average daily prison population rarely rose above 12,000. The key figure in the Prison Commission during the inter-war period, though never the chairman, was Alexander Paterson. Paterson had taken the route from university at Oxford to working in the slums of Bermondsey, after which he published an influential account about poverty and crime in the district, *Across the Bridges* (1911). He aspired to replacing prisons with training or rehabilitation designed specifically for an individual offender and he sought particularly to ensure that no one under 21 years was imprisoned. With this in mind he pressed forward with developments in the borstal system. He was keen to provide training that would mould the young offender into a responsible citizen; he sought borstal staff among young men, often university trained, but with wide experiences especially as teachers or voluntary workers. A model of this type was W.W. (Bill) Llewellin, Eton and Oxford educated, a devout Christian with a good war record and with voluntary experience of the casual wards provided for tramps. In May 1930 Llewellin led a 130-mile march of 43 borstal boys and 9 staff from Feltham in Middlesex to Lowdham Grange near Nottingham where, under the supervision of local tradesmen, the boys built the first open borstal. Others followed, together with the first open prison for adults established at New Hall, near Wakefield, in 1936. But grim, closed prisons remained, often with a rank-and-file staff that was wary of the reformers. Indeed, the *Prison Officers' Magazine* objected when Paterson was appointed to the Prison Commission in 1922.[17]

Dartmoor Prison had an unenviable reputation in the prison estate. Originally built to house prisoners-of-war during the Napoleonic wars, it had been re-established as a convict prison in 1850; the Victorians believed that it would be ideal for invalid convicts because of what they considered the bracing climate of the Devon moor. In keeping with the decline in prison inmates, the number of convicts held in the prison fell from 670 in 1923 to 440 nine years later. But it was no longer seen as a place for invalids; rather it housed some of the country's toughest offenders and recidivists. Nor was the site particularly popular among prison officers, primarily it seems, because of its bleak and remote setting and because of a belief that officers were sent there as a result of being under suspicion elsewhere. In January 1932 tensions within the prison were brought to a head following an assault on a prison officer with a stick inlaid with a razor blade, the discovery of an escape plan and a succession of poor meals, the preparation of which appears to have been deliberately sabotaged. The mutiny was eventually suppressed by armed prison officers supported by the county police and with two companies of infantry in reserve. An official inquiry by Herbert du Parcq, KC, the trial of 32 inmates for their part in the mutiny, and contemporary press reports, pointed to problems arising from a new kind of criminal type, specifically 'the "motor bandit" or "gangster" class', and to some 'irregularities and worse' among a few prison officers. But while prisoners complained at their trial about brutality and the poor diet, the judge kept the proceedings focused on the disorder and the damage. Moreover du Parcq saw no systemic problems and urged that there was nothing questionable, and no cause of the trouble to be found in 'the more humane and reformative treatment of prisoners which has been the aim of prison administration in this country'.[18]

It is significant that du Parcq accepted the appropriateness of the liberal penal system; it is also interesting that he was prepared to point towards some misbehaviour by prison officers. What he did not acknowledge, and in the context of the time this is unsurprising, was the effect of incarceration on the convicts, the issues emanating from power relations within the prison and, specifically in this context, the systemic attitudes and behaviour of prison officers. The officers were often men with military experience; the prison service gave them the opportunity for continuing a life of service in uniform. Discipline went with that life. But the liberalisation policies of Ruggles-Brise and Patterson contributed, in many respects, to a growing disgruntlement and a class-dominated job-consciousness among the prison officers. They found themselves increasingly squeezed out of clerical posts since, as a group, they were not considered sufficiently able or educated for the position, and from 1930 these posts were recruited by the usual open competition for the clerical grades of the Civil Service.

'A cartoon of the Dartmoor Mutiny of 1932'

This cartoon was drawn on toilet paper by one of the prisoners. It subsequently came into the possession of Prison Officer Trask who is illustrated and who, allegedly, gave an order to open fire during the disturbance. (*Source*: John Foulkes. Reproduced by permission of the family of Mrs B.L. Foulkes)

The closure of prisons led to a shortage of staff quarters, especially as officers that continued to serve following a closure had to move to a new posting. The closures also meant a reduction in opportunities for promotion and this was aggravated by a dislike of the men appointed as borstal housemasters. The housemasters did not have to wear uniform; they shared the liberal ideas of the Prison Commission, they were believed to get the best resources and, especially annoying, they appeared to be favoured when it came to promotion.[19]

It would be wrong to assume that, as a body, prison officers took out their frustrations on their charges, but the prison structure enabled the officer considerable discretion in enforcing order and the regulations in the manner that he (and in women's prisons, she) considered appropriate. E.W. Mason, imprisoned for conscientious objection during the Great War, commented from personal experience: 'It is remarkable how efficiently the official mind can neutralise reforms intended to benefit prisoners, so that prisoner continues to suffer that which the reform was intended to remove.' Officially, talking and smoking began to be permitted during Ruggles-Brise's chairmanship of the Prison Commission, yet some officers found ways to limit these privileges. A convict might be told to stop talking by an officer; if he spoke again he was reported, not for talking but for disobeying an order. In women's prisons there were supposed to be bells to summon a female officer if needed; but the bells were often out of order, and some officers took a considerable time to respond.[20] All of which ran counter to the thinking of Alexander Paterson who famously remarked that: 'Men are sent to prison as a punishment, not for punishment.' But then the prison officers' magazine commonly expressed the opinion that, in many respects, the prisoners – 'the pampered scum', according to one – were better cared for by the system than the officers themselves.[21]

Attempts to develop liberal penal policies continued for several years after the Second World War; significant here were the efforts of reform groups, notably the Howard League, many of whose educated and professional membership had close ties and privileged access to senior civil servants and the Prison Commission.[22] The privilege of five-days' home leave on parole, already a feature of the borstal system, was extended to other prisoners in 1951. Two years later selected prisoners were allowed to do normal civilian work away from the prison; their wages went towards their keep – they still had to sleep in prison – and towards the maintenance of their families. There were attempts to improve association and training among prisoners; and all the while there were continuing attempts to keep people out of prison. The Criminal Justice Act of 1967 introduced the suspended sentence and parole; three years later the Administration of Justice Act ended imprisonment for debt. But disgruntlement of the prison officers continued. They still believed that their livelihood and well-being came second to that of the prisoners, and an official report on their pay and conditions published in 1958 described the conditions in some places as 'Dickensian'. Moreover, the report went on, while 'substantial improvements have been made for the prison population with the emphasis now on training and rehabilitation . . . parallel improvements have not been made for the staff'.[23] At the same time the number of assaults on staff increased, and not just on staff. The extension of prisoner association was claimed to have led to the growth of the convict 'barons' who ran the prisons, largely by monopolising the supply of tobacco, through violence and intimidation and without regard to the staff. Such barons, however, had been identified at least as early as the beginning of the 1940s.[24]

The rise in crime following the war led to a steady increase in the number of people held in prison. In 1950 the average daily prison population was around 20,500; ten years later it had risen to 27,000 and it 1965 it was around 29,000. This meant that, from the late 1950s, the average prison population began to exceed what was called the 'Certified Normal Accommodation'. Many prisoners were forced to live three to a cell that was intended for one, and whereas by the 1960s few prisoners came from homes where there was no internal sanitation, few of the Victorian prisons that continued to be the basic housing stock of the system had toilets in the cells and this necessitated the unpleasant task of inmates 'slopping out' their chamber pots each morning. '[M]y own cell was unlocked', remembered one prisoner following his first night inside,

I took a tentative glance outside. Men carrying chamber pots, basins and buckets, trooped past. Emptying my slops into the stinking chamber, I followed them and joined a long queue that was forming at the recess in which were a lavatory and a large sink, with a cold water tap, into which the men emptied their chamber pots. The stench was nauseating and soon the stone floor was swimming with spilt urine and water.[25]

Prison heating was rudimentary; one criminologist recalled interviewing a prisoner in Wormwood Scrubs one evening during the winter of 1955–6 when the water in the man's enamel jug had a thin sheet of ice over it.[26] In addition the Victorian brickwork was often in a poor state of repair and this was brought home in dramatic style in November 1966 when George Blake, who had been given the astonishing sentence of 42 years for espionage, escaped from Wormwood Scrubs Prison by kicking a hole in brickwork around a window. While the annual number of escapes and attempted escapes fluctuated, the number of men making attempts was proportionately four times that of the inter-war period.[27] Moreover Blake's escape came shortly after those of the train robbers, Charlie Wilson from Winson Green Prison in Birmingham and Ronnie Biggs from Wandsworth Prison in August 1964 and July 1965 respectively.

The rise in the numbers sent to prison had already led to the creation of new prisons, often on the sites, and in the buildings of former military bases. The concerns about escapes led to the setting-up of an inquiry into prison security chaired by Lord Mountbatten. The resulting report advised the introduction of a four-part categorisation of male prisoners ranging from Category A, the most dangerous, to Category D, those men that might be trusted and therefore allowed to spend their sentence in an open prison. Mountbatten also proposed a single, high security prison for those in Category A, but a subcommittee of the Advisory Council on the Penal System that was chaired by the academic, Sir Leon Radzinowicz, suggested instead a system of dispersal for these men around other, selected and secure prisons. The Home Office, which had taken direct control after the abolition of the Prison Commission in 1963, opted for the dispersal system, but from the late 1960s and through the 1970s, the prison system was beset with problems. While the rhetoric of treatment and training remained among the administration, the realities were restricted by the needs of security. The new prisons were insufficient to alleviate the problem of overcrowding, and the conditions of the old prisons still necessitated the misery of slopping out. At the same time the Prison Officers' Association became notorious for its militancy, for working to rule and opposing any liberal change. Some of its members were also notorious for their brutality towards prisoners. There was a wave of disorder and rioting culminating in trouble at Hull Prison in 1976 which rivalled that in Dartmoor 40 years before. The Hull riot grew in severity when prisoners found the personal records kept on them, none of which, they protested to a subsequent public inquiry, appeared to have anything positive to say about any man.

Details of the prisoners' outrage at these records, together with accounts of the violence meted out to prisoners at Hull both before and after the riot were made public by the third of three reports into the incident. The first report, an official investigation by the Chief Inspector of the Prison Service, was dismissed by many as a whitewash. The second, organised by John Prescott the MP for the area in which the prison stood, raised broader questions about the national situation. The third, chaired by John Platts-Mills QC, was a public inquiry set on foot by PROP (Preservation of the Rights of Prisoners) and established because of concerns about the official investigation and the belief that the prisoners needed the opportunity to voice their dissatisfaction.[28] PROP was one of the first of a series of campaigning groups to appear during the 1970s and 1980s that stood up for prisoners' rights. Radical Alternatives to Prison (RAP) was established in 1970. It was formed by ex-prisoners, people connected to the prison service and a clutch of radical criminologists. It challenged the whole concept of incarceration and its journal, first published in 1979, significantly took as its title *The Abolitionist*. RAP's members were critical of both the official line that tended to play down many abuses in the system and the liberal penal reformers such as the Howard League whose aspirations were to improve the prison system. They stressed, in particular, the systemic failure of penal policy to reform and rehabilitate those that were incarcerated. They also drew attention to the overwhelming proportion of the poor, the disadvantaged, the mentally ill and people from ethnic minorities among those 'warehoused' by the country's prisons. INQUEST was set up in 1981 to publicise and organise investigations into deaths in custody.

Again it involved radical academics, this time uniting with the friends and families of individuals that had died suddenly, sometimes inexplicably and violently in police custody or in prison. RAP had always given space to the growing numbers of women sent to prison during the 1970s and *The Abolitionist* regularly addressed the problem. Women in Prison (WIP) was the fourth of these pressure groups; first established in 1983 it campaigned on behalf of women in prison, highlighting, among other things, the appalling state of the accommodation in which they were housed.

The arguments, and the problems over prisons and penal policy, continued to the end of the century and beyond. The tough law-and-order stance of Margaret Thatcher's government increased the number of prisons and prison places, but its insistence on longer sentences and reduced opportunities for parole for those deemed most dangerous and violent ensured that overcrowding continued. 'Threeing up' in a cell built for one, and 'slopping out' remained routine in the old prison stock throughout the 1980s. Difficult and recalcitrant prisoners, especially among women, were given psychotropic drugs to make them pliant; the typical drug, Chloropromazine (marketed in Europe as Largactyl), was known among prisoners as 'the liquid cosh'. Anxious observers, including liberal criminologists, urged the need for a new investigation along the lines of the Gladstone Report.[29] In the early 1980s two prison governors took the unprecedented step of writing to the press about the sorry situation. The governor of Wormwood Scrubs labelled his establishment a 'large penal dustbin' and protested that he 'did not join the prison service to manage overcrowded cattle pens'.

As it is evident that the present conditions in prison seem likely to continue and as I find this incompatible with any moral ethic, I wish to give notice that I, as the governor of a major prison in the United Kingdom, cannot for much longer tolerate, either as a professional or as an individual, the inhumanity of the system within which I work.

His colleague, at Strangeways Prison in Manchester, wrote in similar terms emphasising the Victorian origins of his institution and its present 'overcrowding and squalor'.[30] Her Majesty's Inspectorate of Prisons, which had been established within the Home Office in 1981 but separate from the Prison Service, also began to take a critical line. This was especially the case when Judge Stephen Tumin was appointed as Chief Inspector in 1987.

During 1988 to 1989 a new peak of some 50,000 people in prison was reached, and on 1 April 1990 Strangeways exploded. The prison had been built in the mid-Victorian period to house 970 men. Early in 1990 there were over 1,600 inmates ranging from men on remand to Category A prisoners; there was also a wing housing sexual offenders, people who were never popular in prisons – 'You're called a nonce because, they say, "Oh, you've been up to nonsense". The most despised nonces are the child molesters'.[31] Most prisoners in Strangeways were kept locked in the cells for most of the day. In the case of the Category A men this could be for up to 22 hours; they were let out briefly to slop out and for a short period of exercise. The prison officers in Strangeways were noted for their aggression and brutality; in addition the liquid cosh was used. A new organisation, the Prisoner League Association which campaigned for prisoners' rights, was active among the inmates and one of the sparks that ignited the riot was the removal of a local organiser to Hull Prison. The disorder continued for 25 days. It started with a riot and ended as a roof-top protest. One prisoner, a man held on a charge of indecent assault and buggery, died following admission to hospital after being attacked by other prisoners, and the tabloid press treated its readers to fabricated stories of drug-crazed inmates 'butchering perverts'. Prisoners elsewhere heard the news on radios and trouble flared in other prisons. It took four years and a cost of £55 million to make Strangeways, rechristened as HMP Manchester, inhabitable once again.[32] The report of a judicial inquiry into the events, chaired by Lord Justice Woolf, was much quicker.

The Woolf Report, published in February 1991, fell into the liberal tradition and was highly acclaimed by many contemporaries.[33] It offered an agenda for the prison system that balanced the needs of security with the requirements of a humane regime that recognised that even prisoners had rights. It was followed by a White Paper, *Custody, Care and Justice*, which took a similar line. The two publications coincided with a steady fall in the number of prisoners, from an average of 47,000 towards the end of 1991 to 42,200 at the end of the following year. There were some reforms. In April 1996 the last slopping out regime in England, at Armley Prison in Leeds, was ended but, by that time, the prison population was, once again, on the increase. More seriously, the Conservative government had lurched back to promoting a policy in which the prison regime was designed to be tough. The Home Secretary, Michael Howard, had told an appreciative party conference that 'prison works' to the extent that it kept serious offenders off the streets. And while he urged that fewer fine defaulters be imprisoned, Howard also demanded longer sentences for serious offenders and recidivists. At the same time he both forced the resignation of Derek Lewis, the Director General of the Prison Service Agency who had been

A prisoner on the roof of HMP Strangeways, 1980

A prisoner makes a personal statement on the roof, stripped of slates, of HMP Strangeways during the riot of 1980. (*Source*: Ged Murray)

brought in from the private sector with much fanfare, and did not renew the appointment of Stephen Tumin as Chief Inspector of Prisons; Tumin was replaced with a former soldier. New tough policies for prisons and prisoners received a further impetus from two spectacular escapes in September 1994, during which a prison officer was shot, and January 1995.

In the run-up to the General Election of 1997 both major parties sought to out-do each other with a rhetoric of punitive populism. The new Labour government experimented with alternatives to prison such as curfews on offenders verified by electronic tagging devices, and it spoke of the need to embrace the socially excluded, particularly the poor, often ethnic minority families on run-down inner-city estates. Jack Straw, the first Home Secretary in Blair's government, and his successors also embraced the slogan that prison worked; but much to his irritation he found that Judge Tumin's replacement, General Sir David Ramsbotham, was as independently minded and as critical of the system and its estate as his predecessor had been. By the end of the century the prisons held an average monthly total of almost 65,000. In 1992 there had been 90 persons per 100,000 of the population in prison; in 1999 the number had risen to 125. This was a higher proportion than any of the other countries of Western Europe with which the United Kingdom was usually compared.

The Labour government also followed the new kind of managerial policies introduced under the Conservatives which gave the prison service a plethora of mission statements, visions, targets and key performance indicators. It also maintained the policy of contracting out prison services to private companies; the first prison whose management was contracted out by the Home Office, the Wolds, had opened in April 1992. Conservative politicians during the 1980s had supported privatisation primarily because of their faith in market economics and their belief that state-run institutions suffered from high costs, shortages in investment and an overall inadequate supply. But some of the liberal reformers had also been sympathetic in the belief that private companies would provide a means of removing what they saw as one of the principal barriers to reform, the Prison Officers' Association. Labour had opposed privatisation in opposition, but once in power the party recognised the prohibitive costs of renationalising the few prisons that had been privatised.[34]

Penal reformers had been optimistic at the beginning of the twentieth century and their efforts over the century had not been without success. They had seen the abolition of capital and corporal punishment and some of the more pointless practices and fiercest discipline of the prison system. Prisons had closed, and the borstal system, with its blend of public school,

Boy Scouts and muscular Christianity had appeared as the apogee of the reforming ethos. But in the aftermath of the Second World War the borstal had faltered, as the institution had become more integrated with the prison system. Its ethos no longer struck a chord with either the prison elite or the public; the age of borstal inmates was lowered from 17 to 15 years, its training facilities declined, its staff went back into uniform and the whole system grew more like a formal prison. In 1982 the label 'borstal' was replaced by 'youth custody centres', but the new institutions rapidly became stigmatised for bleakness and brutality with high levels of suicide and self-harm among the inmates. It was much the same with the variety of detention centres that were experimented with during the 1950s and 1960s, the institutions designed to give juvenile offenders a 'short sharp shock' in the 1980s, the 'boot camps' of the mid-1990s and the secure units run by local authorities or private bodies from the 1970s. At the end of the century Britain had more young people incarcerated than any other country in Europe, often in unsuitable conditions that seem to have fostered recidivism rather than rehabilitation.[35]

The prison stock as a whole was gradually improved in the last quarter of the century, but mainly as a result of prison disorder rather than any humanitarian pressure. Similarly prisoners' rights began to be acknowledged, with increasing and articulate channels for publicity and for bringing forward for public censure those responsible for offences towards inmates. At the beginning of the century penal reformers had worried about prisons making offenders worse rather than reforming them, but they had faith that reform and rehabilitation were possible. Those reformers also had the ear of policy makers and were to become dominant in the administration of the system. At the end of the century such reformers were still to be found, and many of their aspirations were still to be found in the visions, mission statements and targets of the system, as well as in the criticisms of Judge Tumin and General Ramsbotham. But their voices were commonly drowned by the punitive demands of a tabloid press and by politicians who preferred to go with the punitive flow and to respond to sudden emergencies by playing to the gallery with instant, tough responses, rather than leading with well-considered policies developed after reflection.

References and notes

1 **Kelly Grovier**, *The Gaol: the story of Newgate, London's most notorious prison*, London: John Murray, 2008.

2 The point is generally missed in this traditional narrative that the capital
   statutes that were introduced during the eighteenth century often dealt with
   offences in particular places; thus while the Riot Act of 1715 made rioting
   a capital offence, other statutes made it a capital offence to destroy or
   damage particular property in a particular place during the course of a riot.
   Clive Emsley, *Crime and Society in England, 1750–1900*, 4th edn, London
   and Harlow: Longman, 2010, p. 264.

3 These figures are drawn from the *Judicial Statistics for England and Wales*,
   but for wider discussions see, *inter alia*, **George Riley Scott**, *The History of
   Corporal Punishment*, 10th impression, London: Torchstream Books, 1954,
   pp. 59–65; Victor Bailey, *Delinquency and Citizenship: reclaiming the young
   offender, 1914–1948*, Oxford: Clarendon Press, 1987, pp. 59–61 and 104–7.

4 Quoted in Bailey, *Delinquency and Citizenship*, p. 108.

5 *Report of the Departmental Committee on Corporal Punishment
   (The Cadogan Committee)*, Cmd. 5684, London: HMSO, 1938.

6 *Parl. Debs. (Commons)*, 4 November 1943, col. 847.

7 Bailey, *Delinquency and Citizenship*, pp. 277–8.

8 **Andrew Davies**, *The Gangs of Manchester*, Preston: Milo Books, 2008,
   pp. 310–11.

9 The next four paragraphs are based principally on **Elizabeth O. Tuttle**, *The
   Crusade against Capital Punishment in Great Britain*, London: Stevens and
   Sons, 1961; **B.P. Block** and **John Hostetter**, *Hanging in the Balance: a history
   of the abolition of capital punishment in Britain*, Winchester: Waterside Press,
   1997; **Victor Bailey**, 'The shadow of the gallows: the death penalty and the
   British Labour government, 1945–51', *Law and History Review*, 18, 2 (2000)
   pp. 305–49.

10 The Howard League for Penal Reform was formed in 1921 by an
   amalgamation of the Howard Association (which took its name from John
   Howard, the great prison reformer of the eighteenth century) and the Penal
   Reform League.

11 See, for example, *Parl. Debs. (Commons)*, 13 July 1983, cols. 882–986.
   During this debate there were six separate divisions; on each occasion those
   favouring restoration were defeated, on average, by more than 100 votes.

12 **Christopher Harding**, 'The inevitable end of a discredited system? The origins
   of the Gladstone Committee Report on Prisons, 1895', *Historical Journal*, 31,
   3 (1988) pp. 591–608.

13 **W.J. Forsythe**, *Penal Discipline, Reformatory Projects and the English Prison
   Commission, 1895–1939*, Exeter: University of Exeter Press, 1990, chap. 3;
   Anne Logan, *Feminism and Criminal Justice: a historical perspective*,
   Houndmills Basingstoke: Palgrave Macmillan, 2008, pp. 110–15.

14 See, for example, *Parl. Debs. (Commons)*, 4 June 1937, cols. 1315–70.

15 **Alyson Brown**, *English Prison Society: time, culture and politics in the development of the modern prison, 1850–1920*, Woodbridge: Boydell Press, 2003, pp. 112–14.

16 **Stephen Hobhouse** and **A. Fenner Brockway** (eds), *English Prisons Today*, London: Longman, Green and Co., 1922. For borstal developments in the period see Bailey, *Delinquency and Citizenship*, pp. 227–55.

17 **J.E. Thomas**, *The English Prison Officer since 1850: a study in conflict*, London: Routledge and Kegan Paul, 1972, p. 153.

18 *Report by Mr Herbert du Parcq, KC, on the Circumstances Connected with the Recent Disorder at Dartmoor Prison*, London: HMSO, 1932–33, Cmd. 4010; quotations at pp. 6 and 32; **Alyson Brown**, 'The amazing mutiny at the Dartmoor convict prison', *BJC*, 47 (2007) pp. 276–92.

19 Thomas, *English Prison Officer*, pp. 166–72.

20 **Alyson Brown** and **Emma Clare**, 'A history of experience: exploring prisoners' accounts of incarceration', in **Clive Emsley** (ed.), *The Persistent Prison: problems, image and alternatives*, London: Francis Boutle, 2005, pp. 56–7. The Mason quotation comes from **E.W. Mason**, *Made Free in Prison*, London: Allen and Unwin, 1918, pp. 210–11.

21 **S.K. Ruck** (ed.), *Paterson on Prisons*, London: Frederick Muller, 1951, p. 151; for the prison officer's comments see Thomas, *English Prison Officer*, p. 200.

22 **Mick Ryan**, *The Acceptable Pressure Group: a case study of radical alternatives to prison and the Howard League*, Farnborough: Teakfield, 1978.

23 *Report of the Committee on Remuneration and Conditions of Service of Certain Grades in the Prison Services*, Cmnd. 544, London: HMSO, 1958, p. 20.

24 Thomas, *English Prison Officer*, pp. 190–91; **Philip Priestley**, *Jail Journeys: the English prison experience since 1918*, London: Routledge, 1989, pp. 48–9. For an allegation, at a Prison Officers' conference, that 'barons' had organised 'a whip-round to pay for an attack on a warder', see *Daily Express*, 23 May 1942, p. 4.

25 Priestley, *Jail Journeys*, p. 23, quoting Anthony Heckstall-Smith, *Eighteen Months*, 1954.

26 **Terence Morris**, *Crime and Criminal Justice since 1945*, Oxford: Basil Blackwell, 1989, p. 140.

27 The figures for escapes and attempted escapes can be found in Thomas, *English Prison Officer*, pp. 172–4 and 185–7.

28 **J.E. Thomas** and **R. Pooley**, *The Exploding Prison: prison riots and the case of Hull*, London: Junction Books, 1980, p. 60.

29 Roy D. King and Rod Morgan, *The Future of the Prison System*, London: Gower, 1980, p. 8.

30 *The Times*, 19 November 1981, p. 19; *Daily Telegraph*, 30 November 1981.

31 Priestley, *Jail Journeys*, p. 50, quoting James Campbell, *Gate Fever: Voices from a Prison*, 1986.

32 Eamonn Carrabine, *Power, Discourse and Resistance: a genealogy of the Strangeways prison riot*, Aldershot: Ashgate, 2004. For some of the more ridiculous press reports see *The Sun*, 2, 3, 4 April 1990.

33 *Prison Disturbances, April 1990*, Cm. 1456, London: HMSO, 1991.

34 Trevor Jones and Tim Newburn, 'Comparative criminal justice policy-making in the United States and the United Kingdom: the case of private prisons', *BJC*, 45, 1 (2005) pp. 58–80; Richard Harding, *Private Prisons and Public Accountability*, Buckingham: Open University Press, 1997. In spite of the novelty of contracting out prisons, it had not occurred to the Prison Department of the Home Office to undertake any monitoring or evaluation of the Wolds until approached by a group of academic criminologists. The Home Office eventually agreed to their proposal and the assessment was published as Keith Bottomley, Adrian James, Emma Clare and Alison Liebling, *Monitoring and Evaluating the Wolds Remand Prison and Comparison with Public-Sector Prisons, in Particular H.M.P. Woodhill*, London: Home Office, 1997.

35 See, *inter alia*, Barry Goldson and Eleanor Peters, *Tough Justice: responding to children in trouble*, London: The Children's Society, 2000; John Muncie, 'Juvenile justice in Europe: some conceptual, analytical and statistical comparisons', *Childright*, 202 (2003) pp. 14–17.

CHAPTER 11

Some conclusions

Written history is concerned with change through time; much of the contemporary debate about crime is also concerned with change through time. Any historian writing about crime cannot avoid engagement with contemporary debates and being sucked into the issue as to whether crime is 'worse', 'more prevalent' or 'more violent' than in the past. A quarter of a century ago Geoffrey Pearson drew attention to the way in which generation after generation in Britain looked at what is now termed antisocial behaviour by young people and pronounced that in their immediate present, such behaviour was far worse than in their past.[1] And the problem of the rose-tinted spectacles persists.

The question of whether crime increased or declined over the twentieth century is, essentially, a statistical problem that, as demonstrated in Chapter 2, the available statistics cannot answer. The figures are suggestive of an overall increase for most of the century, but rising more sharply in the second half; there appears also to have been some levelling-off and even a slight decline at the close. That is about as far as any serious broad assessment of the pattern can go, although other sources might be exploited for a picture of certain kinds of crime. A detailed analysis of the admissions to hospital casualty wards, for example, might provide a more nuanced picture of change in the extent of interpersonal violence, but finding a satisfactory run of such sources covering an extended historical period may be difficult.[2]

In the same way that it is easy to assert, from sensational press reporting and personal anecdote, that crime increased across the century, it is equally easy, and equally risky, to insist that things have changed very little. Young people, particularly young males, had posed problems in earlier centuries, and they continued to commit vandalism and petty thefts throughout the twentieth century. Similarly individuals of all kinds have always been prey to the temptations offered by opportunity. Entrepreneurs could be found that were prepared to make available, for a price, things that were prohibited by law or that were in short supply and sometimes restricted by, for example, rationing. Other offenders showed themselves to be supremely adaptable to social and technological change; at the beginning of the century they rapidly showed an ability to use cars; at the end of the century they were using the internet. Some communities considered certain forms of lawbreaking to be acceptable. Dockers, for example, often had few qualms about appropriating items from cargoes; yet these same communities did not sanction theft from family and neighbours. These communities had inhabited the same streets for generations and were essentially stable; some had traditions that made them considerable problems for law enforcers, others considered themselves to be more respectable and behaved accordingly. As a result of the blitz and then the enthusiastic demolitions of the post-Second World War planners, many of these communities were broken up as their streets and homes were flattened and redeveloped. The new estates that sprang up in their place appear often to have housed a much more transitory population; the old-style, tough masculinity was perpetuated among new generations of young men but the communities were less stable while the offending, arguably, became more serious and dangerous as these young men dabbled in drugs and the marketing of drugs, and as they fought violently, sometimes with lethal results over their marketing territory.[3]

Young males from the poorer sections of society continued to constitute a majority of those processed by the criminal justice system, although there appeared also to be an increase in the number of young women offenders in the closing decades of the century. The number of female offenders grew from a very low base in comparison with their male counterparts, and at least some of this increase may have been the result of the police and victims becoming more prepared to act against criminal behaviour by women and girls. The social origins of the majority brought before the courts helped to feed the old positivist notions of criminals as outsiders driven by some form of pathology. The media and other commentators expressed outrage at corporate and white-collar offenders, particularly those able to play the system and to 'get off' with limited sanctions like Roger Levitt and the Guinness directors. But the media and other commentators also had difficulty in integrating offences committed by otherwise respectable members of society with the traditional, common-sense form of criminality that focused almost entirely on murder, robbery and rape. The overall knowledge about crime and criminals increased enormously over the century, and particularly following the research that emanated from the academic, sociology-based discipline of criminology that emerged increasingly from the 1960s. Yet, for all the increase in knowledge and the financial contribution of central government to the research that underpinned it, at the turn of the millennium, many academic criminologists were gloomy about the direction of government policy and the forces driving it.

Throughout the century crime both evolved and maintained its shape according to circumstances. New laws made new offences, or reshaped the description and the punishment of old ones; new laws also decriminalised some behaviours; and changes in the wider culture shaped the way in which certain offences were viewed and reported. At the beginning of the century, for example, while alcohol was regarded by many as a cause of crime, there was little concern about the use of other forms of narcotic. A few intellectuals dabbled with drugs, and opium dens were a feature of many waterfronts where they catered particularly for Asian seamen and the few others who used the drug. As far as the British government was concerned the widespread trafficking and use of drugs was an imperial, not a domestic problem. There was a scare during the First World War about the use of drugs among soldiers, but particularly among soldiers from overseas. In the inter-war period drugs, particularly cocaine, were used by some of the wealthy frequenters of nightclubs in London's West End and sensational stories, like the deaths of Billie Carleton and Freda Kempton and the existence of their exotic nemesis Brilliant Chang, occasionally hit the headlines; but the problem, such as it was, was small-scale and most of the illicit drugs available on the domestic market for recreational activities had been purloined from licit sources, such as pharmacies, rather than being trafficked from overseas.[4] During the 1950s and early 1960s illicit drugs were generally considered by the police to be a problem among the growing immigrant communities, although increasingly white youth, especially students, were found to be among the recreational users of cannabis. They were said to pick up the habit by frequenting cafés, dance halls or jazz clubs with their Afro-Caribbean bands.[5] Parts of the 1960s Hippie culture celebrated the use of amphetamines, stimulants that, to their adherents, were 'mind-expanding'. At the same time others began experimenting with other forms of drug such as heroin which, up until the 1960s, had also been an addiction largely confined to a few members of the middle class who commonly got the drug on prescription from a general practitioner.[6] A few, often student travellers, were caught trying to bring small quantities of different drugs into the country for their own use, and for friends and acquaintances. But by the early 1970s entrepreneurs were beginning to see opportunities for considerable profit by providing drugs to suit whatever the market wanted. As noted in Chapter 5, Charlie Wilson, one of the Great Train robbers, graduated from prison into becoming one such entrepreneur; and he was murdered in Spain a decade later. The addicts' need for ready money with which to buy illicit drugs may have fostered some theft and, by the last decade or so of the century, the supply and use of drugs were seen primarily as a crime problem rather than one of addiction. The sale of drugs on the street provided some youths on the poorest estates with opportunities for making more money than a dead-end job; the gangs in which they worked provided communities for friendship and support. But there was also the need to protect territory and, as the century drew to a close, this was increasingly done with weaponry that became more and more available on the black market from the collapsed Soviet empire, and from 'souvenirs' brought back in soldiers' kitbags.

The growing concerns about the use of drugs and the impact on crime almost coincided with the more liberated attitude towards sex. Together with the growth of a vociferous and powerful feminist movement, this changing attitude appears to have encouraged a greater preparedness to report rape and sexual assaults; it also fostered changes in the way that victims were treated by elements of the criminal justice system, most notably the police and prosecuting counsel in the courts. Similarly, the new attitudes to sex appear to have made people more aware of, and less reticent about reporting incidents of paedophilia. The problem here was that, at the close of the century, the fear of the paedophile encouraged the more populist tabloids to demand the naming, shaming and publication of the residential addresses of those convicted. Such identification, the *News of the World* trumpeted disingenuously, was 'ABSOLUTELY NOT [to be] a charter for vigilantes'.[7] But there were readers that appear to have seen the naming as precisely such a charter and attacks followed on those identified, and sometimes on people wrongly identified. It has always been easy to blame the media for inaccurate and sensational reporting. There were factual inaccuracies reported at the beginning of the century as well as at the end, and if people had refused to buy newspapers that sensationalised stories then probably newspapers would have ceased to sensationalise stories. The public is as much responsible for the media it gets as is the media for reporting sensation.

Yet if the public gets the media that it wants, the public's perception and understanding of crime is greatly influenced by the media, as well as by the documentation prepared by the bureaucracies that have been established to deal with crime. Bureaucracies have a problem when their aims become subordinate to their procedures. The nineteenth and twentieth centuries saw an intensification of the bureaucratic procedures of the institutions of the criminal justice system. Initially this was lost in the elite's and the respectable classes' celebration of, and faith in the English system – although when talking in constitutional terms the system was more commonly reputed to be British. In their understanding, the British constitution was an unwritten instrument that had evolved over time, avoiding the violent upheavals of continental Europe and the untrammelled egalitarian democracy of the United States; it boasted 'the best police in the world' and, generally less overtly stated, the best legal system and the best prison system in the world. These beliefs were combined with a continuing faith in Enlightenment ideas of humanitarianism and progress, and a largely Whig perspective on historical development that envisaged a broadly consensual community on a steady track to an improved future. Yet beneath the rhetoric, the criminal justice institutions were more often concerned with containment rather than solving the problem of crime and criminal offenders. If the system appeared to work this was, at least in part, because so few individuals or groups with any political clout or national voice set out to challenge it or to query its effectiveness. Things began to change in the aftermath of the Second World War.

The statistics collected by criminal justice institutions revealed a sharp rise in criminal offending and in cases coming to court from the 1950s. In the more critical and egalitarian age that emerged during the 1950s and 1960s faults were increasingly found in the British system and in what was came to be known as 'the establishment'. The drive for greater centralisation of the police had been common to most major political parties since the mid-nineteenth century, both because it appeared a better way to ensure uniformity and also because it seemed more sensible to understand the police officer as a servant of the Crown rather than as a servant of local government. The legal profession maintained its independence of the government, but the courts in which it functioned had become more formal since the late eighteenth century. There had been much less local opposition to the centralisation of the prison system than to that of the police, and consequently centralisation had been achieved relatively quickly during the Victorian period. There was also a growing consensus among politicians and management-level criminal justice practitioners that prisons and punishments needed to be moderated. But with the post-Second World War open season on the criticism of institutions and with the rise in the statistics of crime, the apparent consensus on the criminal justice system broke down.

By the early 1970s Britain was still wealthy and influential, but this was not the wealth and influence of the beginning of the century, nor of the inter-war period. It was no longer realistic to claim that British systems were 'the best in the world', though some still did. In the economic malaise of the 1970s, that witnessed a three-day week because of a miners' strike and then a clutch of industrial disputes – labelled 'the winter of discontent' – that brought down a Labour government, crime and the institutions of the criminal justice system increasingly became political issues. At the same time experts, including those in the new and expanding academic discipline of criminology, could find no consensus over the causes of crime, the nature of criminality or the treatment of offenders. And to aggravate the situation still further a sensationalist press, using bigger headlines and colour images, continued to rely upon crime as one of its front-page staples; moreover the decline of the local press, with its column-filling reports of petty offences heard in magistrates' courts, left the impression that crime was overwhelmingly brutal murders, rapes, and attacks on old ladies for their pension money. This impression was strengthened by equally dramatic coverage in television news and documentaries, and by the rougher, more unvarnished representations of crime in films where, sometimes, fact and fiction were blurred.

Rather than perceiving of the institutions within the criminal justice system as the best in the world, by the last decade of the century many appeared to have lost of faith in them. Politicians resisted calls for the reintroduction of the death penalty, yet in other ways their responses were immediate and populist; picking up once again on Andrew Rutherford's distinction among different approaches to criminal justice, a caring credo largely espoused in the first half of the century yielded to a mixture of efficiency and punishment credos. Academic work, funded by government but that did not meet new policy objectives, was stifled. The police found themselves saddled with centrally imposed targets. At times the required measurements and assessments exposed failures; such exposures served to undermine faith in the institution. Bureaucratic institutions find ways to tick the boxes and to manage their evidence to suit those that set the targets; yet the media reporting of sensational crimes served to undermine the claims that policing targets were being met. Politicians also began to issue directives to magistrates and the judiciary; they even followed the tabloid press in publicly criticising those thought to have given sentences that were too lenient. And herein lies perhaps the biggest contrast in criminal justice in twentieth-century England. In the generation before the First World War and on through the inter-war period, the institutions of criminal justice were solidly supported by politicians, by the ruling elite and by the media; occasionally abuses, problems and scandals led to enquiries, but problems were believed to be solved as a result. In contrast, the generation that saw in the new millennium had become used to criminal justice institutions permanently under the microscope and regularly facing criticism from government ministers and the opposition, from within their own ranks, and from the media. Small wonder then, that even when the statistics of crime appeared to level out in the mid-1990s, large numbers of people appear to have been disinclined to believe them.

References and notes

1 **Geoffrey Pearson**, *Hooligan: a history of respectable fears*, London: Macmillan, 1983.

2 A good example, based on contemporary records, of what might be done if the historical material is available can be found in **Jonathan Shepherd**, 'Violent crime in Bristol: an accident and emergency perspective', *BJC*, 30, 2 (1990) pp. 289–305.

3 **Roger Hood** and **Kate Joyce**, 'Three generations: oral testimonies on crime and social change in London's East End', *BJC*, 39, 1 (1990) pp. 136–60.

4 See, for example, **Virginia Berridge**, 'The origins of the English drug "scene", 1890–1930', *Medical History*, 32, 1 (1988) pp. 51–64.

5 See, for example, HO 287/1451 Crime Miscellaneous – drug trafficking.

6 **Alex Mold**, *The Treatment of Addiction in Twentieth-Century Britain*, DeKalb, IL: Northern Illinois University Press, 2008.

7 *News of the World*, 23 July 2000, p. 1.

Further reading: further research

The notes to the thematic chapters are designed to provide the detailed bibliography for this book. This note is merely to highlight some of the broad surveys, the more important texts and source collections, the gaps and where useful work might be done.

The serious academic work on the history of crime which began in the late 1960s focused largely on property offences from the early modern period up to about 1900. From the late 1980s, as work on criminal justice history took its first tentative steps into the twentieth century, research interests in social and cultural history shifted towards gender relations. In consequence, much of the work that has addressed crime in twentieth-century England has had an orientation towards gender and the domestic. A good starting place for anyone wishing to continue in this area is the broad synoptic survey by **Shani D'Cruze** and **Louise A. Jackson,** *Women, Crime and Justice in England since 1660* (Houndmills, Basingstoke: Palgrave, 2009). **Pamela Cox,** *Gender, Justice and Welfare: bad girls in Britain, 1900–1950* (Houndmills, Basingstoke: Palgrave, 2003) is an immensely valuable survey, as is **Alyson Brown** and **David Barrett,** *Knowledge of Evil: child prostitution in twentieth-century England* (Cullompton: Willan Publishing, 2002). **John Muncie,** *Youth and Crime* (3rd edn, London: Sage, 2009), while mainly focused on contemporary issues, has a well-informed and valuable historical perspective. **Anne Logan,** *Feminism and Criminal Justice: a historical perspective* (Houndmills, Basingstoke: Palgrave, 2008) is an important assessment of the growing role played by women in the development of the criminal justice system before the advent of a more active, broader-based and vocal women's movement in the 1970s.

More general surveys of the area include **Terence Morris,** *Crime and Criminal Justice since 1945* (Oxford: Basil Blackwell, 1989), **David J.V. Jones,** *Crime and Policing in the Twentieth Century: the South Wales experience* (Cardiff: University of Wales Press, 1996) and **Eamonn**

Carrabine, Pamela Cox, Maggy Lee and Nigel South, *Crime in Modern Britain* (Oxford: Oxford University Press, 2002). **Edward Smithies** wrote two useful specialist analyses, *Crime in Wartime: a social history of crime in World War II* (London: Allen and Unwin, 1982) and *The Black Economy in England since 1914* (Dublin: Gill and Macmillan, 1984). The former is also the subject of **Donald Thomas**, *An Underworld at War: spivs, deserters, racketeers and civilians in the Second World War* (London: John Murray 2003) but this, for all its readability and lively detail, is short on serious analysis and helpful referencing. There are dozens of books on gangs and well-known offenders such as the Krays and the Richardsons; among the best writers in the genre is **James Morton** – see, for example, his *East End Gangland* (London: Little Brown and Company, 2000). The classic story of a petty East End offender remains **Raphael Samuel**, *East End Underworld: chapters in the life of Arthur Harding* (London: Routledge and Kegan Paul, 1981).

   T.A. Critchley, *A History of Police in England and Wales* (revd edn London: Constable, 1978) is Whiggish in its perspective, but remains valuable, not least for the author's personal insights as a key figure in the Home Office from the 1950s to the 1970s. **Clive Emsley**, *The English Police: a political and social history* (2nd edn, Harlow and London: Longman, 1996) covers the same sort of ground but taking account of more recent research and perspectives, and Emsley's *The Great British Bobby: a history of British policing from the eighteenth century to the present* (London: Quercus, 2009) attempts a kind of collective biography of police officers describing their lives and work experiences. **Mike Brogden**, *On the Mersey Beat: policing Liverpool between the wars* (Oxford: Oxford University Press, 1991) is an important study of the experiences of men in a provincial force and, like **Barbara Weinberger**, *The Best Police in the World: an oral history of English policing* (Aldershot: Scolar Press, 1995) is a lesson in the use of oral history. **James Whitfield**, *Unhappy Dialogue: the Metropolitan Police and black Londoners in post-war Britain* (Cullompton: Willan Publishing, 2004) is a balanced, well-argued account of a contentious subject. **Louise A. Jackson**, *Women Police: gender, welfare and surveillance in the twentieth century* (Manchester: Manchester University Press, 2006) is indispensable for anyone interested in this area.

   Anette Ballinger, *Dead Woman Walking: executed women in England and Wales, 1900–1955* (Aldershot: Ashgate, 2000) is a starting point for those interested in gender and penal policy, though some of its assertions may need qualifying in the light of the work of, particularly, **Lucy Bland, Ginger Frost** and **John Carter Wood**. **Victor Bailey**, *Delinquency and*

Citizenship: reclaiming the young offender, 1914–1948 (Oxford: Clarendon Press, 1987) remains the key analysis of penal policy and juveniles in the first half of the century. **W.J. Forsythe**, *Penal Discipline, Reformatory Projects and the English Prison Commission, 1895–1939* (Exeter: University of Exeter Press, 1990) provides the essential background for understanding penal policy as a whole from the Gladstone Report to the Second World War, and **Philip Priestley**, *Jail Journeys: the English prison experience since 1918* (London: Routledge, 1989) offers vivid vignettes of the prisoner's life behind bars. For the prison officers see, **J.E. Thomas**, *The English Prison Officer since 1850: a study in conflict* (London: Routledge and Kegan Paul, 1972).

Many books that are listed as 'criminology' now also provide some historical perspective, notably the handbooks such as **Mike Maguire**, **Rod Morgan** and **Robert Reiner** (eds), *The Oxford Handbook of Criminology*, (4th edn, Oxford: Oxford University Press, 2007), **Yvonne Jewkes** (ed.), *Handbook on Prisons* (Cullompton: Willan Publishing, 2007), **Tim Newburn** (ed.), *Handbook of Policing* (2nd edn, Cullompton: Willan Publishing, 2008). **Clive Coleman** and **Jenny Moynihan**, *Understanding Crime Data: haunted by the dark figure*, (Buckingham: Open University Press, 1996) is a little old now, but still offers a valuable account of how statistical information is acquired and understood.

Criminology has a key concern to influence policy; the discipline's growth in the concluding decades of the twentieth century means that there is a wide range of publications dealing with specific areas from a contemporary perspective during these years. All of these are useful to both the historian of the period and to the criminologist seeking to understand changing perceptions and policies. While it may be invidious to make a brief selection for specific topics it is worth consulting: **Hazell Croall**, *White Collar Crime* (Buckingham: Open University Press, 1992); **Frances Heidensohn**, *Women and Crime* (Houndmills, Basingstoke: Macmillan, 1985); **Gary Slapper** and **Steve Tombs**, *Corporate Crime* (Harlow and London: Longman, 1999); **Sandra Walklate**, *Gender, Crime and Criminal Justice*, (2nd edn, Cullompton: Willan Publishing, 2004).

There remain significant gaps in the historical knowledge. There is, for example, the need for some serious long-term assessments of property crime in the twentieth century and the development of penal policies particularly since the Second World War. Useful sources for such work are available in, for example, The National Archives and local repositories. Unfortunately the Old Bailey Proceedings end in 1913 and there is no comparable online resource running through the twentieth century, although an increasing number of Metropolitan Police papers are to be found at www.open.ac.uk/Arts/history-from-police-archives. There are also increasing numbers of newspapers available online: *The Times* run for most and *The Guardian* for the whole of the twentieth century. The British Cartoon Archive at the University of Kent at Canterbury is also a valuable source; its collection can be searched online at http://library.kent.ac.uk/cartoons and the British Film Institute has a whole section of its *In View, British History Through the Lens* devoted to Law and Order. This is available through the Shibboleth platform.

Index

Alden, Percy 140
Alderson, John 135
Allan, Lt. Col. W.D. 158
Ambler, Eric 110
anarchists 2, 104–5
Arnott, Jake 113
assault 3–4, 16, 18–19, 20, 33,
        44–5, 74–5, 171, 193, 204,
        215, 219, 230
Association of Chief Police Officers
        (ACPO) 154, 157, 170–1

Baden-Powell, Lord 71, 115
Baldwin, Stanley 8
Ballinger, Anette 189
Battle, Arthur 100
Beeching, Lord 178
Bell, Mary 7, 80–81
Bentley, Derek 206–7
Bevan, Aneurin 97
Beveridge, Peter 133
Biggs, Ronnie 43, 216
The Bill 111
Birmingham 32–3, 104, 123, 143, 163,
        193, 216
Biron, Sir Charles 194
Bishop, Peter 134
black market 3, 95–6, 195, 230
Blair, Tony 10–11, 221
Blake, George 216
Blake, Sexton 89, 110, 112, 114
Blakelock, Keith 163
The Blue Lamp 110, 118, 128, 166
Booth, Charles 139
Borstal 51, 54, 69, 138, 144, 195, 203,
        209, 212, 222
Bowley, Arthur 139

boy labour problem 66
Brady, Ian 124
British Board of Film Censors 113,
        115–16
British Crime Survey 33–4
Brockway, A. Fenner 211–12
Brooke, Henry 207
Buchan, John 112
Bulger, James 7, 10, 64, 81, 127
burglary 12, 22, 33, 26–7, 165, 193
Burke, Edmund 7
Burt, Cyril 68–9, 143
Butler, R.A. 161
Bywaters, Frederick (Freddie)
        125, 205

Cadogan, Sir Edward / Cadogan
        Committee 203–4
Campbell, Sybil 195
Cancellor, Henry 137
Carlton, Billie 119–20, 229
Chang, Brilliant 120, 229
Chapman, Cecil 6, 136–7, 160–1,
        194
Charrington, Brian 58, 101
child abuse / abusers 78–80, 109,
        219, 230
Childs, Gen. Sir Wyndham 165–6
Christie, John 41, 207
Churchill, Winston 155, 192, 210
A Clockwork Orange 116–17
Cole, Harry 135
Confait, Maxwell 163
Conrad, Joseph 105
Cook, Dee 55–6
Cornell, George 44
Court of Appeal 39, 81, 163

courts 15, 27, 29–30, 119, 125
  advocacy in 181, 183–5
  assizes 178, 180, 203
  bias in 186–92
  Central Criminal 119, 178, 180
  Crown 119, 178
  Juvenile 64, 190–1
  magistrates 119, 177–8, 180–1,
    183–4
  martial 24, 95
  quarter sessions 177, 180, 203
  sentencing in 191–6
  witnesses in 185–6
Craig, Christopher 73, 207
crime
  cinema representations 112–13,
    115–17
  definition problem 2–5, 16
  drug dealing 89, 101–3, 120, 220–1
  economic causes 25–6
  homosexuality as 5, 77
  regional variations 32–3
  war and 3, 6, 24–5, 49–50, 66–8,
    94–8
  at workplace 91–2
  see also assault, child abuse, homicide,
    rape, robbery, theft
Crimewatch 123
criminals
  class 6, 55–8, 73–4
  dockers as 72, 91–2, 95, 228
  as entrepreneurs 43, 46, 58–9, 88,
    90–1, 93–4, 97, 99, 101–3,
    228, 230
  gender ratio 63, 228
  habitual / recidivists 8, 48–53
  ideas of honour 42, 44, 138, 228
  immigrants / ethnic minorities labelled
    as 6–7, 45–6, 75, 87, 89–90, 117
  press representations of 109, 121–2
  soldiers as 24–5, 30, 36, 45, 71,
    95, 133
  women as 20, 28, 50, 52–4, 56, 67,
    75, 92–3, 120, 125, 127, 133–4,
    137, 140, 189, 228
  see also media, young offenders
criminology / criminologists 1–2, 12, 20,
    25, 72, 78, 87, 123, 131, 140,
    143–7, 209, 217–18, 229, 232

Crippen, Dr H.H. 186
Crompton, Richmal 71
Crown Prosecution Service 30, 169, 184
Cunningham, Andy 99

Daley, Harry 135–6
Danesfort, Lord 203
Darwin, Charles 140
Delvigne, Margaret Bowman 125
Denning, Lord 126, 189
Dickens, Charles 201
Dirty Harry 112, 128
disorder / riots 4–5, 73–5, 90, 155, 163,
    165, 169–70, 172
Dixon of Dock Green 110–12, 166
Dobkin, Harry 122
doli incapax 64, 81
Downes, David 72
Drage, Geoffrey 140
Drake, Sir Francis 71
Driver, Neville 117–18
Drummond, 'Bulldog' 89, 112
Drury, Kenneth 94
Du Cane, Gen. Sir Edmund 208–9, 212
Duncan, Helen 'Hellish Nell' 5

East, William Norwood 142
Edward, Prince of Wales 125
Edwards, Ronald 'Buster' 41
Elizabeth II 72
Ellis, Ruth 125, 207
eugenics 141–3
Evans, Timothy 41, 207

Fabian, Robert 132–4
Fahmy, Marie Marguerite 185, 189
Field, Simon 26
Fielding, Henry 139
Fitch, Herbert 134
Flying Squad 94, 111, 132, 162, 164
Fowell, Frank 115
Fox, Sydney Herbert 47–8
Fraser, 'Mad' Frankie 138
fraud 55–9
Fu Manchu 89, 134

Galton, Sir Francis 140–1
gangs 28, 41–6, 64–5, 74–5
Garland, David 8

Get Carter 113
Ghost Squad 132, 162
Gladstone, Herbert / Gladstone
    Committee 8, 201, 208–10
Goddard, George 93
Gordon, Dr. Mary 210
Goring, Charles 141–2, 210
Gosling, John 132–3
grassing 44–5
Great Train Robbery (1963) 31, 42–3,
    57, 101
Green, T.H. 139, 209
Greene, Graham 91
Griffith-Jones, Mervyn 187
Grove, Trevor 183
Grünhut, Max 143–4
'The Guildford Four' 126, 163

Haigh, John George 40–1, 122
Hall, G. Stanley 66
Hannay, Richard 89, 112
Haselden, W.K. 182, 186–8
Heath, Edward 53, 99
Heath, Neville 41
Henderson, Arthur 190
Her Majesty's Inspectors of Constabulary
    (HMIC) 153–5, 157–8
Hill, Billy 138, 149
Hindley, Myra 124–5
Hippies 75, 225
Hoare, Sir Samuel 206
Hobbs, Dick 88–9
Hobhouse, Stephen 211–12
Holmes, Sherlock 112
homicide 2–3, 5, 16, 27–8, 40–1, 44,
    46–7, 64, 70–1, 80–1, 99, 110,
    113, 116–17, 124–5, 134–5, 159,
    162–3, 166, 179, 184–6, 189–90,
    202, 205–7, 228, 232
Hornung, E.W. 137
Horwell, John 132–3
Howard League for Penal Reform 8,
    205–6, 215, 217, 223
Howard, Michael 11, 81, 127, 219
Humphreys, Sir Travers 186
Humphries, Stephen 70

Irish Republican Army (IRA) 2, 104–5,
    126, 163, 164, 189

Jacoby, Henry 70–1, 187
Jaeger, Philip 100
Jenkins, Harry 73
Jenkins, Roy 167
Joseph, Sir Keith 53–4
Joynson-Hicks, William 91
judges 126, 178–9, 181, 186–9, 192–3,
    195–6
juries 180–3, 189

Kempton, Freda 120, 229
Kennedy-Cox, Sir Reginald 99
Kiszko, Stefan 163
Kray brothers (Charlie, Reggie, Ronnie)
    43–4, 46–7, 53, 57, 101, 103,
    113, 138
Kubrick, Stanley 116–17

Lady Chatterley's Lover 187
Lane, Lord 126, 189
Lawrence, Stephen 165
Leeds 32–3, 142, 193, 219
Levitt, Roger 58, 228
Lewis, Derek 219
Lindop, Sir Norman 168
Liverpool 32, 69, 74–6, 92, 102, 154,
    167, 193
Llewellin, W.W. (Bill) 212
Lombroso, Cesare 141, 210
The Long Good Friday 105, 113
Low, David 187
Lundy, Tony 162, 174
Lynskey, Judge George Joseph 97–8

McCardie, Justice H.A. 156
McClintock, F.H. 33
M'Naghten Rules 27
McNeile, Lt. Col. Herman Cyril 'Sapper'
    112
Macpherson, Sir William 6, 165
McVittie, Jack 'The Hat' 44
Mafia 87, 90, 103, 105
magistrates
    ethnic minority 180
    memoirs 136–7
    women 179–80
    working-class 178–9
Malcolm, Lt. Douglas 121–2,
    184–5

Manchester 32–3, 39, 44, 64, 76–7, 91, 102, 116–17, 142, 154, 204, 218

Mannheim, Herman 25–6, 32–3, 50–1, 69, 143–4

Manning, Edward 120

Mark, Sir Robert 135

Mason, E.W. 214

Maudling, Reginald 99, 117

media
  crime statistics and 23, 116
  decline of sourcing agencies 119
  influence on criminal behaviour 113, 115–17
  miscarriages of justice and 126–7
  police suspicion of 122–3
  pressures on 109, 119, 147
  stress on sensational (sex and violence) 78–9, 113, 123–5, 230
  use of stereotypes 109, 112–13, 117–22, 125

Messina brothers 93

Metropolitan Police 5–6, 16, 25, 48–9, 54, 64, 73, 93–4, 101, 103–4, 111, 116, 118, 122, 126, 132–5, 153–5, 157, 159–62, 164–6, 170

Meyrick, Kate 3

Mods and Rockers 63, 74

Montgomery, Field Marshal Viscount 5

moral panic 63

Moriarty, C.C.H. 23

Morrison, Herbert 195

motor bandits 99–100

Mountbatten, Lord 216

muggers / mugging 31, 75, 109

Muir, Richard 186

murder, see homicide

Murray, Charles 54–6, 146

National Council for the Abolition of Capital Punishment (NCACP) 205–6

National Council for Civil Liberties (NCCL) 160, 168

National Society for the Protection of Cruelty to Children (NSPCC) 79

Nilson, Denis 41

Normanton, Helena 179

Nottingham 102, 193

Oxford 64, 111–12, 119, 143–4, 209, 212

Pace, Beatrice 125, 190

Paedophile Information Exchange 77–8

paedophiles, see child abuse

Parcq, Herbert du 213

Paterson, Alexander 71, 139, 212–13, 215

Pearson, Geoffrey 227

Peel, Sir Robert 54

Pethick-Lawrence, Emmeline 210

Platts-Mills, John 217

police 4, 6–8, 10–12, 29, 31, 33–4, 44–6, 63–5, 76–7, 78–9, 87, 97, 101–2, 207, 213, 218, 228–32
  corporal punishment and 202, 204
  corruption 90, 92–4
  crime statistics and 10–20, 23–4, 26, 169
  demonstrations / riots and 155, 157, 168–9, 171
  detectives 132–5, 159–62
  discretion 4, 159
  ethnic minority officers 154, 165
  forensic techniques / technology and 48, 159, 165, 167
  informants 161–2
  media representations 110–12, 172
  memoirs 131–6
  'noble cause corruption' 127, 184
  organisation and structure 18, 153–8
  as prosecutors 169, 184
  women officers 8, 29, 154, 164
  see also Metropolitan Police

Pottinger, George 98–9

Poulson, John 98–9

Prescott, John 217

Press Association 119

prison 8, 11, 54, 195
  central for punishment 201, 208–9
  disorders in 213, 216–7, 219
  liberal policy 210–12, 215
  population 212, 215–16, 218–19
  power relations in 213–15
  regimen 216–18
  rights of inmates 217–18

Prison Commission / Commissioners 71,
    73, 141, 201, 208–12, 214–15
Prisons
    Armley 219
    Bedford 209
    Dartmoor 52, 212–13, 217
    Grendon 143
    Holloway 201
    Hull 217
    Newgate 201
    Pentonville 201
    Strangeways 218–20
    Wandsworth 216
    Winson Green 216
    Wolds 221, 225
    Wormwood Scrubs 182, 211,
        216, 218
prostitutes / prostitution 20, 41, 71, 76,
    80, 90, 92–3, 103, 119, 134, 137,
    148, 163, 208
punishment 192–4
    capital 8, 202, 205–8
    community / family 3, 79–80, 138
    corporal 8, 16, 79, 193, 202–5
    fine 187–8
    see also prison

Radzinowicz, Sir Leon 19, 143–4, 216
Raffles, A.J. 138, 149
Ramsbotham, Gen. Sir David 221–2
rape 6, 12, 28–31, 44, 124, 147, 189,
    196, 229, 230, 232
Rentoul, Sir Gervais 137, 194
Reynolds, Bruce 43
Richards, Judge Bertrand 189
Richardson brothers (Charlie and Eddie)
    43–4, 46, 101, 113, 138
robbery 31, 33, 75, 99–101, 118, 138,
    203, 228
Ronson, Gerald 58
Rough Justice 126
Rowntree, Seebohm 139
Royal Commissions
    Assizes and Quarter Sessions (1969)
        178
    Capital Punishment (1953) 206–7
    Criminal Procedure (1981) 163
    Duties of the Metropolitan Police
        (1908) 160

Police (1962) 161
Police Powers and Procedure (1929)
    160–1
Selection of Justices of the Peace (1910)
    178, 190
Ruggles-Brise, Evelyn 209–14
Rutherford, Andrew 8–9, 145, 232
Rutherford, Col. Norman 121–2

Sabini brothers (Darby, Harry, Joseph)
    45–6, 49, 53
Sandbach, J.B. 136–7
Saunders, Ernest 58
Scarman, Lord 165, 170
Scott, Sir Harold 25, 73
Scuttlers 64, 204–5
serial killers 40–1, 46
Shackleton, Lord 5
Sharpe, F.D. 'Nutty' 132–4, 137
Sheffield 32, 91, 166, 193
Silverman, Sydney 206
Simon, Sir John 203
Simpson, Keith 186
Simpson, Wallis 125
Skinheads 174–5
Smith, Maurice Hamblin 142
Smith, T. Dan 99
Spencer, John C. 25, 95
Spilsbury, Sir Bernard 186
Stanley, Sidney 97
Statutes
    Administration of Justice (1970)
        215
    Betting and Gaming (1960) 91
    Children (1908) 205, 211
    Children and Young Persons (1922)
        205
    Children and Young Persons (1933)
        64
    Crime and Disorder (1998) 170
    Criminal Justice (1948) 145, 204
    Criminal Justice (1967) 215
    Criminal Justice Administration (1914)
        211
    Health and Safety at Work (1974)
        171
    Inebriates (1898) 211
    Jury (1949) 181
    Jury (1974) 181

Statutes *(continued)*
  Local Government (1972) 156
  Mental Deficiency (1913) 211
  Murder (1957) 27
  National Insurance (1946) 57–8
  Police (1964) 156
  Police and Criminal Evidence (PACE)
    (1984) 163, 169–70
  Police and Magistrates' Courts (1994)
    156–7, 169
  Police (Health and Safety) (1997) 171
  Prevention of Crime (1908) 192
  Prevention of Crimes (1871) 48
  Prison (1898) 209
  Probation of Offenders (1907) 210
  Regulation of Investigatory Powers
    (2000) 162
  Sex Disqualification (Removal) (1919)
    179, 181
  Sexual Offences (1965) 5
  Sexual Offences (Amendment) (1976)
    29–30, 189
  Street Betting (1906) 90
  Street Offences (1959) 94
  Theft (1968) 22
  Witchcraft (1724) 5
Straw, Jack 221
Sutcliffe, Peter 59–60
The Sweeney 111–12

Taylor, Howard 19–20
Teddy Boys 74, 109
Thatcher, Margaret 10, 169, 207, 218
theft 3, 5, 16–17, 23–5, 27, 31, 64, 69,
    72, 91–2, 95, 113, 126, 187,
    227–8, 230
Thompson, Edith 125, 205, 207
Thompson, Edward (E.P.) 1
Thompson, Robert 81
Thwaites, Ron 185
Triads 90, 103
True, Ronald 71, 187
Tumin, Stephen 218, 221–2

Turnbull, Dr. G.M. 186
Turner, J.W. Cecil 144

underclass 54–6
Unit Beat Policing 166–7

Venables, Jon 81
Viccei, Valerio 120–1
Virgo, Wallace 94

Waddy, H.T. 194
Wagner, Rupert 100
Wainwright, John 16, 135, 184
Wallace, Edgar 110, 116
Wallasey 68, 193
Warren, Curtis 'Cocky' 58, 101
Watson, John 72
Webb, Beatrice 139
Webb, Sidney 139
West, Fred 41
West, Rosemary 41
White, Alfred 46
Wilcox, Herbert 116
Wilde, Oscar 186
Wilkins, Leslie 72
Wilson, Charles 101, 216, 230
Wilson, Harold 156, 178
Wilson, Field Marshal Sir Henry 104
Woodcock, Sir John 163
Woolf, Lord 219

Yakuza 103
Yardies 46, 90, 162
Yorke, Jane Rebecca 5
Young, Jock 146
young offenders
    American influence on 68, 118
    fault of parents 63, 69
    gangs 64–5, 74–5
    murder by 70, 80–1
    petty offending 64–5, 72, 75
    statistics of 66–7
    war and 24, 65–8, 72, 75